20-
14415
AF881603

Cheap and Easy Internet Access

-Macintosh-

LIMITED WARRANTY AND DISCLAIMER OF LIABILITY

ACADEMIC PRESS, INC. ("AP") AND ANYONE ELSE WHO HAS BEEN INVOLVED IN THE CREATION OR PRODUCTION OF THE ACCOMPANYING CODE ("THE PRODUCT") CANNOT AND DO NOT WARRANT THE PERFORMANCE OR RESULTS THAT MAY BE OBTAINED BY USING THE PRODUCT. THE PRODUCT IS SOLD "AS IS" WITHOUT WARRANTY OF ANY KIND (EXCEPT AS HEREAFTER DESCRIBED), EITHER EXPRESSED OR IMPLIED, INCLUDING, BUT NOT LIMITED TO, ANY WARRANTY OF PERFORMANCE OR ANY IMPLIED WARRANTY OF MERCHANTABILITY OR FITNESS FOR ANY PARTICULAR PURPOSE. AP WARRANTS ONLY THAT THE MAGNETIC DISKETTE(S) ON WHICH THE CODE IS RECORDED IS FREE FROM DEFECTS IN MATERIAL AND FAULTY WORKMANSHIP UNDER THE NORMAL USE AND SERVICE FOR A PERIOD OF NINETY (90) DAYS FROM THE DATE THE PRODUCT IS DELIVERED. THE PURCHASER'S SOLE AND EXCLUSIVE REMEDY IN THE EVENT OF A DEFECT IS EXPRESSLY LIMITED TO EITHER REPLACEMENT OF THE DISKETTE(S) OR REFUND OF THE PURCHASE PRICE, AT AP'S SOLE DISCRETION.

IN NO EVENT, WHETHER AS A RESULT OF BREACH OF CONTRACT, WARRANTY OR TORT (INCLUDING NEGLIGENCE), WILL AP OR ANYONE WHO HAS BEEN INVOLVED IN THE CREATION OR PRODUCTION OF THE PRODUCT BE LIABLE TO PURCHASER FOR ANY DAMAGES, INCLUDING ANY LOST PROFITS, LOST SAVINGS OR OTHER INCIDENTAL OR CONSEQUENTIAL DAMAGES ARISING OUT OF THE USE OR INABILITY TO USE THE PRODUCT OR ANY MODIFICATIONS THEREOF, OR DUE TO THE CONTENTS OF THE CODE, EVEN IF AP HAS BEEN ADVISED OF THE POSSIBILITY OF SUCH DAMAGES, OR FOR ANY CLAIM BY ANY OTHER PARTY.

Any request for replacement of a defective diskette must be postage prepaid and must be accompanied by the original defective diskette, your mailing address and telephone number, and proof of date of purchase and purchase price. Send such requests, stating the nature of the problem, to Academic Press Customer Service, 6277 Sea Harbor Drive, Orlando, FL 32887, 1-800-321-5068. APP shall have no obligation to refund the purchase price or to replace a diskette based on claims of defects in the nature or operation of the Product.

Some states do not allow limitation on how long an implied warranty lasts, nor exclusions or limitations of incidental or consequential damage, so the above limitations and exclusions may not apply to you. This Warranty gives you specific legal rights, and you may also have other rights which vary from jurisdiction to jurisdiction.

THE RE-EXPORT OF UNITED STATES ORIGIN SOFTWARE IS SUBJECT TO THE UNITED STATES LAWS UNDER THE EXPORT ADMINISTRATION ACT OF 1969 AS AMENDED. ANY FURTHER SALE OF THE PRODUCT SHALL BE IN COMPLIANCE WITH THE UNITED STATES DEPARTMENT OF COMMERCE ADMINISTRATION REGULATIONS. COMPLIANCE WITH SUCH REGULATIONS IS YOUR RESPONSIBILITY AND NOT THE RESPONSIBILITY OF AP.

Cheap and Easy Internet Access

-Macintosh-

Bob LeVitus · Jeff Evans

AP PROFESSIONAL
AP PROFESSIONAL is a Division of Academic Press, Inc.

Boston San Diego New York
London Sydney Tokyo Toronto

AP PROFESSIONAL

An Imprint of ACADEMIC PRESS, INC.
A Division of HARCOURT BRACE & COMPANY

ORDERS (USA and Canada): 1-800-3131-APP or APP@ACAD.COM
AP PROFESSIONAL Orders: 6277 Sea Harbor Dr., Orlando, FL 32821-9816

Europe/Middle East/Africa: 0-11-44 (0) 181-300-3322
Orders: AP PROFESSIONAL 24-28 Oval Rd., London NW1 7DX

Japan/Korea: 03-3234-3911-5
Orders: Harcourt Brace Japan, Inc., Ichibancho Central Building 22-1, Ichibancho Chiyoda-Ku, Tokyo 102

Australia: 02-517-8999
Orders: Harcourt Brace & Co. Australia, Locked Bag 16, Marrickville, NSW 2204 Australia

Other International: (407) 345-3800
AP PROFESSIONAL Orders: 6277 Sea Harbor Dr., Orlando FL 32821-9816

Editorial: 1300 Boylston St., Chestnut Hill, MA 02167 (617)232-0500

Web: http://www.apnet.com/approfessional

This book is printed on acid-free paper. ∞
Copyright © 1997 by Academic Press, Inc.
All rights reserved.
No part of this publication may be reproduced or transmitted in any form or by any means, electronic or mechanical, including photocopy, recording, or any information storage and retrieval system, without permission in writing from the publisher.
All brand names and product names mentioned in this book are trademarks or registered trademarks of their respective companies.
United Kingdom Edition published by
ACADEMIC PRESS LIMITED
24–28 Oval Road, London NW1 7DX

LeVitus, Bob.
Cheap and easy internet access for Macintosh / Bob LeVitus, Jeff Evans.
p. cm.
Includes index.
ISBN 0-12-445580-8 (alk. paper)
1. Internet (Computer network) 2. Macintosh (Computer)
I. Evans, Jeff, 1955- . II. Title
TK5105.875.I57L484 1996b
384.3'3--dc20

96-27715
CIP

Printed in the United States of America
97 98 99 00 IP 9 8 7 6 5 4 3 2 1

Contents

Introduction

So what's with the title? Why this book? How could we be so presumptuous as to assume that there needed to be yet another Internet-related book?

Do you want the truth? We took a look around the bookshelves of our local Barnes & Noble (and Book People, and Borders, and B. Dalton, and BookStop, and so on) and decided it was our duty to single-handedly squash the trend among writers and publishers to crank out 750-1000 page Internet tomes and call them starter kits and tour guides (sorry Adam and Michael). We felt it was time for a no-nonsense book that gets you going without trying to explain everything about everything about the Internet. One that doesn't fill countless pages with screen shots of World Wide Web home pages you could care less about. And one that saves you time, money, and effort in the bargain. We like to think of Cheap & Easy Internet Access as a kind of "Steal This Book" (Abbie Hoffman's epic '60s anarchist cookbook) for the net-surfing set.

Who Cheap & Easy Is For

It's for the penny-pincher in all of us. If you're a student with limited Internet access, or if you're just finishing college and about to lose your free Internet account, or if you're a bargain hunter who doesn't want to pay a premium for customer support you never get anyway, or you're just plain cheap, you probably want some cheap and easy Internet access. Which makes Cheap & Easy Internet Access (the book) perfect for you.

We're going to take you beyond how to get on the Internet and how to find and use Internet surfboards like Netscape and Eudora. We'll do that, of course, but our plan is to turn you into a raging beast of an Internet power user, able to sniff out bargains and discounts, saving money and time every time you connect.

This book is for anyone who wants to learn to connect to the Internet cheaply and easily, from rank beginners to experienced power users. We've tried our best not to overwhelm you with complicated instructions and useless information about how to configure software or learn UNIX commands that no one needs or uses anymore. (You'll have plenty of opportunities to waste time and get useless information once you're connected. If that appeals to you, there are several Web sites that specialize in providing the latest in information overload, such as The Well-Connected Mac WWW site at **http://www.macfaq.com/faq/Macintosh.html.** You name it, it's there.)

Another point worth noting: Cheap & Easy Internet Access doesn't limit itself to a single service provider like many other books. We're provider agnostic. Rather than recommend one over another, we cover many of the major national Internet providers such as UUNET, PSI, and Netcom, plus offerings from CompuServe, America Online, and Prodigy. We also cover how (and why and when) to consider a local Internet service provider (ISP) as well as opening the door to the whole Internet bulletin board system (BBS) scene.

Beware, though, there will be trade-offs from time to time. For example, we might recommend that you choose an Internet provider who is a little more expensive but who distributes a killer connectivity package. Please trust us. Cheaper isn't always better. Our goal in this book is to help you figure out which service is best for you, then how to use it effectively and efficiently.

How to Get the Most out of Cheap & Easy

The first thing you need to do is choose an Internet provider. We're going to show you in Chapter 1 how it all works and who the players are. You need to know what to look for, what questions to ask and what answers to expect. You need to know when it's better to use a major online service like America Online (AOL), CompuServe, or Prodigy and when it really does make more sense to use a local mom-and-pop Internet provider in your neighborhood. You'll learn that and more in Chapter 1.

Getting connected and configuring your Mac to surf the Net can be a real drag if you don't know what you're doing. Chapter 2 will walk you through this process, step by step. Luckily, many Internet providers are starting to make what used to be a nightmare a real no-brainer by including pre-configured software in their package, so it's easier these days than it used to be. We're going to give a quick lesson in what hardware and software you need to get up and running.

You need to know how to set up and surf the World Wide Web with a browser such as Netscape or MacWeb. You need to know how to use your browser to do file transfers and read newsgroups. You need to know how to do Internet E-mail with programs like Eudora or Claris eMailer, and you may need Telnet to log into the Internic to search for a domain name. And all of that is in Chapter 2. But here's the big secret: Those few things are all you really need to surf the net like a pro. Everything else is for geeks. By the end of Chapter 2, all your essential Internet software should be up and running smoothly.

Of course, if you're a geek like us, you'll find lots of other cool stuff at our WWW site:

`http://www.cheapandeasy.com`

where you can always download the latest versions of Fetch, Newswatcher, IRC, MacWAIS, MacWeather, Turbogopher, and everything else under the sun. But remember what we just told you: You don't really need 'em.

We are big fans of simplicity. Take it from us. We've been using the Net big time for almost 2 years now. The last thing you need to be doing is messing around with 20 different apps, all with their own subtle nuances that make them just a little bit better at doing a particular task such as a file transfer. Forget it. You'll never see the light of day or moon at night, let alone find the time to check out anything useful or entertaining on the Net. You'll be forever configuring and downloading the latest versions of everything. Relax. We're professionals. You can trust us. It's up to sick puppies like us to try everything and bang around on every piece of software and preference settings there is and then let you know what's best. We want you to have a life. We want you to have fun. We bear the pain so you don't have to. So the easy way is always going to be to follow our advice.

Chapter 3 tells you how to shop for the best deal. We'll show you some great sources for pricing information and teach you how to compare apples to apples. And in the best "Steal This Book" tradition, we'll tell you who to call to try to hustle free access, how to get a better deal, how increase the monthly base time allowance that most Internet providers offer without paying more, and much more. You'll also get some tips on how you can learn who is the best provider in your area. Finally, we'll teach you what questions to ask and what gimmicks to watch out for.

Speaking of fun. You're going to love Chapter 4: "Great Deals on the Net." We cruised around and found some fantastic sites for you to check out for incredibly great deals. You name it, you can get it wholesale on the Net. T-shirts, wine, flowers, hardware, software, shrubs and vintage guitars it's all out there. You just gotta know where to look. That's what Chapter 4 is all about—where to go if you're looking for deals.

Finally, you'll find some great appendices at the back of Cheap & Easy. OK, so there's a glossary as in everyone's computer book, but the rest of our appendices—Internet Service Providers; FreeNets; Mailing Lists, Newsgroups, WWW and FTP Sites; Internet BBSs; Zines, Rags & Online Buys—are extremely useful, and designed to make your life on the Internet easier.

Our Promise to You

We promise to make you self-sufficient. That's the name of the game. It takes a little time and patience to filter through all the hype, tools, and options and start using the Internet effectively, but that's what this book is all about. Stick with us and you'll soon be surfing with total impunity.

Cheap & Easy Internet Access is about trying stuff out, having fun, and learning to use the Net. It's also about doing it better, or cheaper, or easier. We promise all of that, plus where to get everything you'll ever need to surf the net (most of it is on the CD-ROM that comes with the book) and how to get connected to the Internet itself.

Thanks for deciding to buy our book and spend a little time with us—and for bearing with our jokes and irreverent style. At the end of the day we hope you'll be as wide-eyed and enthusiastic as we are about the Internet. And believe us, you're going to have a blast as soon as you get jacked in and pointed in the right direction.

So have at it. And while you're out there, don't forget to visit the Cheap & Easy WWW site at:

http://www.cheapandeasy.com

One last thing—please send us your feedback on this book and our Web site. We care. Here are our e-mail addresses:

Bob LeVitus: levitus@powercc.com

Jeff Evans: jevans@versa.com

chapter 1

Internet Service Providers (ISPs)

What Every Mac Nethead Needs to Know about Who's Zoomin' Who

The first question we always get when we speak to user groups or friends about the Internet is: "Where do I start? I don't have a clue." Well settle in—this book's for you. It's not like you were born with the knowledge or can cognize it by reading your genetic code with some ancient technique of meditation or something. We tried that and all we got was a headache. The fact is, most people aren't on the Internet yet. Most aren't even online with a service like America Online, CompuServe, or Prodigy. Many don't have a modem, let alone know where to plug it in.

We've heard of studies indicating that only 1–2% of all computer users had access to the Internet. It's not like Internet access is ubiquitous or anything. Yet. It is the case, however, that about 30% of all people who have computers have a modem. And sooner or later some of them are going to figure out where to plug it in and how to turn it on. The point we're making is that while it may seem that everyone is "jacked in to the Internet" except you, that's hardly the case. Since it's only a matter of time, though, there's no time like now. So hang tough—you'll be jacked in soon.

A Brief Aside About Demographics and Statistics

By the way, if you ever want more information about the Internet's demographics or statistics, we're big fans of a couple of sites on the Net. The first is updated regularly by the Georgia Tech Research Corporation. Once we show you how to use your WWW software in Chapter 2 you can visit it at:

http://www.cc.gatech.edu/gvu/user_surveys/User_Survey_Home.html

Hey! We're off to a good start. It's free. You can't beat that! And, other than the fact that that's a tough address to type, it was pretty easy, too. Think of this as the beginning of a beautiful tradition of cheap and easy. (We make it even easier—the CD-ROM that accompanies this book includes a special file called "cheesy.html" that you can use with Netscape to quickly get to every site mentioned in the book.)

There are a couple of other sites that publish Internet demographics — kind of. One we like a lot is by O'Reilly & Associates and Trish Information Services. You can find it at:

`http://www.ora.com/survey/`

What you get for free at this site is a succinct executive summary with some nice pie and bar charts. (The surveys themselves cost a boatload and are the kind of things advertising agencies and big corporate muckity-mucks salivate over.)

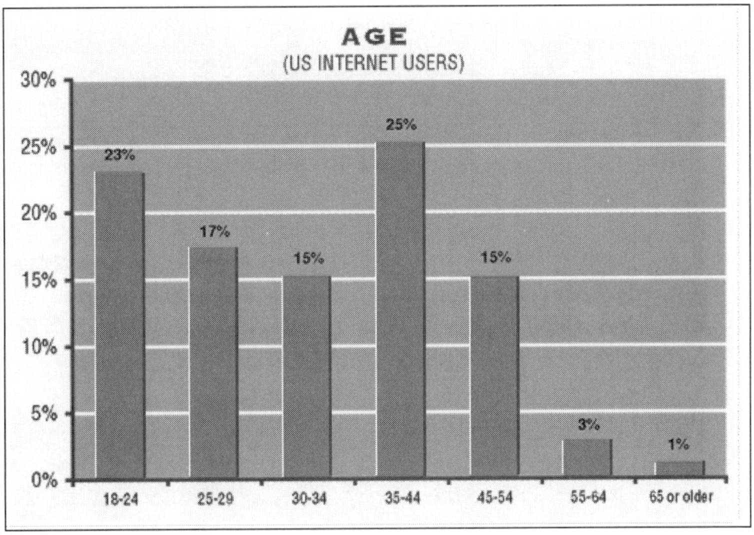

Figure 1.1: Average age of U.S. Internet users. Source, O'Reilly & Associates, 10/1/95.

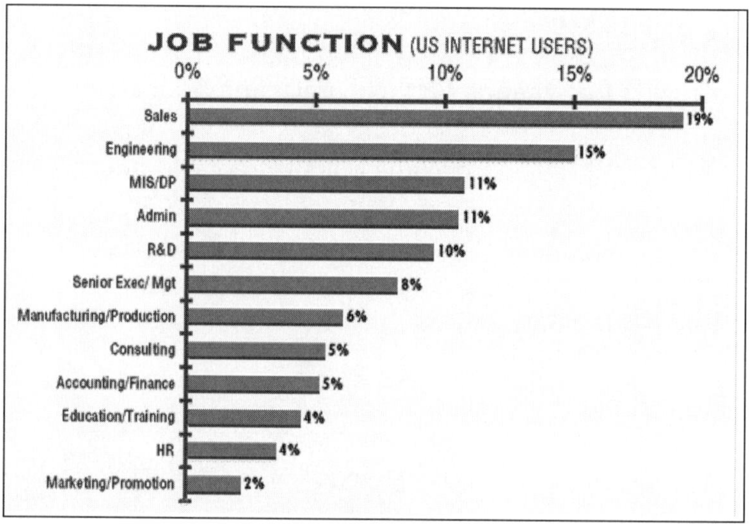

Figure 1.2: Job types of U.S. Internet users. Source, O'Reilly & Associates, 10/1/95.

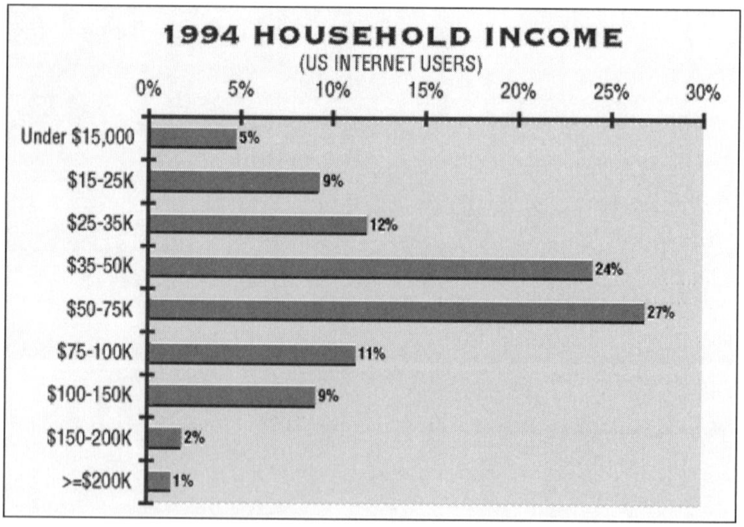

Figure 1.3: Income of U.S. Internet users. Source, O'Reilly & Associates, 10/1/95.

Where to Start

There are two paths to choose from when you decide to become a denizen of the Internet. One is get your connection from a commercial online service like AOL, CompuServe, or Prodigy. The other is to go with a straight Internet service provider (ISP) such as Netcom, PSI, or UUNet.

Let's take a look at what each of them has to offer. Keep in mind that a lot of what follows—especially pricing—will be out of date later this afternoon. That's why we provide phone numbers and e-mail addresses for the six services. If you're really serious about getting service as cheaply as possible, you need to contact each of the about-to-be-mentioned services for its current pricing (and software offerings and even, perhaps, support policies). Really. It changes almost daily.

Commercial Online Services

America Online

8619 Westwood Center Dr.
Vienna, VA 2218
800.827.6364
FAX 703.448.0760
info@aol.com
www.aol.com

America Online, Inc., based in Vienna, VA, is one of the nation's fastest-growing providers of online services, offering services such as e-mail, conferencing, software, and computer support to over 4 million members at affordable rates. For $9.95 per month for 5 hours of use ($2.95 per hour for each additional hour) and no setup fee America Online (AOL) is currently among the least expensive Internet solutions.

AOL offers 28.8Kbps maximum dial-up connectivity and 166 POPs (points of presence) nationwide. All cities offer connectivity at 14.4Kbps, with 9.6Kbps also available. AOL users have the option of connecting via TCP/IP only through SprintNet but not directly.

The standard suite of Internet tools is available on AOL, including Archie, FTP, Gopher, Telnet, and Usenet. The Usenet reader now accesses more than 20,000 groups. AOL offers the ability for users to download selected groups for offline reading, a feature absent in all other commercial online services. Search functions such as Veronica (gopher sites), Archie (FTP sites), and DejaNews (Usenet newsgroups) are straightforward and intuitive, enabling easy searching of other Internet resources. There are plenty of forums on which to discuss and find out more about the Internet.

AOL includes a basic but functional browser to access the World Wide Web. AOL's browser is currently HTML 2.0 compliant, with plans to support HTML 3.0 in the near future. It offers the standard browser functions such as back, forward, home, reload, images, stop, and the ability to build a list of favorite places. Currently, AOL members do not have the capability to store individually created Web pages on AOL's server.

AOL Growing Pains

AOL is well known for sporadic service to some customers. They are experiencing growing pains, with frequent "service too busy to complete that request" messages and occasional difficulty maintaining a connection. Bob connects via 28.8 Global Village Platinum modem to seven different services including AOL. His AOL connection is easily the most troublesome.

That said, AOL is probably least expensive way to get on the Internet. And though service can sometimes be spotty, when it's good, it's pretty good. Hopefully, it'll be better by the time you read this.

If you can make a reliable connection, AOL is a good choice. Its non-Internet (sometimes called "proprietary") content is broad and deep, its discussion boards are lively, its chat rooms are legendary, and its client software package—all free—is mostly intuitive. You can't beat it for $10 a month.

CompuServe Information Service

5000 Arlington Centre Blvd.
PO Box 20212,
Columbus, OH 43220
800.848.8199
70006.101@ compuserve.com
www.compuserve.com

CompuServe Information Service, while being known for its online services before the Internet boomed, has regrettably less to offer than America Online or Prodigy in terms of customer service and Internet access. However, members can enjoy full, uncencored access to FTP, Telnet, Usenet, and the World Wide Web more at competitive prices. CompuServe offers either a basic rate of $9.95 per month for 5 hours of basic service or a better rate which includes unlimited services plus 20 hours of Internet use for $24.95 per month ($1.95 per hour thereafter) through the Internet Club.

CompuServe offers dialup access speeds of 9.6Kbps, 14.4Kbps, and 28.8Kbps worldwide in addition to direct PPP access to the Internet. There are currently 420 POP (points of presence), but 14.4Kbps connectivity is available in only 300 cities and 16 cities offer 28.8Kpbs.

CompuServe's host of Internet tools include FTP, Gopher, Telnet, and e-mail as well as their own browser, NetLauncher (Mosaic based). NetLauncher allows members to set up hotlists or browse through the numerous stored pages. Other conveniences include the ability to scroll through documents as they load and to view the status of each document in a status bar at the bottom of the page. However, the user must launch a separate session to use the browser, therefore missing out on the integrated feel of AOL or Prodigy. CompuServe is rumored to be working on integration of their proprietary content and content on the Web, which could change things considerably. Before making any decision, ask about CIM 3.0, the client tool rumored to contain many new Internet features.

CompuServe's Web site (www.compuserve.com) has an Internet searching mechanism which allows the user to search by keyword over 50 different engines. Currently, CompuServe members do not have the capability to store individually created Web pages on CompuServe's server.

Prodigy

445 Hamilton Ave.
White Plains, NY 10601
914.448.8000
freetrial@ prodigy.com
www.prodigy. com

Prodigy offers its members competitive rates for relatively reliable access at $9.95 per month for 5 hours of use ($2.95 per hour thereafter). Also offered is Prodigy's new 30/30 plan which costs $29.95 per month for 30 hours of usage and $1.00 per hour for Internet access. Additional hours are again $2.95 each. Both 9.6Kbps and 14.4Kbps access are available, with 28.8 making an appearance in 10 cities so far.

Prodigy leads the commercial online services in World Wide Web access with a Web browser, which remains an easily accessible, affordable onramp to the Internet. It is integrated into the service; however, the browser and the online service cannot be used simultaneously.

Prodigy's Internet access focuses on the World Wide Web, integrating Gopher and FTP into the browser instead of keeping them separate (as AOL and CompuServe do). Extensive assistance is available on the World Wide Web through tutorials and tours and links to popular search engines such as Lycos, Web Crawler, and Yahoo. Parental control features include alerts that go off when the browser leaves the predefined list of pages. As a valuable feature, Prodigy provides ready-made fill-in-the-blank templates for quick and easy creation of personal Web pages, which can be stored on its servers at no extra charge. This is definitely the easiest, cheapest way to put your (albeit limited) page on the Web.

National Internet Service Providers

NetCom Internet Services

3031 Tisch Way
San Jose, CA 95128
800.353.6600
FAX 408.556.31853
info@netcom.com
www.netcom.com

NetCom Internet service is fully scalable, from simple dial-up access to high-speed dedicated data lines. A personal dial-up account for individuals includes full Internet services such as the WWW, FTP, Telnet, Usenet, and e-mail.

New users who are eager to get online but still need a little help doing so will find NetCom's approach most gratifying. The tools that NetCom distributes to accomplish that goal include NetCruiser, which is a graphical user interface intended to open the Internet to a new generation of computer users. Its simple point-and-click interface allows new users to roam the vast, worldwide Internet without knowing a single UNIX command.

NetCruiser is easy to install and allows users to connect to and cruise the Internet in a matter of minutes. NetCruiser includes tools that allow users to connect to Usenet news and to send and receive e-mail by simply clicking icons and selecting options from pull-down menus. NetCruiser also supports the two major Internet browsing tools, World Wide Web and Gopher, as well as Telnet for remote access and FTP for file transfer.

Best of all, NETCOM claims to deliver complete Internet access solutions for the lowest individual and commercial usage costs in the industry. So go ahead—make 'em live up to it!

NETCOM's extensive network around the United States includes over 200 POPs. Though some NetCom users complain about slow e-mail transmission rates and peak time inaccessibility, NetCom is a hard deal to beat. They had just started adding ISDN access to their service as of this writing, so if you have the bucks ask them if it's available where you live.

Interramp/PSI

510 Huntmar Park Dr.
Herndon, VA 22070
800.827.748
800.450.4200
interramp-info@psi.com
www.psi.net

PSI brings the newbie as well as the seasoned Internet user flexible, high-speed access with AOL-esque ease of use. With plans to reach over 200 POPs, InterRamp provides a simple, inexpensive way to access the power of full TCP/IP access, 28.8Kbps dial-up speed, or ISDN using software that the user is free to choose. InterRamp provides native support of TCP/IP applications and software, unlike the commercial online services' limited Internet access.

PSI does have a service similar to the commercial online services—kind of—called "PipeLine USA" that offers competitive rates of service and connectivity at $19.95 per month for unlimited use. Alternatively, InterRamp's full-fledged TCP/IP service goes for $9.00 for 9 hours or $29.00 for 29 hours ($1.50 per hour thereafter). Go with the full-fledged TCP/IP service. We think it's a better deal and you'll get up the full-bore Internet learning curve faster.

InterRamp works with anything that will run over a TCP/IP connection including Finger, FTP, Gopher, IRC, PING, and Telnet. And InterRamps's free trial is really free: they provide a 7-day, no obligation account which expires at the end of the trial period with no strings attached if you don't dig it.

PSI provides basic but not spectacular tools to help the user take advantage of the latest Internet applications such as the World Wide Web, Gopher, and WAIS. In order to access these tools, PSI provides each user with a PPP dialup access to the Internet, an e-mail account, an unlimited Usenet account, and access to the InterRamp users home page. Their "Internet Valet" software bundle is easy to configure and use.

AlterDial/UUNet

3060 Williams Dr.
Fairfax, VA 22031-4648
800.488.6384
703.206.5601
info@uu.net
www.uu.net

UUNet brings reliability and sound service to users who know what they want and are not intimidated by the technology requirements of setting up their own software. AlterDial offers excellent connectivity and a great software package called "MacPack" with clear step-by-step setup instructions. New Internet users should be wary of jumping into an account with UUNet based on the lack of coddling the company provides to subscribers. But if you get their MacPack and read the docs you'll be home free. UUNet's price structure is a bit higher than that of the competition, with a $25.00 setup fee and $30.00 per month for 25 hours ($2.00 per hour thereafter). The trade-off is reliability in connectivity: users have less use for customer service when the service is reliable. Every AlterDial POP provides 28.8Kbps and ISDN connectivity and will intervene in the users' efforts to establish ISDN with their phone company.

For businesses, UUNet's AlterNet is the way to go: they specialize in leased-line connections for businesses which require full-time access. AlterNet's direct TCP/IP access allows users to choose TCP and Net applications other than what's provided in the MacPack.

Customer support again works best for the seasoned Internet user, however basic connectivity customer service is available 24 hours per day.

Comparison Charts

Commercial Online Services

	America Online	CompuServe Information Service	Prodigy
Address	8619 Westwood Center Dr. Vienna, VA 22182	5000 Arlington Centre Blvd. PO Box 20212 Columbus, OH 43220	445 Hamilton Ave., White Plains, NY 10601
Phone	800.827.6364	800.848.8199	914.448.8000
Fax	703.448.0760	N/A	N/A
E-mail	info@aol.com	70006.101@compuserve.com	freetrial@prodigy.com
URL	www.aol.com	www.compuserve.com	www.prodigy.com
Tech support hours	24 hours, 7 days	7am-2am M-F, 12am-10pm Sa-Su	24 hours, 7 days
Max speed	28.8Kbps	28.8Kbps	28.8Kbps

	America Online	CompuServe Information Service	Prodigy
POP	166	420	325
ISDN	ø	ø	4
28.8Kbps	166	16 cities	10
14.4Kbps	All	300 cities	All
9.6Kbps	√	√	√
Dial-up	√	√	√
TCP/IP	ø	√	ø
800-number access	√	√	√
Software	America Online	NetLauncher	Prodigy
Standard TCP/IP stack	√	√	ø
Setup	None	None	None
Per month	$9.95	$9.95(basic)	$9.95
Hour limit	5	5	5
Per hour	$2.95	$2.95 (basic)	$2.95

National Internet Service Providers (ISPs)

	NetCom Internet Services	InterRamp/PSI	AlterDial/UUNet
Address	3031 Tisch Way San Jose, CA 95128	510 Huntmar Park Dr. Herndon, VA 22070	3060 Williams Dr. Fairfax, VA 22031-4648
Phone	800.353.6600	800.827.7482	800.488.6384
Fax	408.556.31853	800.450.4200	703.206.5601
E-mail	info@netcom.com	interramp-info@psi.com	info@uu.net
URL	www.netcom.com	www.psi.net	www.uu.net
Tech support hours	24 hours, 7 days	24 hours, 7 days	24 hours, 7 day
Max speed	28.8Kbps	28.8Kbps	28.8Kbps
Points of Presence (est)	200	150	100
ISDN	6 and growing fast	150	All
28.8Kbps	All	75	All
14.4Kbps	All	150	All
9.6Kbps	All	150	All
Dial-up	√	√	√
TCP/IP	√	√	√
800-number access	√	Ø	√
Software	Netcom Cruiser	Internet Valet	MacPack
Standard TCP/IP stack	√	√	√

	NetCom Internet Services	InterRamp/PSI	AlterDial/UUNet
Setup	$25	$9.00-$50.00`	$25
Monthly	$19.95	$29	$30
Hour limit	40	29	25
Per hour	$2	$1.5	$2

So What Do I Do Already?

On the surface, the basic difference between the commercial online service and the Internet over the last few years has been that the online services have had ease of use, abundant content, and local phone call access from almost anywhere in the world. Just under the surface is the fact that they are big private telecommunications networks that have poured tons of money into infrastructure that is now being short-circuited by the Internet itself.

Until Internet publishing via the World Wide Web came along, the Internet never pretended to be anything other than a big network of computers used by nerds. The Net was (and still is) a big, organic anarchy of networks linked together by the common protocols of the UNIX operating system on which it is based and has its origins. People, researchers, and companies sent files and e-mail across it and shared info with each other electronically. Content for public consumption was never much the issue until recently. But now it's a REALLY BIG DEAL. In other words, hypertext and the World Wide Web really upset the whole enchilada.

And so today the line between traditional online services and the Internet is becoming increasingly blurred. Local number access to the Internet is becoming the norm for ISPs (ISPs aren't stupid), while online services in turn are starting to convert their huge telecommunications network toward providing direct access to the Internet.

With the advent of the WWW as a vehicle for publishing content for public consumption and internal corporate use, the die is cast. You can see the truth of this in the fact that Microsoft and Apple basically decided to blow off Microsoft Network and E-World as private online systems and to make their services Internet based using the World Wide Web. And America Online, CompuServe, and Prodigy better figure out how to fit in and fully integrate the Internet with the best netsurfin' software available or they will disappear like dinosaurs.

The power of the press belongs to those who own the presses, and the Web gives that power to almost anyone with an interest. Many people who in the past have developed content for the private online systems and who have thousands and thousands of visitors to their online forums on CompuServe, AOL, and Prodigy are starting to think: "Hey, wait a minute. I can go buy Bob and Jeff's *WebMaster Macintosh* book, set up a Web site, and do this myself." It's like the desktop publishing revolution all over again.

But we digress from the point. That is, unless you have a specific need for some content that exists only on one of the commercial online services, there is no reason to do anything other than get a full-blown Internet account. Given the tremendous amount of cool stuff on the Internet, it's hard to believe that you won't be able to find almost anything you need there. Plus, an ISP lets you choose your own weapons, which means you can use better tools if you know of them; CompuServe, AOL, and Prodigy pretty much sentence you to the software they provide.

Things used to be worse. Much worse. In the old days, all service providers provided was a temporary password and a phone number. It took the Internet geeks a while to figure out that the average person doesn't care about or want to configure complicated software, much less figure out what we need and download it from somewhere. (Where's the logic there?) We want to get on with the work. Or fun. We're Mac users, for gosh sake! But it's only recently that Internet providers have started to offer simple software installers that make life easy. All three of the aforementioned ISPs do. You just turn on your modem, double-click on a icon, and blammo, you're connected to the Internet and 20–30 million other people.

The bottom line: probably the only reason we can think of to go with a commercial online service as your Internet access provider is that none of the ISPs have a local access number where you live. Unless you really and truly want features like chat rooms (AOL), threaded message forums and surcharged databases (CompuServe), or the thrill of doing business with Sears and IBM (Prodigy), ISPs are the better way to connect to the Internet.

The BBS World

There's a whole other world of online systems that you may have heard of called bulletin board systems, or BBBs for short. Austin, Texas alone has over 200 of them.

A BBS is usually an online system with a few modem lines and content that is of specific interest to the subscriber. There are environmental ones, entertainment ones, PC user groups, etc. They tend to be very inexpensive at the cost of busy phone lines, little customer support, and limited content. But check them out sometime.

There are many excellent BBSs. There are some really good ones accessible directly from the Internet. We think the best ones are those that run on FirstClass software. They tend to have the best user interface and are the easiest to use and find your way around.

There are others. We like FirstClass.

There is a list of FirstClass systems and other BBSs accessible via the Internet in Appendix E. We've included some instructions to help you get started. The software you need to connect to a FirstClass system is included on the CD-ROM that came with Cheap & Easy.

We probably won't get to talk much more about BBSs, but we wanted you to have a glimpse into another fascinating microcosm of the Internet.

To Surf and Provide: The Internet Service Provider Story

We're not ever going into business as Internet providers—there is just not enough money in the world. But it's useful to know a little about what their business is all about and how it works, when it comes to choosing a service provider for your own account. So now that we've made the case for why you should use an ISP and not a commercial online service for your Internet connection, here's how to choose the right one for you.

Competition among all the Internet providers is a boon for the rest of us to enjoy. It means cheaper access and better service. The trick is to figure out what you need to know to pick the right one for you. There might be one in your area charging only $5 a month for unlimited access. Sounds great, but they may not be in business next month. Or you may spend hours and hours trying to get their modem to work with your modem. Or worse, constant busy signals. Some small, local Internet providers have stared raising their rates for these very reasons. Watch out for that when you shop. Ask about rate protection.

We're busy. If it were us we'd pay a little extra for the peace of mind of knowing that a big national Internet provider is more likely to be around longer. And provide some level of support for what they sell. But before you can intelligently choose an Internet provider, there are some questions you need to ask and answers you need to hear. Just because you see an Internet provider's ad plastered in every magazine and newspaper in town doesn't mean they're any good. In fact, beware of most Internet service companies that make a lot of marketing noise—especially a local or regional provider. They often lack the technical expertise to run the show. We guess they figure that's something they can always add after they get all those eager new customers.

Not.

Running an Internet service business is no small task. It requires a lot of UNIX and system administrator expertise to keep it up and running smoothly.

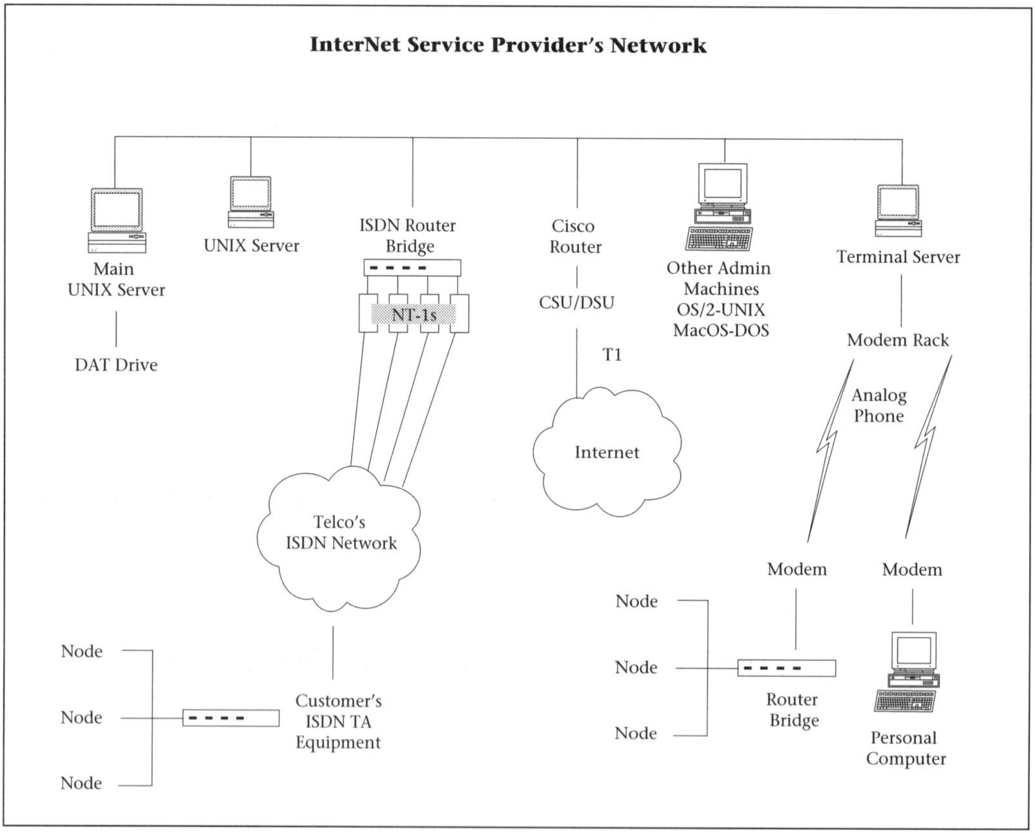

Figure 1.4: Internet site layout. Tomorrow's Technologies, Austin, TX, January 1996.

Top 10 Questions to Ask an ISP—OK, So It's Not Exactly 10

With the help of our friends who run an Internet training business called Learning Curve we've put together the important questions to ask when choosing an Internet service provider (ISP). They've got great training programs for all levels of expertise and after we teach you how to get your e-mail up and running you can send an e-mail to them at info@learningcurve.com for details.

Some of these questions will make more sense once you know what they mean by the time you finish Chapter 2. It's kind of a chicken-and-egg thing. You just have to trust us that these are the questions and answers you need to deal with.

Yeah, it's kind of a bummer that you can't start at the beginning of something and go step by step. But you need to get an Internet account before you can connect to an Internet account. And in order to connect smoothly to an Internet provider you need to have a provider whose setup lets that all happen smoothly.

Relax. It isn't a test. At least not for you... We're going to give you the answers you should be listening for too.

Access Questions

1. Do you support SLIP, PPP, or both?

   You want both or PPP. PPP is better. We'll tell you why in Chapter 2.

2. What is the speed of your connection to the Internet (full T1, fractional T1, or ISDN)?

   Faster is better. Full T1 fastest, ISDN slowest.

3. Do you offer "full Internet access?" (That is, Internet e-mail and full access to Internet services including the Web.)

The answer to this needs to be an unequivocal yes.

4. What speed of modems do you have? 14.4Kbps? 28.8Kbps? Or a mix? If it's a mix, which ones am I more likely to hit, or do you have separate phone numbers for each speed? Is the cost different?

   You'll find that 28.8 is getting more common and indicates a provider who has the beans to afford better equipment and invest in the future. You should not pay extra for 28.8.

   (None of the above matters, of course, if you're using a 14.4 or slower modem. If so, we recommend strongly a 28.8, which we consider the bare minimum for enjoyable Web surfing.)

5. Does the account come with the ability to put my own WWW page on the Internet. If so, what are the limits?

   If you never plan to have your own Web page, of course, this question doesn't matter. But if you do, we suggest you buy our book WebMaster Macintosh (subtle plug, eh?), which teaches you everything you need to know to set up your own WWW site. One of the things you'll learn is that it sometimes makes more sense to park your pages at your provider's site. It's nice to know in advance that they can do it and what they charge.

6. Do you register domain names for personal users/ business users?

   If you want a personal or business e-mail address like jevans@evans.com or bob@levitus.com instead of the one you get from your Internet provider (j7t8@mailpop.is.net or jeff@outer.net), you need domain name. It's easier to have your Internet provider apply for it than do it yourself. It's going to cost you $50–$200/year, depending on your

Internet provider, to register and keep your domain name active. It used to be free if you did it yourself. Not any more. Bummer, huh.

Support Questions:

7. Do you have a "no busy signals" policy?

   This means they have figured out the math of how many modems per user they need to keep customers satisfied. See what they'll promise.

8. Do you have tech support personnel versed in my platform (MacOS)?

   If they are UNIX heads who have an attitude about beginners and only answer what you ask without pointing out everything else you need to know, find a different provider.

9. Is documentation included?

   Good documentation is a must even with everything you're going to learn in this book. And do all of us a favor and read it.

10. How is tech support available? (Telephone? e-mail?) During what hours?

    Telephone is best. If you can't make a connection, e-mail is a problem. Try to suss out if the tech support is going to be friendly. Ask for a referral and talk to someone else who uses them. Better still, call tech support yourself prior to making a commitment. See how long it takes them to answer. See if they can answer one of the above questions.

It's a real drag when your Internet provider's customer support staff have an attitude and you have a problem you need help with. Better you should try it before you buy.

Cost Questions

11. Do you have a monthly rate, or do you charge by the hour? If there is a monthly rate, what are the limits and the charges for overtime?
12. Are there any "prime time" charges?
13. Is there a "setup" fee? What do you get in return besides an account? What exactly is the "free" software you provide?
14. Is there a free evaluation period?

The answers you get to the cost questions above will help you compare apples to apples.

Landed on the Beach and Bummin'

So, now that you have a notion of the lay of the land, pick an Internet service provider. Choose one with local number access. If you travel a lot, find one who has an 800 number or one with lots of local number access points all over the country. Believe us, you want to be able to jack into the Net when you are on the road or visiting your parents. As soon as they realize you are an "expert" you can forget about playing golf, going to the beach, or just hanging out at their place on a beautiful day in Florida. You'll be loading the Jeopardy and Wheel of Fortune games on a new 5300c PowerBook they had you pick out for them. You want to be able to visit the WWW site at **http://www.man-i-wish-had-one.com** and get some solace.

Seriously, shop around. Ask the questions. Pay attention to the answers. Start with one of the providers included with Cheap & Easy from the list in Appendix G that we struck a deal with for you. Or try one of your local service providers if you like. But go ahead. Be brave and crash right into this stuff. Get an account and get started. Take advantage of free trial periods. That's what they're for.

If you'd rather keep reading or if you're waiting for your modem to arrive, read on. In the next chapter we're going to cover how to get your hardware and software up and running so you can get connected.

Parting Advice on Modems: Faster Is Better

You have a modem already, right? If you don't, or you have an older, slower one, pick up the phone and call any decent mail order place (pick up any Mac magazine) and get yourself a 28.8 modem. Or check out the next chapter, which starts off with a list of great places you can nab a 28.8 modem for about $225.00.

"28.8" refers to the speed of the modem in baud, and 28.8 pretty much pushes the envelope as far as modems goes. If you want faster than that, you need ISDN, which requires special phone lines and adapters.

It's hard to even find a 14.4 modem anymore, not that you'd want one. You want 28.8 for the Net. It used to be you could just deal with hankering after more RAM or a bigger hard drive. These days you also need to hanker after a fast net connection. Speed is king. That old 300 or 2400 baud modem you have is history. Don't even think about it. Though it's possible, you'll hate using anything slower than 28.8 on the Web. And we're not being snobby, we're just saying the way it is. Slow modems suck on the Net. Order your fast new modem by midnight tonight and it will arrive tomorrow. (If you have a modem and network connection already, you can order a fast modem from an online vendor like Cyberian Outpost at **http:// cybout.com**) Hey, why schlepp all the way across town?

chapter 2

Hopping on the Information Superhighway

Hot-wiring Your Car and Finding the Frontage Road

We've sacrificed a few trees telling you all about how to find an ISP that meets your needs as well as your budget. If you haven't found one by now you're not trying hard enough. More important, you can't continue down this road with us until you do. So, if you don't have an ISP get one, NOW!

OK, you've found the perfect ISP (and you thought dating was hard) so it's time to make the connection. You need just a few things to get ready for your jaunt: a computer, a modem, a phone line, and connection software. It's a short list, and getting connected is relatively easy. Let's take a look under the hood of your computer and then talk about what to do once you're ready to pull out of the garage.

Parts Is Parts: Building the Perfect Internet Vehicle

Hardware: The Nuts and Bolts of It All

The most important component of your Internet connection is your computer. Imagine that. Still, we wanted to make sure you knew. You can connect to the Net with just about any machine running the Mac OS, but if you don't have a quality setup then your Internet adventures will be slow, boring, and ultimately frustrating.

Before Apple began licensing the Mac OS to other companies we could have simply made a list of good Mac systems for Internet access. While we're sure many of you still own an actual Apple Macintosh, we know there are just as many running the Mac OS on a clone. Thankfully, this won't affect the way you install or configure your software, since the layout on the screen and the way the system works are the same no matter who makes the computer. What it does mean is that we have to talk about boring things like processor speed and MHz so you will recognize a computer suited for your Internet travels when you see one. Cheer up, at least you'll be able to hold your own in a conversation with the PC/Windoze folks.

In our not-so-humble opinion a good Internet system includes (at least): a 28.8K modem, 200+MB hard drive, 16MB RAM, 75MHz Power PC 601 RISC processor, 256-color monitor, and a mouse. Granted, you can connect to the Internet using a Mac IIsi with 8MB RAM and an 80MB hard drive via a 9600K modem—we know people who do—but it's like riding your bicycle on a cross-country trip and not half as rewarding. If you can possibly avoid it, don't go there.

There are more parts to a computer than we've mentioned, but these are the ones that really matter when it comes to speeding up—or slowing down—your Internet trip. As much as we'd like to take you step by step through the entire setup of your computer, that's not why we're here. If you have problems with a piece of hardware, read the manual (really, even for a Mac) or one of the half-zillion or so computer books filling the shelves of your local bookseller. If that doesn't work, then call the dealer or manufacturer where you bought it.

Modem

Even the most souped-up computer in the world can't cruise cyberspace without a connection to it. This is where your modem and phone line come in to play. A modem is a device that converts computer-generated digital information to an analog signal and transmits the signal via a phone line to another modem, which then converts the signal back into digital format to be interpreted by its attached computer. Pretty slick, huh? Since you're going to be sending and receiving large amounts of information from the Internet you want speed on your side, hence the recommendation that you have at least a 28.8K modem. 28.8K modems facilitate transfers of up to 115,200 bps, which is the uppermost limit a nondigital phone line can be expected to transfer with reasonable accuracy. For faster transfer rates a digital connection, such as ISDN (Integrated Services Digital Network), is required, and that's nowhere near cheap and easy. You can get both internal and external modems, but we suggest you go with an external unit. They're easy to install. Connect a cable to your computer, add a phone line (much easier than taking your computer apart and performing minor surgery), and you're good to go. Most external modems have a handy set of indicators on the front that let you know what's going on at all times and usually a handy guide in the manual to help you decode the flashing lights. And, most important, you have provided your cat with yet another warm place to sleep in addition to the top of your monitor. External modems come in all sizes for all sizes of cats.

The Case for a Second Phone Line

You've seen the commercial: daughter talking on the phone for hours, dad trying to get through to say he'll be working late, and mom becoming more and more irritated as dinner gets colder and colder. The solution, according to the commercial, is to get a second phone line. This commercial may not have sold you on the merits of a second phone line, but we bet we can, if only because we have nothing monetary to gain.

If you plan to spend any significant amount of time online, then you should seriously consider a second phone line. Call waiting and modems don't mix, so callers will get a busy signal while you're hacking away. For half an hour or so it's not a big deal, but any longer and you will have some irritated friends and family.

The good news is phone companies have recently come to realize that there is a large market for second phone lines if they are offered at reasonable rates. It's definitely worth your while to call your local bell and see what sort of incentives and installation deals they have to offer. Soon you can surf in peace, secure in the knowledge your mother-in-law will have no problems getting through to you.

Hard Disk Space

How much disk space is too much disk space? Surely you jest. There is no such thing. We've started you out with a useful but modest collection of tools that take up very little disk space. Soon, after you've been ensnared by the Web, you come to believe there isn't a hard drive out there big enough to store all the data you simply can't live without. After all, you want copies of all the major browsers and their helper applications, and don't forget about all those cool plug-ins. You collect myriad utilities so you can do all manner of things like tar, zip, stuff, and binhex any and every file. Once you've played on the Net you will invariably want to build your own playground, and for that you need all sorts of multimedia tools. Talk about space hogs. Not to mention the bytes and bytes of video and audio you can download from the Internet. A good rule of thumb is that the cooler something is the bigger it is, and you want all the cool stuff, right? As a new netizen you can probably get away with a 200MB hard drive, which leaves you with about 100MB of free disk space depending on the applications you install. The day will come (sooner than later) when your hard disk is stuffed tighter than the Thanksgiving turkey. Go ahead and invest in a higher capacity drive now and save yourself the headache and cost of upgrading later. A gig or two should do ya'.

Fragmentation Is Not Your Friend

Have you ever noticed your otherwise trusty and speedy computer is all of a sudden slow and sluggish? Have you tried to run a single program and received an Out of Memory error? Think back on your recent computing activities. Have you opened and closed many programs? Your RAM may be fragmented. Have you had your machine for a while, saving and deleting regularly? Your hard disk may be fragmented. Fragmentation occurs when RAM or hard disk space is used over and over again. When your computer is done with either type of memory it doesn't put it all back in a nice, neat pile; but it leaves it where it found it, basically in little pieces. Soon your computer may not be able to find a single block of RAM large enough to run a program, or it may have to store file information in several little spaces strewn all over your hard drive. Either way, your performance can slow down noticeably.

There are a couple of easy remedies for fragmentation that should perk your machine right back up. Simply restarting your computer clears and regroups your RAM. Any disk-optimizing utility, such as Norton Utilities or DiskExpress, scans your hard drive and puts all your free disk space into a single large block. How frequently you optimize your hard disk is directly related to machine usage. The more you use your computer, the more fragmented your hard disk becomes. So if you have a memory problem of any sort restart your machine first and then optimize your hard disk before you call in the cavalry.

RAM

Just like you can't have too much hard disk space you can't have too much RAM. RAM is the giver of speed. If RAM was a god you would sacrifice to it daily. Get the picture? Technically RAM, or random-access memory, is the computer's high-speed, short-term memory and is accessed at a much faster rate than the hard disk, and we've already agreed faster is better. Every application needs a certain amount of RAM to function properly, and as applications get bigger they demand more RAM. You want at least 16MB of RAM in your machine because many Internet applications, most notably Web browsers, run much faster when they have plenty of RAM.

All Mac OS machines can have their RAM upgraded, but you can't just run out and buy the first cheap RAM you see. Some computers require SIMMs (single inline memory module) while others need DIMMs (dual inline memory module), pin sizes vary, and RAM has to be combined in very specific ways. RAM speed is measured in nanoseconds (ns), and in this one case less is better. RAM rated at 60ns is preferable to that rated at 150ns. Your best bet if you are buying a new machine is to order a RAM upgrade at the time of purchase. If you are an experienced user and you have already opened up your computer and tinkered with it, without blowing it up, you can probably go to a dealer or mail order catalog and find the specific combination you need to upgrade to your desired MB yourself. The best, and safest, bet is to take your CPU to either the place you bought it or a reputable computer store and let them perform the upgrade for you.

Virtual Memory for the RAM Impoverished

The Mac OS has a nifty little addition to its memory management system called Virtual Memory. In a nutshell, you can assign part of your hard disk space to act as RAM. Remember we said that RAM is accessed faster than a hard drive, so Virtual Memory will be slower than RAM but not as slow as a hard drive. If you have extra disk space and you don't want to invest in RAM you can go to the memory control panel (Figure 2.1), switch on Virtual Memory, assign it hard disk space, and restart. There is a limit on how much hard disk space you can allocate to Virtual Memory, which varies from machine to machine.

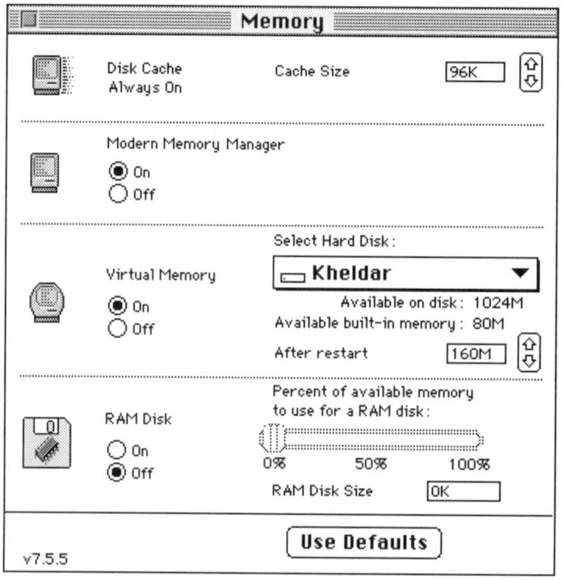

Figure 2.1: Memory control panel.

So what will Virtual Memory do for you? First of all it helps stop those annoying Out of Memory messages you get when you try to run too many programs at one time. Also, some programs, such as Netscape, require less RAM if Virtual Memory is turned on. Conversely, there are some programs that don't like Virtual Memory, and you may have to turn it off (and restart) to get maximum performance from them.

The bottom line is Virtual Memory is not equivalent to RAM but is an acceptable substitute until you can add RAM to your machine.

CPU

The CPU, or central processing unit, of a computer is very aptly named. It is responsible for all the calculations your machine performs, and the faster your CPU is the better your computer performance is. CPU technology is constantly evolving and improving, so each generation of CPUs is more powerful than the last. If you're running the Mac OS then you have either a 68K-based computer (produced only by Apple beginning with the MacII series) or a PowerPC-based computer (produced by Apple and clonemakers). While it is possible to connect to the Internet using a 68K-based machine, like the IIsi mentioned at the beginning of the chapter, you are going to be much better off with a PowerPC. The basic PowerPC processor is the 601, followed by the 603, 603e, and the 604 and 604e. Regardless of who manufactures a machine it will be labeled PowerPC, so you can be certain what type of processor you have. You probably also noticed there is a second attribute associated with the CPU, MHz, which indicates the clock rate of the CPU. Yep, you guessed it, the more MHz the better. We've recommended 75MHz, but you can get CPUs that run as fast as 180MHz, and the developers are promising higher speeds very soon. In all reality you can do just fine with a 120MHz processor. If you've looked at computer prices and specs at all you will have noticed that higher MHz is usually coupled with higher processor speeds. If you've got money to spend, stop at a 120MHz 604 (or even a 601) and spend your money on RAM, it will serve you better in the end.

Monitor

Your monitor is your window to the Internet. Through it you see dazzling graphics and movies, move through virtual worlds, and interface with other cyberjunkies all over the world. You want a monitor that supports at least 256 colors, and if you've invested in a computer in the last 3 or 4 years yours probably does. The newest monitors on the market support millions of colors, although some applications require you view in 256 colors only, but that can be set with the click of a button in the monitor's control panel. Unless you're trying to add a new monitor to an old Mac system you shouldn't have any color problems.

The only other monitor issue to address is size. While a 15 inch monitor will probably do, you can usually get a 17 inch for just a couple of hundred dollars more. A larger monitor makes viewing, organizing, and manipulating information easier and more comfortable. Yeah, we know the old SEs had dinky little monitors and people got by back then, but they had no choice—you do.

Mouse

Once upon a time there was a mouse, plain and simple, the only one of its kind. Now there are light pens, track balls, cordless mice, mice for kids, and ergonomically correct mice—just to name a few. If you choose a device other than the standard one that comes with your CPU, make sure to read the manual (yes, again) and install any related software. Regardless of what shape it takes you need some sort of input device. You can't "click" anywhere without one.

Software

The hard part (ha ha) is over and you've built your well-oiled Internet surfin' machine. It's time to move onto software, your steering. It's pretty straightforward: to connect to the Internet you need Internet connection software - duh. But—and there's always a but—we need to have a little talk about your system first.

The Mac OS

Before we can go any further you need to determine what version of the Mac OS you are running because that directly affects how you connect your computer to the Internet. We'll start with the easy scenario. You have a PowerPC and are running system 7.5.3. This also means you are running Open Transport and will configure your connection software as such. Now, for everyone else.

We have included system 7.5.3 on the CD-ROM accompanying this book. If you have a PowerPC and are running any other Mac OS, now is a good time to upgrade your system. Read the installer information and come back when you are done. You now fit the first scenario. Sit tight.

If you have a 68K-based system, one of the MacII family computers, you may not want to upgrade to system 7.5.3 unless you have significantly increased your RAM and disk space. If you read the installer information and decide to go ahead and upgrade, then do so now, and you too will be part of the Open Transport group. On the other hand, if you want to stick with your current system, be it 6.X (shudder) or an early system 7, you will need to drop the Mac

TCP control panel from the CD-ROM into the control panel's folder in your system folder and restart.

Internet Connection Software

Your computer is assembled and ready to go, and you've determined what version of the Mac OS you are running, so you are all set to connect. Internet connection software simply allows your computer to talk to your ISP. You have a couple of options when it comes to setting up this software. You can either do it yourself with the FreePPP software and TCP/IP-compatible applications (like Netscape and Eudora) we've included on the CD-ROM, or you can let one of several commercial packages do it for you. Both ways have their positive and negative aspects, and we'll explore them thoroughly, although we highly suggest jumping in with both feet and doing it yourself.

Do It Yourself: Getting TCP/IP Working on Your Own

The Internet is a worldwide network—this means that many different kinds of computers in many places are linked together in order to share information. But for the computers to communicate they need to speak a common language. The common language, called a protocol, of the Internet is TCP/IP. This is a fairly complicated subject and the full interworkings of TCP/IP are at best useless to the casual Internet surfer, so we won't bore you with all the details. However, there are a few tidbits which just may interest you. For instance, TCP/IP is the reason the Internet is so robust. It is a powerful networking protocol which is able to transmit data rapidly, route around slow or broken links, and handle synchronous transmission.

To work on the Internet you must have your computer on the Internet. This may seem to be a difficult problem if you are not a computing superpower, but it does have a reasonable solution. You need to have a direct connection to the Internet and a translation program to speak TCP/IP for you, since your computer's operating system isn't built on TCP/IP.

A direct connection to the Internet is established by using your modem as a network interface. This is done by connecting to your ISP with a communications protocol (PPP or SLIP) to open a pathway for TCP/IP packets to travel to and from your computer. Once you've made the connection you are on the Internet.

What Are PPP and SLIP?

PPP stands for Point to Point Protocol, and SLIP stands for Serial Line Internet Protocol. That explains it, right? Not. Basically, these are modem protocols used to establish a network connection to the Internet. Usually PPP is easier to set up and is a bit more stable, so it is the protocol we have chosen to include on the CD-ROM and walk you through configuring.

To get your computer speaking the lingua franca of the Internet, your connection software uses a networking interface called TCP/IP. Mainly it is a collection of protocols, translators, and control processes which allows your computer to communicate with the rest of the Internet. As a user of the Mac OS you are using either Mac TCP or Open Transport, both of which incorporate TCP/IP. All you have to do is configure TCP/IP to work with PPP and PPP to work with your ISP. It's like a giant chain.

Earlier we said you could either configure your connection software yourself or let one of several commercial packages do it for you. Be brave and daring—do it yourself. It's not that hard, really, and you'll know more when you're done. Besides, we'll be with you every step of the way. Now is a good time to mention that the configuration for every ISP is just a little different from all the others, but they are all based on the same principles and types of software. We can't anticipate the requirements and quirks of every ISP, but we have made an effort to lay out the best overall setup procedure. If you run into problems call your ISP, they know more about their system than anyone.

Before we start, go find the stuff your ISP sent you via snail mail, you'll need it. There should be a sheet of information that lists things like "Domain name," "Nameservers," "SMTP server," and other cryptic but necessary bits of information. Alternately, your ISP may have provided you with a step-by-step guide to configuring your system to work with their system. Their guide should be similar to ours, and between the two you can get your system ready to go. Regardless of what form your ISP information is in, put it where you can find it.

One last thing you need to do, before you get down to the business of configuring your system, is make sure Mac TCP or Open Transport and FreePPP are installed. At the beginning of this chapter we discussed the software you need based on the system you are running as well as your memory resources. As a quick refresher, or—shame on you—in case you conveniently skipped that part, if you're running system 7.5.3 (it's on the CD-ROM) you'll find TCP/IP is part of your system, as is Open Transport, and you can skip directly to the section on Open Transport—do not pass go, do not collect rent. If you're running a system other than 7.5.3 you'll need to drop Mac TCP (it's on the CD-ROM too) into the control panel's folder in your system folder and restart.

For any system, to install FreePPP click on the FreePPP installer icon and let the software do the work. When it asks you if you want to configure Mac TCP for FreePPP, say yes. Trust it, it knows what it's doing. Now you're ready to begin tinkering.

Mac TCP

Open up the Mac TCP control panel (Figure 2.2), click the FreePPP icon, and then click "More..." to get to the real meat of the control panel. Don't worry that your IP address is blank or "0.0.0.0"; that fixes itself later.

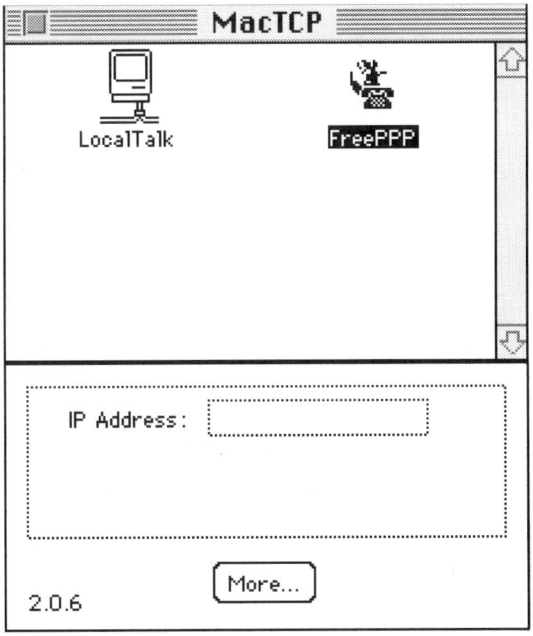

Figure 2.2: Mac TCP control panel.

You don't need to mess with most of the stuff in the TCP control panel configuration window, and doing so only delays your road trip. Control your impulse to see "What happens if I...." Just say no.

It takes just a few simple steps to configure Mac TCP. Grab that information sheet we told you to keep where you could find it and then (working top to bottom and left to right):

1. Choose Server in the Obtain Address box.

2. Enter the Gateway number provided by your ISP.

3. Make sure Class in the IP Address box is set to C. Just click on the drop menu and select C.

4. In the Domain Name Server Information box enter the domain name identified by your ISP as a Domain Name Server (or perhaps just Nameserver) in the box under Domain followed by the address (a set of numbers in the form of xxx.xxx.xxx.xx) in the box under IP Address. Your ISP may have more than one DNS server listed. In that case just add any additional ones in the same way, and make sure to click the Default radio button next to the first one.

   When you're done, your control panel should look like Figure 2.3.

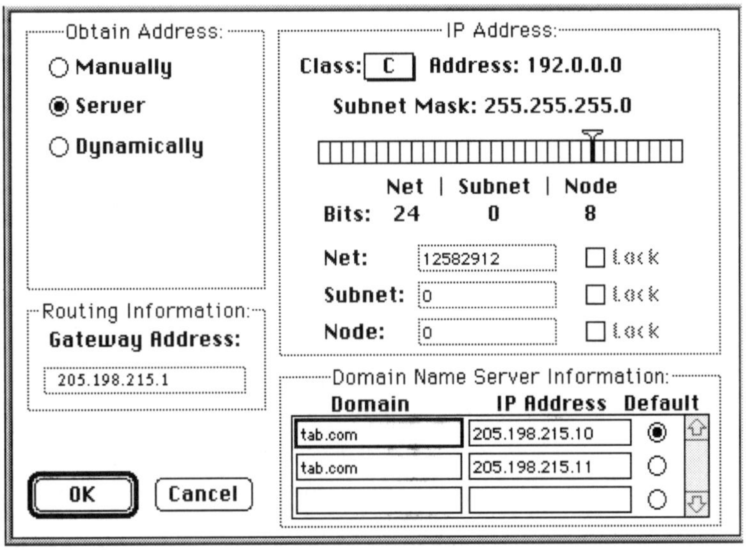

Figure 2.3: Mac TCP configuration.

That's it! You're done configuring Mac TCP. Click on OK, close the Mac TCP control panel, and restart (even if your machine doesn't ask you to, it's a good idea). You're such a pro. We'll make a power user out of you yet. You can skip the section on configuring TCP/IP with Open Transport and move on to configuring FreePPP.

Open Transport

First a word of advice: don't use Open Transport (OT) unless you're running version 1.1 that comes with system 7.5.3; all the earlier versions are just a little too unstable for our taste, and besides, since it's on the CD-ROM you have no excuse. That said, Open Transport makes working with your Mac easy as pie. Follow these few simple steps and you'll be on your way.

1. Open the TCP/IP control panel.

2. You should be in Basic user mode. To make sure, go to the Edit menu and choose the User Mode option. You'll see a window like the one in Figure 2.4.

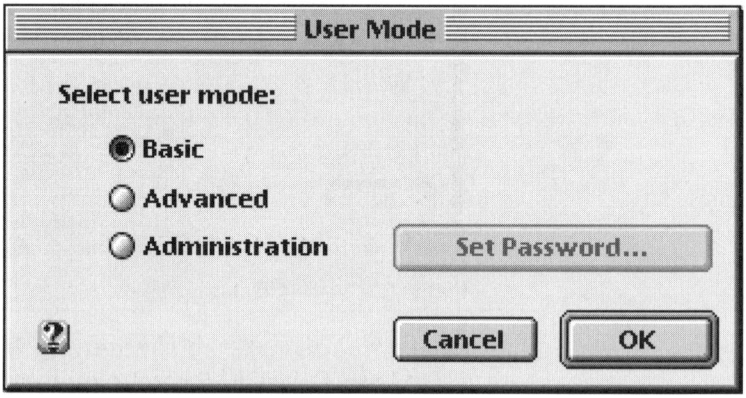

Figure 2.4: TCP/IP User Mode window.

3. Back in the TCP/IP control panel (Figure 2.5), choose MacPPP under Connect via and Using PPP Server under Configure.

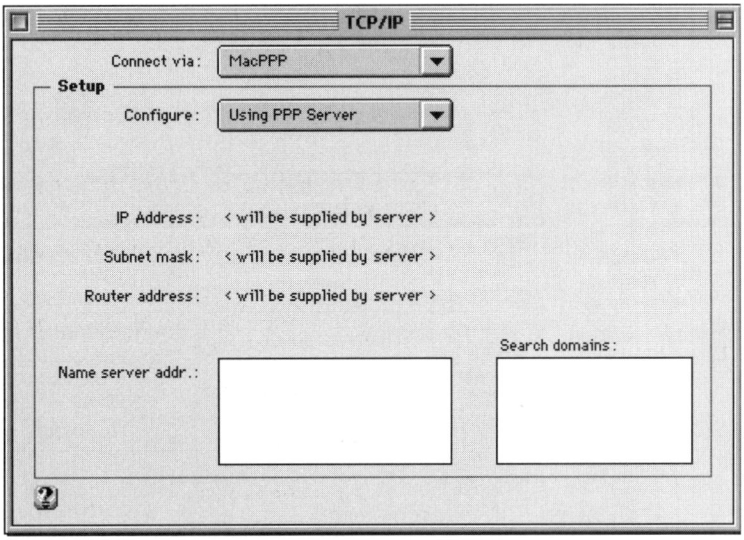

Figure 2.5: Open Transport TCP/IP control panel.

4. Your IP Address, Subnet mask, and Router address will be supplied by the server, hence the phrase <will be supplied by server> (funny how that works), so you couldn't enter anything here even if you wanted to.

5. Using the information supplied by your ISP, enter their domain name (apple.com is an example of a domain name); it should be on the information sheet somewhere, in the Search domains box. If your setup has a box for Ending domain just leave it blank.

6. In the Name server addr.: box enter the address or addresses (numbers in the form of xxx.xxx.xxx.xx) identified by your ISP as Domain Name Servers or just Nameservers.

7. Click "OK" and you're on your way to FreePPP.

DNS: The Universal Translator

So you're watching basketball on Sunday afternoon and one of the ubiquitous "I Love This Game" ads is playing. The announcer's final message to you is "Visit on the Web at http://204.201.32.31." Yeah, sure, next time you're surfin' the Web you'll remember that number. NOT! But, http://www.nba.com is a whole other ball game (pun intended).

You can thank the invaluable domain name system (DNS) for translating those bunches of numbers into the easy-to-remember and catchy names devised by Web developers. Without DNS, http://www. apple.com would be http://17.254.3.21, a rather nondescript set of numbers, don't you think? Or imagine trying to remember http://205.216.146.104 every time you wanted to do a search at Yahoo? We don't even know what our ISP's IP addresses are.

Of course, there are other uses for the DNS system, including providing an infrastructure for the dissemination of addresses, but that really matters only to ISPs. And in case you were wondering, domain name servers are the repository of IP address/identity matches. When you tell your computer you want to visit http://www.webedge .com to check out the coolest new Mac tools, you might as well be speaking Greek to it. The domain name server takes one look at the URL, translates it into http://206.160.218.22, the number addressing scheme your computer understands, and you're on your way.

FreePPP

The next bit of tweaking you'll be doing involves the FreePPP software you installed earlier. You might have noticed that a new folder appeared on your hard disk entitled FreePPP. There might also be a FreePPP backup folder, ignore it for now. You might also have noticed that there is a new addition to your menu bar (Figure 2.6) right next to the Finder on the far right.

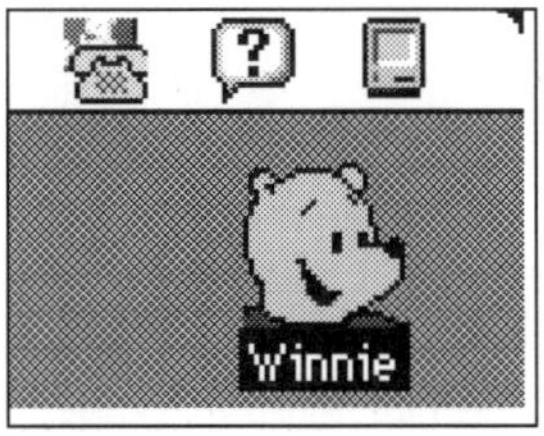

Figure 2.6: FreePPP menu icon.

If you click on it you get the FreePPP drop-down menu. You can choose FreePPP Setup from inside the FreePPP folder on your hard disk or from the drop-down menu. When you do you'll see a window that looks like Figure 2.7.

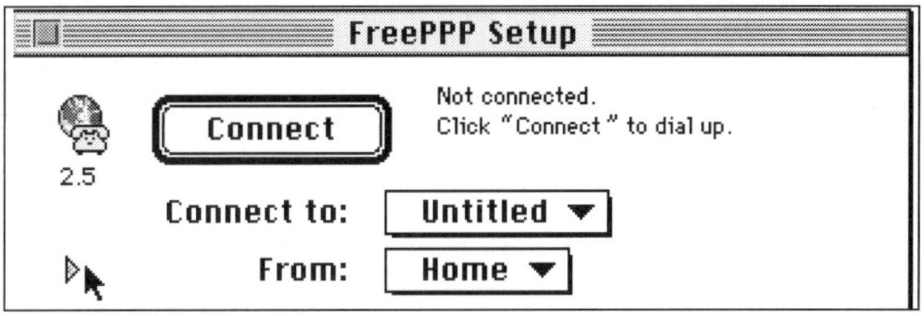

Figure 2.7: FreePPP setup window.

Click on the small triangle (next to the arrow in the picture) to get the extended version of the window (Figure 2.8).

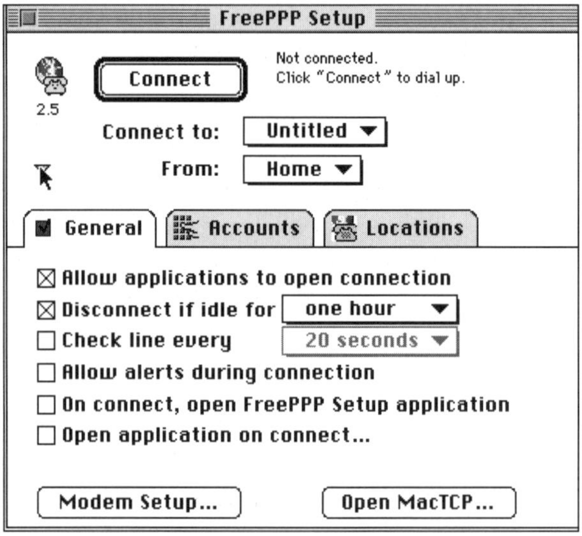

Figure 2.8: FreePPP setup general controls.

Now, unlike the setting in the Mac TCP folder, you can make some adjustments to the FreePPP settings based on your personal preferences. We'll briefly describe what each of the options does and you can make your own decisions about your setup.

Allow applications to open connection lets you connect to your ISP from a TCP application, such as Netscape Navigator, without first going through the FreePPP connection dialogue. We recommend selecting this option because it simplifies your connection process and saves you time. Why open up the FreePPP Setup, click on Connect, and then Open Netscape when you can simply start up Netscape and have the computer do the rest? Easier is better.

Disconnect if idle for X minutes is another recommended option, especially if your ISP charges you for connect time. Say you're sitting at home, wandering the Web, when suddenly, the man/woman (we're not making any stereotypical assumptions here) of your dreams calls—assuming you have a second phone line—and says they want to meet you right then. Are you going to think about disconnecting from the Net as you run around like the proverbial beheaded chicken? We doubt it. What a bummer to come home after spending hours with your newfound love to discover you were logged on the whole time and running up your bill. Somehow we don't think your ISP will credit your account. So choose your time limit to make sure you're covered if you forget to log off. You never know when your phone will ring.

Check line every X seconds monitors the status of your line for stability of connection and packet transmission after a specified time. Nice but not necessary. You can go either way on this one.

Allow alerts during connection simply allows your Mac to let you know about things like the time and problems with applications while FreePPP is making a connection. Your choice.

On connect, open FreePPP Setup application is sort of redundant. You've selected Allow applications to open connection (to expedite your connection, no less) and now when you start a Web or e-mail or any other Internet session the FreePPP Setup window appears? We don't use it, but feel free to if you think it's necessary.

Open application on connect... is the reverse of Allow application to open connection. After you choose Open Connection from the FreePPP Setup window and a connection is made, then a selected application (it asks you to select this application when you click the box) will open. Once again, your call.

Once you've chosen those general features you want to enable click on the Modem Setup button in the lower left-hand corner. The window you see will look like the one in Figure 2.9.

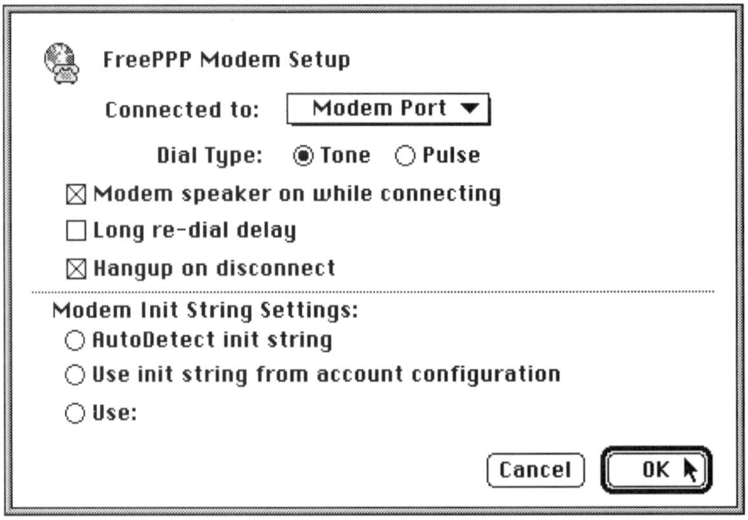

Figure 2.9: FreePPP modem setup.

This window, while fairly straightforward, may be different for everyone depending on their modem. Unless you have a strange hardware configuration, your modem is connected to your modem port and your phone dials via tone not pulse (wow, they still make pulse phones?). You may or may not want to listen to your modem dial, so choose "Modem speaker on while connecting" depending on your preference. The "Long re-dial delay" causes the modem to wait longer between redials when your ISP's number is busy. Don't select it.

Things start to get sticky down in the Modem Init String Settings section. The modem init string is a set of commands that configure a modem for things like hardware handshaking, high-speed transfers, and better compression. If you don't have a clue and/or have a slow modem (9600K and slower), then choose AutoDetect init string and go on. If you happen to have a faster modem (14.4K or 28.8K) and your modem manual handy (geek), then you might take a look and see if they have a suggested init string. If so, choose the Use init string from account configuration button and we'll fill the actual string in later. Unless you're an experienced modem user, don't choose the Use section and write your own string. You could stall yourself before you even leave the driveway if you're not careful. When you're done setting up your modem click OK to return to the FreePPP Setup window.

Now choose the Accounts tab from the FreePPP Setup window. One of the nice features of FreePPP is you can store information for multiple Internet accounts (believe it or not there are those of us who have more ISP accounts than kids, cars, and dogs combined), as well as add, modify, and delete account information. Clicking on the Accounts tab will bring up a window that looks like Figure 2.10.

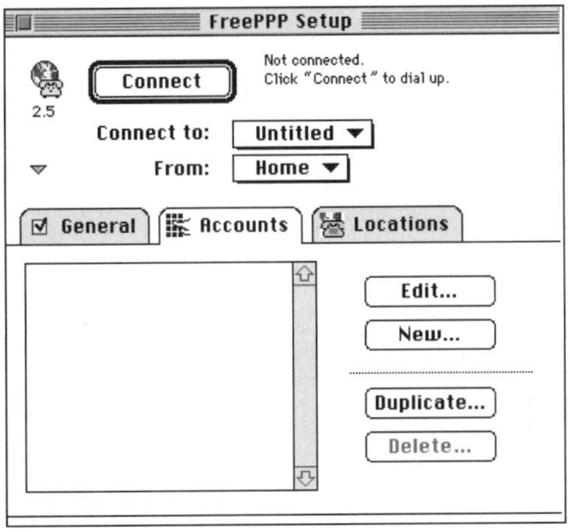

Figure 2.10: Accounts setup window.

There shouldn't be any accounts currently configured, so choose New and a new Account window will appear (Figure 2.11).

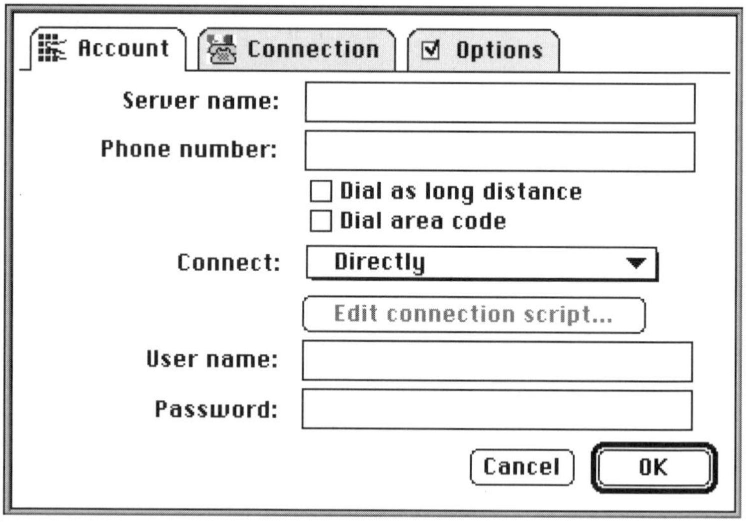

Figure 2.11: Account configuration window.

It's like elementary school—fill in the blanks. From your ISP information (what, you thought we were done with that? Get real) fill in the server name, the phone number, your user name, and your password. Unless you're dialing long distance (since this is a book about cheap and easy connectivity we doubt you would want to pay the LD charges) there's no need to choose either the Dial as long distance or Dial area code box. You want to connect directly and don't even think of messing with the connection script, unless your ISP tells you to and then it's their responsibility.

Next choose the Connection tab. Remember when we talked about init strings for modems a couple of paragraphs back? We're going to come back to that here. The Connection window should look like Figure 2.12.

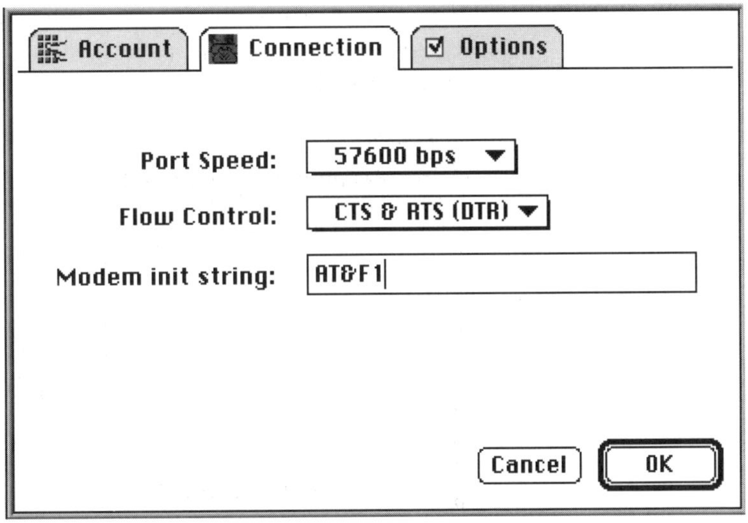

Figure 2.12: Connection configuration window.

The settings in this window are largely dependent on your modem and machine speed. Here are few guidelines to help you decide what settings are best for you, but there's no way we can account for every possible computer-modem combination. Fast Macs, like PowerPCs and AV machines, and fast modems, 28.8K and faster, can handle port speeds of up to and even over 114,200 bps, but other computers are happier with 57.6Kbps as a port speed, and we all want happy computers. If you have a 28.8K or 14.4K modem then you want to choose CTS & RTS (DTR) for your Flow Control. For slower modems, 9600K and lower, look at your manual and see if there is a recommendation. You may need either CTS or RTS (DTR) or none at all. If you have a slow modem and no manual just choose none, it's safer that way. You really don't want to know what all those letters stand for; if you did you'd still have your modem manual. Just go with us on this one.

We're not going to go in depth about init strings here either. Suffice it to say the string AT&F1 will configure many high-speed modems, from Hayes to Global Village and many in between, for a high-speed connection. If you've got a slow modem then you chose Auto Detect Init String back when you set up your modem and could care less about this discussion. Thanks for sticking with us, we're done now—with this part anyway. Onward to the Option tab.

Now this is where it really gets tricky. Make sure you pay close attention to everything we say or your entire FreePPP setup will be destroyed and this book will self-destruct. In the Options window (Figure 2.13) leave all three blanks, well, blank (or filled with those oh-so-catchy phrases provided for you), and make sure Assign by PPP server is selected by IP address. Click OK.

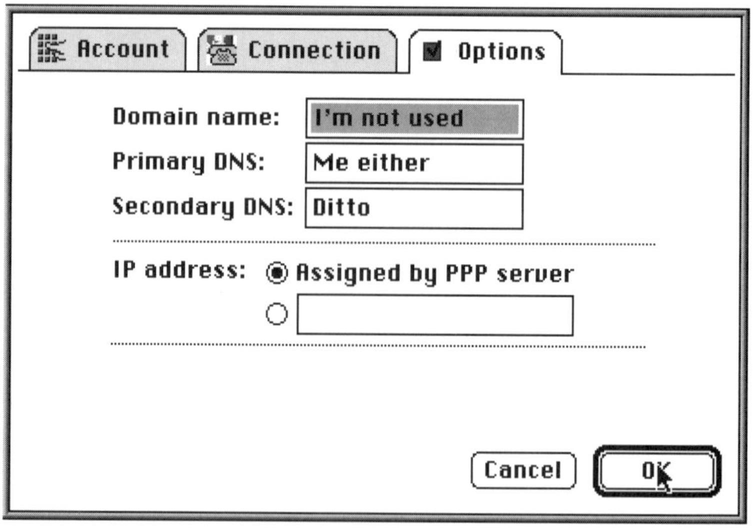

Figure 2.13: Account options window.

Ha. We had you sweatin' there for a while. If you're reading this the book didn't self-destruct, so you must have made it through the Options setup just fine. Hey, give us a break, we had to add some bit of humor to what would be an otherwise dull configuration session. Does it help if we say April fool?

Since you clicked OK (and didn't blow anything up) in the Account Options window you've been returned to the main FreePPP setup window and it's time to deal with our last tab, Location. One of the way-cool things about FreePPP is you can preconfigure it for separate locations, just like for separate accounts, if you log on from different places consistently. Obviously, this is most useful for portable computers, unless you make a habit of carrying your desktop unit with you everywhere you go (build those muscles). For now we're going to assume you're connecting from home.

The Locations window looks so much like the Accounts window we're not going to kill any more trees to show you a picture of it. Just choose Home and click the Edit button. The Location Setup window (Figure 2.14) does all kinds of useful and fun things, although you'll probably leave most of them alone. There are two notable exceptions. First, you can give your location a cool name, like "Bob's Beaudacious Abode" or "Jeff's Jammin' Cyberspace." "Home" works fine too.

Also, you can set the "Dial prefix" to disable call waiting, usually by typing in *70, which is a very good thing because the beep from an incoming call will kill your PPP session. When you've spent 3 hours downloading the latest version of Doom and you have only 5K to go when someone beeps in and destroys both your connection AND your download, you'll understand why we suggest disabling call waiting. Is any phone call more important than Doom? We didn't think so.

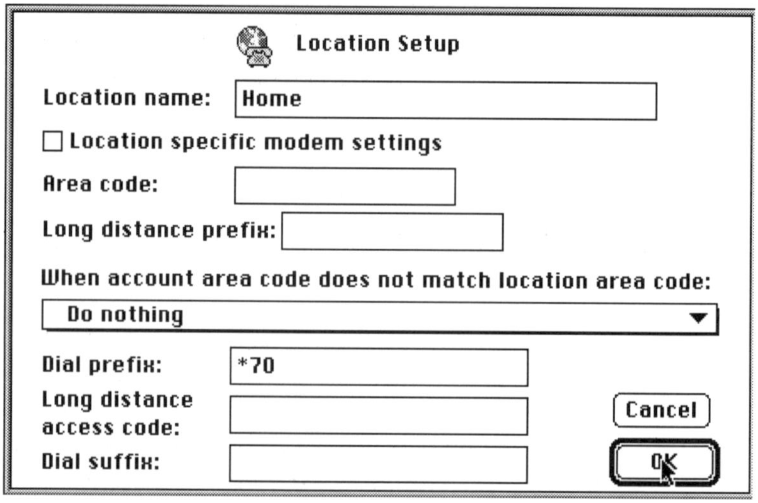

Figure 2.14: Location setup window.

Once you click on OK...wait...believe it or not...YOU'RE DONE. You can return to the FreePPP Setup page, click on the little triangle to condense the window, and then try to connect by clicking the Connect button. (Now that's what they mean when they say "intuitive.") Now is the time to find out if you're having any connection problems beyond busy phone lines and line noise. If you are, then reread this section on configuring FreePPP and if all else fails call your ISP. You may need some weird init string or modem configuration we couldn't have anticipated in a zillion years. Hopefully, though, if we're as good at this as we think we are, you'll be connected and ready to move onto the killer Internet apps you've been hearing so much about. Oh yeah, you don't have to go through this rigmarole every time you connect to the Net. Just go to the FreePPP menu bar icon and choose Open PPP Connection and you're ready to go. Conversely when you're tired of hanging out in front of your computer and are off to find a life, you can choose Close PPP Connection from the very same menu. It's so easy it's almost scary.

If you've set up your Mac using the information in this section you can skip all the way to the next chapter. See, perseverance does have its rewards.

A Little Help from Your Friendly ISP

We mentioned earlier that every ISP is just a little different and it is sometimes necessary to tweak your settings just right to connect. Anticipating this, many ISPs have their own installation packages that provide the software they recommend for use with their services, as well as a step-by-step guide or a preconfigured file to expedite getting your connection up and running. OuterNet, a local provider here in our excellent hometown, has such a package that doesn't miss a beat during the installation process. From the very first double click of the mouse on the installer you know what to expect (figure 2.15).

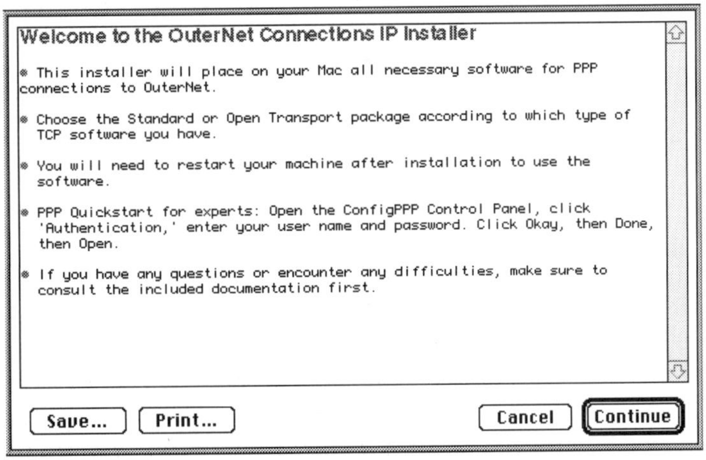

Figure 2.15: Outernet Installer instructions.

The installer application allows you to choose what tools are installed on your computer based on what version of the Mac OS you are running. If you aren't running 7.5.3 you install their preferred PPP software, but if you do have 7.5.3, and consequently Open Transport, you install the Open Transport configuration file. Once you have all the necessary equipment there is a nifty README file (Figure 2.16) that explains exactly, step-by-step, how to configure your connection on either system.

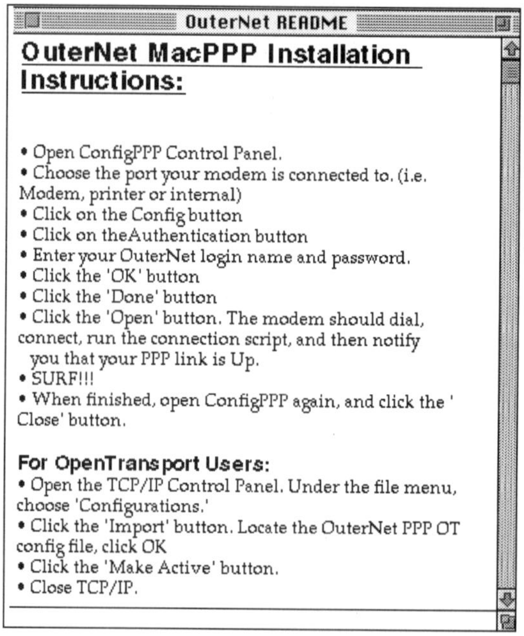
OuterNet README

OuterNet MacPPP Installation Instructions:

• Open ConfigPPP Control Panel.
• Choose the port your modem is connected to. (i.e. Modem, printer or internal)
• Click on the Config button
• Click on theAuthentication button
• Enter your OuterNet login name and password.
• Click the 'OK' button
• Click the 'Done' button
• Click the 'Open' button. The modem should dial, connect, run the connection script, and then notify you that your PPP link is Up.
• SURF!!!
• When finished, open ConfigPPP again, and click the ' Close' button.

For OpenTransport Users:
• Open the TCP/IP Control Panel. Under the file menu, choose 'Configurations.'
• Click the 'Import' button. Locate the OuterNet PPP OT config file, click OK
• Click the 'Make Active' button.
• Close TCP/IP.

Figure 2.16: OuterNet configuration instructions.

The TCP/IP configuration file is a perfect example of why such an installation package is so useful. Rather than entering your TCP/IP information yourself and running the risk of misconfiguring your setup, all you do is import the settings file provided for you and you're set. Even we can't make it simpler than that.

Hired Help: Commercial Packages and ISP Setups

It's pretty obvious that we advocate setting up your Internet connection yourself. Just in case you were a little intimidated by the whole process, or simply don't have time to fiddle with your computer for hours on end like we do, you can resort to one of the bundled Internet utility/connectivity packages available on the market. These packages do most of the work, with just a little input from you, and include whole suites of Internet applications to boot. While the market is swamped with packages of this sort we've chosen three to look at: Internet Valet, The Apple Internet Connection Kit, and Total Access. We were even kind enough to include Total Access on the CD-ROM.

Even though we've provided you with information about these three packages, you'll want to do a little research of your own before you commit the cash and purchase one. Each package contains different sets of applications, some better than others. Keep in mind that the minimum requirements for any package are just that, minimum. Plan on needing twice as much RAM and hard disk space to run any of the packages effectively. Honestly though, you can find all the applications you need on our CD-ROM and on the Internet itself, making it possible for you to create a custom Internet connection environment specifically suited to your needs.

Internet Valet

Software Ventures Corporation
2907 Claremont Avenue
Berkeley, CA 94705
510-644-3232
FAX: 510-848-0885
E-mail: valet-info@svcdudes.com
MSRP: $29.95
Minimum RAM required: 2MB
Disk storage required: 8MB
System required: 7 or higher

Internet Valet offers 14 days of free and unlimited use with PSI, a national ISP, and can also be configured for a PPP connection with any other ISP. A simple configuration utility that launches after installation spares users the sometimes frustrating setup of Mac TCP and PPP. The package includes tools for Web browsing, e-mail, news, FTP, gopher, and Telnet and makes all of them accessible on a handy floating pallet.

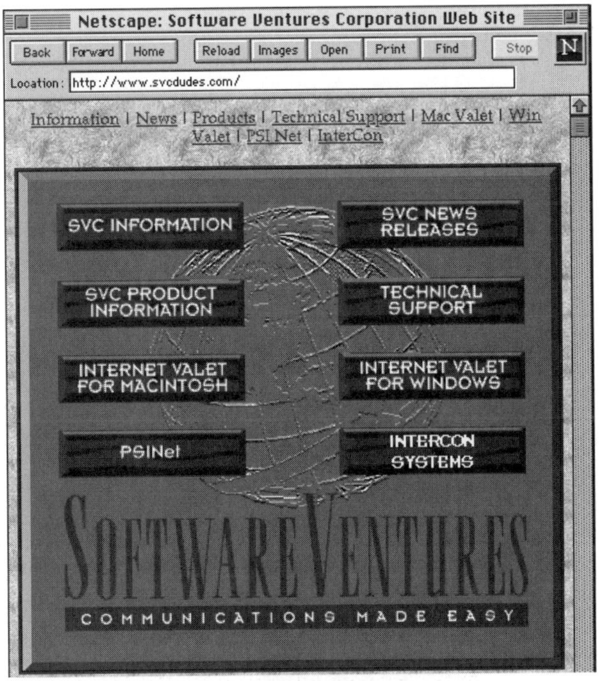

Figure 2.17: Software Ventures homepage at http://www.svcdudes .com/.

Apple Internet Connection Kit

Apple Computer, Inc.
1 Infinite Loop
Cupertino, CA 95014-2084
800-538-9696
FAX: 800-462-4396
MSRP: $50.00
Minimum RAM required: 8MB
Disk storage required: 10MB
System required: 7.5 or higher

Apple's connection package provides a good set of Internet tools (all of which you can download on the Net yourself, BTW) but has its share of connectivity problems. While it's relatively simple to connect directly from the software to one of the ISPs supported by Apple, connecting to any other has its difficulties. Still, there is something to be said about the convenience of having utilities for browsing, e-mail, news, FTP, compression, telnet, QuickTime, and PDF all in one place.

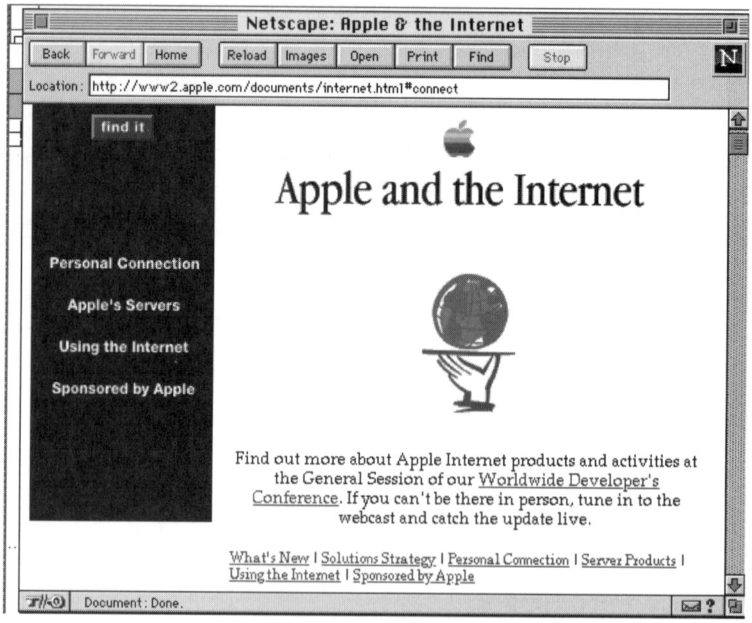

Figure 2.18: Apple Internet page at http://www2.apple.com/documents/Internet.html.

Total Access

EarthLink Network
3100 New York Drive
Pasadena, CA 91107
1-800-876-3151; 1-818-296-2400
Sales: 1-800-395-8425
MSRP: $25.00 setup fee; $19.95 per month unlimited access
Minimum RAM required: 2.5MB
Disk storage required: 7MB
System required: 7 or higher

Total Access is an example of a connection package specifically created by an ISP for connection to their services. EarthLink has reasonable rates and their connection software is simple and straightforward. A word of warning for all PowerPC/Open Transport users. Total Access is not compatible with OT and you will have to call EarthLink for instructions on how to configure your machine manually. They include a browser and e-mail as part of their setup. A credit card is necessary to sign up with EarthLink after installation.

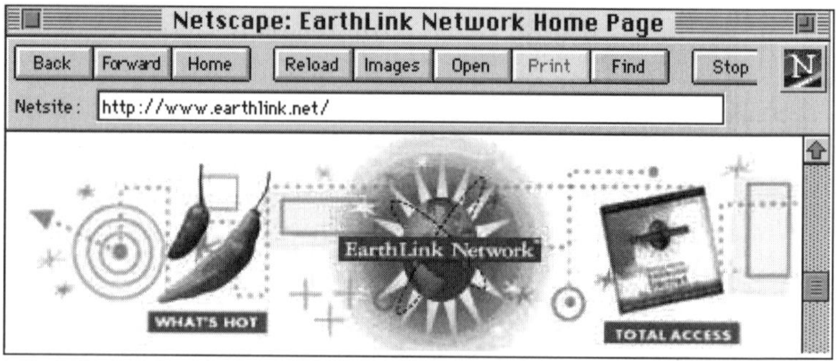

Figure 2.19: EarthLink homepage at http://www.earthlink.net.

Where to Turn for Help?

Help! The cry for mercy and relief is often screamed in vain, especially when you don't have this handy list we have so generously compiled for you. But before you rush off, consider what you need to know or do before you seek help.

- Make sure you have a real problem: Check to see that the problem is repeatable. Once you make that determination, write down the steps you need to make the problem occur.

- Know your system: A technical support representative will need information about your computer—its hardware components as well as setup and configuration.

- Know your enemy: The person you speak with on- or offline may not be the designer or programmer of the software which is causing you problems, so they are not responsible for the problem. They are there to help solve the problem. Don't take your wrath out on them. Try to make that person a partner instead of an enemy.

Now that you have a few simple ground rules regarding technical support, all you need to do is get some!

Online

The best Internet help is often available on the Internet. If your problem deals specifically with getting an initial connection, you should skip to the Offline section. If you are not familiar with any of the online services listed here, consult the next chapter, where we introduce each service and list some of the top utilities used to access them.

Web Sites

The World Wide Web is the largest collection of information available to anyone with an Internet connection. There is so much information that locating exactly what you need can sometimes be difficult. The key to finding relevant information on the Web is using search engines efficiently.

A search engine is a Web site that is designed to collect data about the information available on the Web and store it in a database. We introduce you to two of the larger search engines, Yahoo and AltaVista, in Chapter 4. Check 'em out. They make sorting the myriad Web information much easier.

When you access a search engine you provide a query string for which to search this stored database, and the background programs return matches. Each search engine on the Web (there are over 50) uses a different method to gather and search information. You should always use more than one engine when researching a topic. Here are a few points to keep in mind as you look for information:

- Be as specific as possible when providing search strings.
- Be sure to spell everything correctly and use proper capitalization.
- Try synonyms, related words, and even alternate the form of the words.
- Read the search tips provided by most engines geared specifically to the kind and organization of their information.

Some Internet-savvy software developers have created Web sites with good technical support information, and they may even list the URL in their documentation or README files on the diskettes or in the archives. Take a look through the materials available; you may save time by jumping straight to their site instead of searching worldwide.

E-mail : Tech Support

E-mail is not the most expeditious form of online technical support, mainly because you have to wait until the support staff reads your message and responds. Requesting information by e-mail can be very time-consuming and frustrating, especially if you have an emergency or are extremely impatient. We highly recommend looking for a Web site, Usenet postings, or even asking someone on IRC (see below) before seeking help by e-mail.

Once you decide e-mail is the way for you, you hit a significant roadblock: finding out the technical support e-mail address. Unless it is listed in the materials that came with the software, you probably will have better luck giving them a call and asking for the address instead of rooting around on the Net for it. On the other hand, if you are going to call them anyway, why not go ahead and talk with them on the phone?

E-mail: Listservs

Unlike e-mail to tech support, e-mail to a listserv can provide both timely and accurate answers to just about any problem. A listserv is a remailer that takes an e-mail message sent to an address and forwards it to anyone subscribed to the listserv. There are listservs for just about anything, from computers to ancient history. Listservs are similar to Usenet in that they create a community of people with a common interest in discussing issues, trends, problems, and solutions. They are different from Usenet because they are e-mail based and can have criteria for subscribing and posting. Most of the time you must be a list subscriber to post messages. This makes a good case for subscribing before you actually have a problem so you are familiar with the other members of the list, as well as the culture of the list. Many listservs are moderated to keep discussions focused on the list topic. Quite often if you have a problem you can send a message to the list and begin to receive replies within the next few minutes, especially if your situation is urgent. Someone on the list may have had the same problem and can tell you in no time flat how to fix it. For a searchable, comprehensive list of listservs point your browser at Liszt **(http://www.liszt.com/)**.

Usenet

Usenet postings can often get your answers immediately, especially if others have encountered similar problems and have posted the information for all to see. To look for technical support information Usenet, you'll need to locate one or more relevant newsgroups and then find and read their FAQs. Once you are familiar with the topics of a group and the etiquette for postings, you can search through the thousands of message headers looking for a keyword or phrase. (Most Usenet utilities provide a FIND function to look for keywords in the header and sometimes even the message body.) If your search proves successful, great; but if you don't find anything relevant, you may need to post a request.

Always be sure you are complying with the guidelines of a newsgroup's FAQ limitations before attempting to post. Improper postings can result in e-mail floods, flaming, bad karma, and even quivering in small animals. Post a short direct message requesting help or information, give it a focused heading with good keywords, and indicate the preferred means of contact—either by a follow-up Usenet posting or by e-mail. Now wait; you'll need to check your e-mail or the newsgroup periodically to see if anyone was kind enough to answer your plea. If you do receive several responses via e-mail, it is always polite to post a follow-up message summarizing the responses you received and how you ultimately solved your problem, so other can benefit from your newfound knowledge.

IRC

IRC (Internet Relay Chat) provides one of the quickest and most enjoyable methods of getting help and information, but the reliability of the information you get can be highly questionable. On IRC you can "chat" with people from all over the world, in any age group and with many levels of computer knowledge. Take time to look for a channel which is close to the subject you need help with. Then join the channel and read the conversations. If your request falls in line with the tone of the current channel environment, ask your question. Be prepared to be ignored or given false information. You'll need to use common sense and caution when following information gained via IRC. There are no truth restrictions on IRC, so anyone can mislead you about anything. But don't let this discourage you; many people enjoy providing solid information and relevant help to others. With luck, you will encounter such an entity.

Offline

Getting help offline for a computer-related problem is similar to getting help about any other type of service or product—you either make a call, go to a place of business, read a book, or talk to a friend.

Tech Support

Tech support is often given a bad rap; however, this is not necessarily the fault of the technician who handles your call. Here are a few things to keep in mind when contacting technical support by phone:

- Make sure you contact the right tech support for the right problem. Don't call 1-800-SOS-APPL with a Netscape problem.
- Speak clearly and be polite.
- Answer all questions as specifically and directly as possible—it is OK to say, "I don't know."
- Be prepared to be put on hold for as long as it takes.
- Write down the solution or information given to you.

You can usually find technical support numbers in the product's documentation. Other places to search are computer magazines or books with vendor glossaries. You can also try calling local computer stores or national information (1-900-555-1212) to ask for a number, if you know the company name.

Local Computer Sales and Repair

Most local computer software stores and computer hardware repair centers have well-trained staff members who may be able to help you. But since computer repair and sales are their business, they may not want to give free help over the phone. Take a walk through your yellow pages for computer retail and service/repair shops near you.

Books

There are hundreds of great books about troubleshooting and repairing computers. Many are focused on a single computer platform or product, which makes their content highly relevant. If you don't already have a few good general computer reference or repair books handy, it's a good idea to see what your bookstore carries. With the wide variety of software and hardware available today, it is difficult to recommend a single title that encompasses all the materials we discuss in this book. Speak with one of the salespersons at your bookstore and ask if they have materials which relate to your system and products.

Geeks, Dweebs, the Kid Down the Street, and Other Experts

The Internet is a breeding ground for "geeks." Almost anyone associated with computers, communications, and high-end business has to have contact with and knowledge of the Internet. You probably know a few of these people: they are in your office, down the street, or the kid in your upstairs bedroom. Never underestimate the fortitude of a young genius who spends all day in front of the game box. He may already know the solution to your problem and can fix it before you can blink. They have something weird going on in their genetic code.

If all these support avenues fail, you are beyond help. Give it up and go home. Oh wait, you are home....

chapter 3

Surf's Up

Finding the Right Board for the Right Wave

Because we are equal opportunity cliché abusers (and frankly we're bored with the information superhighway thing) we turn to the "surfin' the Net" metaphor to provide us with a vehicle (oops!) for discussing the installation and configuration, of Internet service utilities. Before you run away screaming at the mere mention of installation or configuration, be comforted—compared to getting connected to the Internet your next few setups are a piece of cake.

The Internet is an ocean of information and your Internet service utilities are your surfboard. So what exactly do we mean when we say Internet service utilities? These are the applications that give you access to one of the many Internet services, like FTP, e-mail, and the Web. There are as many of these utilities out there as there are fish in the sea—OK, maybe not quite that many, but sometimes it seems like it—with more being tossed into the fray each day. Our self-appointed duty in this chapter is to help you wade through the numerous utilities without getting pulled under. We will look at the major Internet services and the best utilities available to access them, and even help you through the installation and configuration processes.

When the first utilities were created and released they tended to focus on one particular Internet service, such as Web browsing. The latest trend in utility development is creating applications that give you access to multiple services in one package. This approach definitely has its good and bad aspects. The old saying "jack of all trades but master of none" is a good way to describe some of these multipurpose packages. While they do lots of things, they don't do any of them particularly well. The question then becomes, do you want to have one so-so Internet utility package that does it all or several well-focused, high-quality ones? Granted, configuration of one package is definitely easier than configuration of six or seven, and the utilities in a multipurpose package are all designed to work together, reducing the chances of conflict significantly. We will look at utilities that fall into both categories and you will be able to choose the ones that fit your needs and quirks best. The sky—or rather your hard disk space—is the limit.

Surfing 101: The Basics

There are a few terms and concepts you need to be familiar with before you dive head first into the Internet. After all, you wouldn't try to catch a wave without knowing which end of your board was up.

URLs

You know that the Internet is a worldwide network of computers that speak a common language, TCP/IP. From all the hype about the Internet you suspect that there is an enormous amount of information to be found and fun to be had. You're right. The question now is how do you get to the goods? To access any information on the Internet you need to know its Uniform Resource Locator (URL). A URL is the address of any give file on the Internet, comprised of several different parts, in a particular order, just like an address on a postal letter. Let's dissect this particular URL to see how it works.

http://www.w3.org:80/hypertext/WWW/Addressing/Addressing.html#top

|-1-|--2–|-3|——4——|—5—|-6-|

There are six pieces to this URL:

1. Protocol/data type

   This will be the name of the protocol or service types used to access the data. The protocols you may come across include:

   - ftp://—FTP or file transfer resource
   - gopher://—gopher resource
   - http://—hypertext http resource, i.e., a Web document
   - mailto://—causes a compatible browser to launch an e-mail utility
   - news://—Usenet newsgroup
   - telnet://—causes a compatible browser to launch a Telnet utility
   - WAIS://—a WAIS resource, which is usually spawned off to a helper application
   - file:///—indicates a local file with syntax: file:///<drive name>|/<path>/<filename>

2. Domain name
   The domain name of the host computer.

3. Port address
   In most cases, port addresses are automatically selected by the protocol/data type being used. However, when a port is specifically listed it is wise to include it.

4. Directory path
   The directory path, document tree, or symbolic pathway.

5. Object name
   This is the actual name of the file, object, or resource.

6. Spot
   This indicates a specific internal anchor within a Web document. It allows direct linkage to a point within a long document.

You are probably asking yourself why we spent so much energy going into gory detail about the guts of a URL. On occasion you may have to parse the URL, i.e., break the URL down into its component parts, to use some utilities. Most Web browsers can handle all of the URL types we just listed, which means you can cut and paste a full URL into the browser to load the document or resource. However, many Internet service utilities are not able to use a fully qualified URL; you have to break the URL down manually and feed it bit by bit to the utility. For example, some FTP utilities cannot use the URL `ftp://ftp.netscape.com/navigator/3.0/3.0b4/mac/standard/Netscape3.0b4Installer.hqx`.

Instead, you first have to connect to the site ftp.netscape.com, change directories until you reach /navigator/3.0/3.0b4/mac/standard/, then select and retrieve the file "Netscape3.0b4Installer.hqx." Luckily, most Web browsers can read the entire URL and FTP the file right to your desktop. Score one for multipurpose utilities.

Network Load: She Canna' Go Any Faster, Captain

"Network load" is the term used to describe the condition of a network (or a portion of it) when it is working at full or near full capacity. Network load results in local (if not overall) slower performance and response time. The Internet is a mind-bogglingly huge network with uncountable connections and routes through which to direct information. As a whole, the Internet is able to handle just about any amount of use and abuse thrown at it. But individual computers and subsections of the Internet can experience network load when too many users try to access the same resources. When this occurs, communication can become slow or completely interrupted. In fact, so much network load can be placed on some systems that it causes them to disconnect themselves from the Internet altogether or "fail"—obviously, this is not a good thing. You will encounter Internet network load during your surfing—it's a fact, so prepare yourself for it.

Just as Panama City Beach, New Orleans, and Colorado get overcrowded at especially popular times of the year (spring break, Mardi Gras, and winter), so, too, an Internet site can be so popular that it becomes too busy to let you in. When this occurs you will experience: 1) extremely long transmission times, 2) interrupted and canceled transmissions, or 3) service time-outs, 4) messages about the current load, or 5) no information or access to a site whatsoever. When you encounter network load, you have a few options in dealing with it: 1) wait and try again later, 2) look for an alternate site or mirror, 3) give up. Usually, you will encounter network load only around extremely popular sites or locations where new software has just been released (e.g., Netscape and Microsoft).

Also keep in mind that the speed of the computer being used to serve up information, as well as the speed of your computer and connection, affects download time. As you spend more time on the Internet you will discover those sites that are notoriously slow, which mirrors are the best for downloading the latest beta version of this or that, and when the low traffic times are—here's a hint: during single-digit hours in the AM.

Mirrors

Many Internet FTP sites which experience a high level of network load are often mirrored. To mirror a site is to dynamically copy the contents of one system to another, creating an exact duplicate of the original. Most mirrors are automatically updated on a daily or weekly basis. Often, when you try to gain access to an FTP site which is too busy to grant entry, the system's mirror sites will be listed. Simply use one of the mirror domain names or IP address to gain access to the files located elsewhere on the Internet. Throughout the rest of this chapter we'll frequently refer you to the major archive sites, all of which are mirrored in several other places. So that we only have to do this once, here is a good list of software-rich FTP sites:

mirrors.aol.com

mirror.apple.com

wuarchive.wustl.edu

sumex-aim.stanford.edu

ftp.amug.org

ftp.pht.com

Internet Service Utilities

You have a connection, some basic knowledge, and a burning desire to surf. The only thing left is to assemble your personal suite of Internet service utilities, configured for maximum comfort and ease. We have included a set of utilities on the CD-ROM accompanying this book, but will by no means limit our discussion to these few. As you peruse the information on specific utilities for each service you will find:

- A general description of the utility, the current version at publication time, the system requirements to run it, and where to find it (on or off our CD-ROM)
- A glance at any nifty features it might have
- Things we like and things we don't like about it (in our not-so-humble opinions)
- Installation and configuration instructions
- A few handy tricks and tips we've come across—learn from our mistakes and accidental discoveries

I Know It's There: Why Your Hard Drive Should Not Look Like Your Bedroom

Now is as good a time as any for us to revert to parent mode and give you the "clean your room" lecture. Seriously, though, you are about to enter a whole new realm where an incalculable amount of cool, and maybe even useful, software is just waiting for you. But, if your hard disk is mess and you have so many files and folders on your desktop you can't even see your background pattern, you need to take a few minutes and clean house. After all, if you can't find your copy of the latest "killer app" what good will it do you?

For now you may just want to create a couple of basic folders for Internet applications and offline utilities. Later, when you start to accumulate more and more files, you will probably want to break these down even further, depending on your own sense of organization. The other folder we recommend you create is a downloads or temporary folder. Almost all the utilities we will be discussing allow you to designate where the information you retrieve from the Internet goes, and, if you don't, they all have a nasty habit of hiding it from you in the deep, dark recesses of your drive. If all of your downloads end up in one place on your hard drive you will never have to search in vain for the file you just waited three hours for.

General Installation Instructions

If you are retrieving files from the Internet they will most likely be self-extracting archives. This means that when you run, open, or execute them they automatically decompress their contents, usually creating multiple files. You may have begun with "app.bin.hqx" and ended up with "app.bin," "app.sea," and the actual installer as well. See why we recommended a good hard drive organization scheme? In the downloads folder you have the original file plus any other files it creates to get to the installer. When you run the installer program you direct it to install the application in the Internet utilities folder, and when the installation is complete you can trash everything in the downloads folder, secure in the knowledge you're not throwing out anything the application needs to run.

The nice thing about installation programs is that they put all the right parts in all the right places. Some programs don't have installer programs but do include specific directions on how to install the application correctly. Read the manual or you'll be sorry. Now is also a good time to mention how important it is to install an application rather than copy an already installed application from another source. Quite often there are extensions or additions to your system folder you don't even know about that are integral to the functionality of the application, and if you don't have them it might not work at all.

Some files will also automatically start their own install/setup program after decompressing themselves; many companies are incorporating this feature into their latest releases of software. If in the installation instructions for a utility, we state that you have to execute the install/setup program, but the self-extracting archive does it on its own, don't be alarmed, be happy. This is evidence that the software company is making their software easier to use—an end devoutly to be wished.

On occasion a file will not be uncompressed after you download it and you will have to do it yourself, which is not a big deal thanks to a whole host of freeware and shareware utilities. In the section on offline utilities we'll take a closer look at these must-have compression tools.

Remember when you installed your connection software? What comes after installation? You got it, setup and configuration. On to the fun stuff.

The World Wide Web

The World Wide Web is the most versatile, powerful, and popular Internet service. It is a standardized method of accessing and transmitting Internet resources with a wonderful, colorful, and easy-to-use GUI (graphic user interface). This interface, called a Web browser, has the ability (or at least the potential) to handle every type of resource on the Internet, either through built-in support, the use of a plug-in, or via some of the helper applications we're going to describe shortly.

How to Use the Web

Web browsers access the information on the Internet by using URLs (remember those?) and are designed to parse a URL automatically, grab the information, and display it for you. Usually you can cut and paste a URL into the "open location" window or the location bar to access whatever the URL has to offer.

The browsers listed here will load their company's homepage the first time they are used. Often there is a "getting started" page or hotlist of cool sites to visit. Just in case you don't find what you want on the preloaded homepage, take a look at the section in which we discuss search engines.

Web Browsers

Netscape

Netscape is the number one Web browser in use today, even though it wasn't the first to be developed. Designed by Netscape Communications Corporation, it is available either as an off-the-shelf software product or as a downloadable shareware product. Netscape is free to educational institutions and other nonprofit organizations, as detailed in their licensing agreement. Unlike many Internet utilities, Netscape is available for almost all platforms, from Macintosh to UNIX, and all the screwy Windoze versions in between.

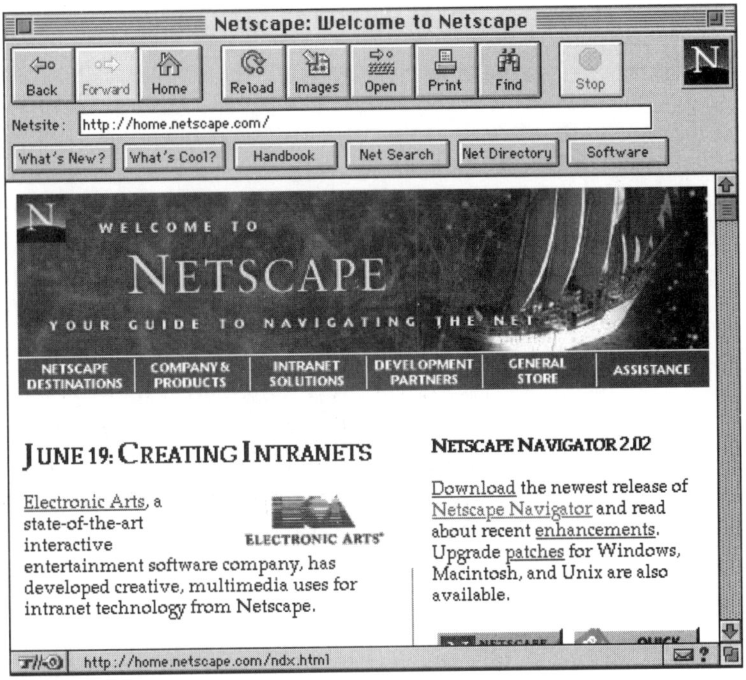

Figure 3.1: Netscape Navigator 2.0.

VERSION AND SYSTEM REQUIREMENTS

The current full release version is 2.0, although the 3.04 beta is available for use at your own risk. Unless you are very familiar with the Mac OS, are comfortable resolving conflicts and troubleshooting, and don't mind frequent system crashes, we suggest you avoid beta releases as they are often more trouble than they are worth. Netscape 2.0 requires a 68K-based computer or better, running system 7 or later, 4MB of RAM required with 8MB recommended, and 2MB of disk space.

WHERE TO FIND IT

We have included Netscape Navigator on the CD-ROM, but in case you don't have a CD-ROM drive (how do you manage to survive?) you can obtain the browser from the Netscape Web site if you have any other Web browser: http://home.netscape.com/comprod/mirror/index.html. If you have only an FTP utility, you can retrieve Netscape from ftp.netscape.com or one of the mirrors. The Netscape software sites are high-traffic areas. If the site is too busy, it will give you a list of alternate sites where the software can be found. Your best time to grab the software is between the hours of 11 PM and 7 AM.

NIFTY FEATURES

Netscape has hundreds of built-in features, not to mention its numerous configurations with add-ons, plug-ins, and helper applications. Instead of listing them all, which is done at: `http://home.netscape.com/comprod/products/navigator/version_2.0/datasheet.html` We have included just a few highlights.

Netscape 2.0 has an advanced bookmark utility, supports multiple simultaneous windows, has streaming audio and video support, intelligent e-mail capabilities, Usenet threading and posting, security, drag and drop compatibility, Java support, and is able to send and receive files.

WHY WE LIKE IT

Netscape is easy to use, simple to master, and looks nice without sacrificing speed, features, or compatibility. Why anyone would even consider using any other browser is a mystery we may never solve. Everything we can think of or would want in a browser Netscape has and does it with style. Some of our favorite features are spawned FTP sessions, fast page display, and file upload capabilities.

WHAT WE DON'T LIKE

We found it hard to name anything about the Netscape Navigator we are displeased with. However, as we didn't want to give you the idea it was perfect, we came up with a few things we think are missing. Netscape does not have a lifetime history file, only a current session history file. An old version of Netscape did have a lifetime history file, but obviously that wasn't a hereditary feature. This makes locating that one page you saw last week impossible unless you added it to your bookmark list (which you didn't since you didn't think it was that important at the time). Netscape has also opted not to include any local help files, not even operational basics. If you want help you have to go online and access their Web site's database of help files, and they are often more confusing than helpful. You can purchase the commercial or "Gold" version to get a printed manual (and don't forget the shiny box!), but we prefer having something useful in that little Help menu item other than site links.

INSTALLATION AND CONFIGURATION

Installing Netscape is about as hard as microwaving a TV dinner. Double click on the installer icon, choose easy install from the drop-down menu in the upper left-hand corner, select the folder you want the application to live in, and let the installer do its "thang." You don't have to restart your machine after installing Netscape and the browser starts up automatically after install. A window pops up that allows you to continue your setup now, continue your setup later, or skip the whole thing by never seeing the message again. The last option is the best choice. Their setup process is designed to sell you more Netscape stuff, ours is designed to get you up and running as quickly as possible.

With the evolution of each version of Netscape the interface has changed a little but the basic functions are still there. Even if you are brave and are configuring one of the current beta releases, the following configuration guidelines should still apply. The setup we outline below is based on our personal preferences for browsing. As you spend more time on the Web you may find any one of several variations to be more your style. Don't be afraid to experiment with, and change, your configuration. One of a browser's biggest advantages is the ability to let the user create a custom environment for viewing and retrieving information.

1. Run the browser.

2. The first time you run the browser the licensing agreement will appear. Read it, and then click on Accept.

3. Make the browser window whatever size works for you.

4. Chose General Preferences under the Options menu.

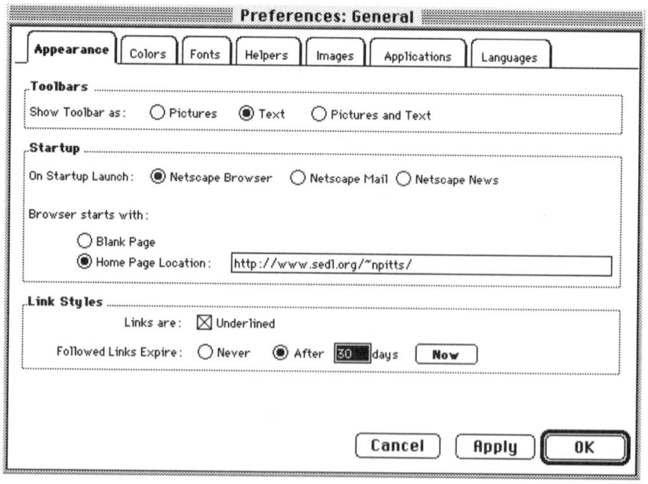

Figure 3.2: Netscape Navigator General Preferences window, Appearance tab.

5. In the **Appearance** section choose the options that you are most comfortable with. We suggest

   Toolbar: Text

   Startup: Netscape Browser and a blank page

   Links: Your call. We prefer ours to be underlined and to expire after 5 days, just in case we have to retrace our steps somewhere a day or two after an initial visit.

6. Don't change anything under the **Color** tab.

7. If you have a hard time reading small type or text on a screen, you may want to enlarge your font size or change your type face for easier viewing in the **Font** section. We recommend Times 14.

8. The **Helpers** settings will take care of themselves for now, so leave them as they are.

9. Under the **Images** tab make sure the "While Loading" radial button is selected.

10. The choices you make in the **Applications** tab will affect almost every browser session you have. You can choose Browse to select any application from your hard drive. Your Telnet application will most likely be NCSA Telnet 2.6, available on the CD-ROM. Don't worry if you don't have a TN3270 application, it's not necessary really. The text editor is a different story. Whenever you choose Document Source from the View menu in Netscape it will use the application you've selected here. We recommend you use a good editor such as BBedit Lite, available from Bare Bones Software at http://www.barebones.com/. Simple Text and Teach Text, the two editors that come with the Mac OS, have very limited functionality and can't

handle large files but will do in a pinch. Finally, choose your download file. This is where Netscape will put any information it retrieves from the Internet for you. We suggest selecting the downloads folder (we discussed this earlier, remember?) so you can always find stuff no matter how many thousands of files you've downloaded or how late at night it is.

11. If you are reading this book you don't need to change any options under the **Languages** tab.

12. Click on OK.

13. In the Options menu open the Mail and News Preferences.

14. The **Appearance** tab needs no changes.

15. Select the **Composition** tab.

16. In the boxes labeled "By default, e-mail a copy of outgoing message to:" place your e-mail address.

17. Select the **Servers** tab.

18. Fill in the correct domain names or IP numbers for your SMTP and POP servers.

19. If you plan on using Netscape as your e-mail utility, you should fill out the rest of the Mail section according to the information provided by your ISP and your preferences.

20. Fill in the correct domain name or IP number for your NNTP server.

21. Select the **Identity** tab.

22. Fill in the information about yourself.

23. If you have already created a signature file, add its pathname with the Browse button. (The signature file will be attached to all outgoing e-mail or newsgroup messages.)

24. If you are using Netscape as an e-mail utility and/or newsreader, you can configure the **Organization** tag to your preferences.

25. Click OK.

26. If you want a larger memory or disk cache, change the settings under the Options Network Preferences **Cache** tab.

27. No changes are needed in the Security Preferences.

28. Deselect the Show Directory Buttons line from the Options pull-down menu.

29. Verify that Auto Load Images is selected on the Options pull-down menu.

30. Select Save Options from the Options menu.

Wasn't that fun—not. But then again, waxing a surfboard isn't the most exciting way to spend an afternoon, but no self-respecting surfer would hit the waves without taking the time to do it.

HOW TO USE IT:

Getting Started: Netscape is a graphical Web browser that allows you to select hyperlinks on screen using a pointing device to jump anywhere and everywhere on the Web. But you do have to start somewhere—click on File Open

Location from the menu bar. In the pop-up box type: "http://www.yahoo.com." (See Search Engines for detailed instructions on the use of Yahoo!) Now you are surfing!

Bookmarks: Bookmarks, sometimes called a hotlist, are stored URLs listed in a pull-down menu. Bookmarks allow you to save the address of a page to which you want to return in the future. Simply click on Bookmarks, and choose Add Bookmark to add the currently open page to your list. Do that now to add Yahoo! to your bookmarks. Now every time you want to revisit Yahoo!, just click on Bookmarks and select the name Yahoo! on the menu. If you need to edit or remove a bookmark, click on Bookmarks and choose Go To Bookmarks; there is a help file there if you need instructions.

HINTS AND TIPS:

Go Home: To get to the Netscape homepage, just click on the "N" icon in the upper right corner beside the location box.

More Menus: Clicking and holding your mouse button down over the browser, you should get a context-based pop-up menu. You can use these menus to "steal" images, download pages, open new browser windows, navigate, and even add bookmarks. Try it, you'll like it!

Mail and Print: From the File menu, you can e-mail a page and its URL to anyone or you can print it, including the graphics, to your local printer.

On Screen Text Selection: One great feature Netscape has adopted is allowing you to highlight or select text within the display window and copy it (<Command-C>) onto the clipboard (from which you can paste it into any other application, usually with <Command-V>).

STOP!: The small stop sign icon has two useful purposes. First, as long as a page is being loaded, it will remain red. Second, when the icon is red, you can click on it to halt the loading, which will allow the browser to display information it has already received.

Images: Images are vastly huge; often the graphics of a page are 100 to 10,000 times the size of the HTML code used to lay out the page. You can speed up the display of the textual portion of a page by turning off the Auto Load Images in the Option menu. If you need to see the images, such as imagemaps or navigation icons, click on the Load Images button or hold the mouse button down over an image and select Load this Image. (The Load Images button is the one with the arrow pointing at an empty graphic icon, right below the Bookmark menu item.)

Microsoft Internet Explorer

Microsoft's entry into the Internet browser race has made a good first showing. Not to be outdone by Netscape, Microsoft has added their own proprietary HTML tags as well as support for most of the popular Netscape extensions. With eyes on controlling the Web as they do the desktop, Microsoft is sure to build power and versatility into their "end-all-be-all" Web browser.

Figure 3.3: Microsoft Internet Explorer 2.01.

VERSION AND SYSTEM REQUIREMENTS

Internet Explorer's current release version is 2.01. It requires a 68K-based machine or better, 8MB of RAM, and 2–4MB of hard disk space. As usual there are new beta versions released pretty regularly and we issue the same caveats as we did for Netscape betas.

WHERE TO FIND IT

You can obtain Internet Explorer from the Microsoft Web site: http://www.microsoft.com/mac/ie/iexplorer.htm. You will need a Web browser to access this page. If you have only an FTP utility, you can retrieve Internet Explorer from ftp.microsoft.com in directory /Softlib/MSLFILES/. Take note that this is a heavily used host and getting connected may be impossible during peak hours.

NIFTY FEATURES

The Microsoft Internet Explorer is a full-featured Web browser, complying with the current standards of HTML and HTTP. With support for most of the HTML 3.0 proposed standards (tables, figures, and math), multimedia (sound, video, VRML), Usenet, and FTP, there is little you will be unable to accomplish with this puppy.

A rather cool extra from IE is the integration of True Type fonts with the Web browser. Previously there was no way for a Web designer to choose what font or fonts their Web page was displayed in. This additional capability promises to add an entirely new dimension to page design.

For all the information about Internet Explorer that is fit to publish (and even some that's not) see http://www.microsoft.com/windows/ie/ieinfo.htm.

WHY WE LIKE IT

Internet Explorer does a very good job of supporting the current HTML standards while pushing the envelope with new features such as the True Type font implementation, mentioned above, the use of sound, and integration of Java applets. Another kudo to Microsoft for not letting the non-standard bells and whistles interfere with the transmission of standard HTML-compliant pages.

WHAT WE DON'T LIKE

We don't like Microsoft's reckless renaming of standard Internet concepts, especially those related to the Web. In Milord Gates' crusade to rule not only the desktop but everything it comes in contact with, Microsoft has gone too far in redefining terms. One of the most annoying examples of this is calling hypertext links "shortcuts." (A shortcut is a faster way to get somewhere, a hypertext link is the direct path to the resource—anyone not working for Microsoft can see the difference.)

INSTALLATION AND CONFIGURATION

Once again after you download the installer just double click on its icon and let the program go to work. Open the application and get comfortable, we have some more surf-board waxing to do.

1. From the Edit menu choose Options.

2. Load the Web site you want the browser to access automatically each time it opens. Make it tasteful, http://www.playboy.com just implies bad things to the uninitiated. Really mom, it's just a place to start, and we only read the articles. Yeah, right.

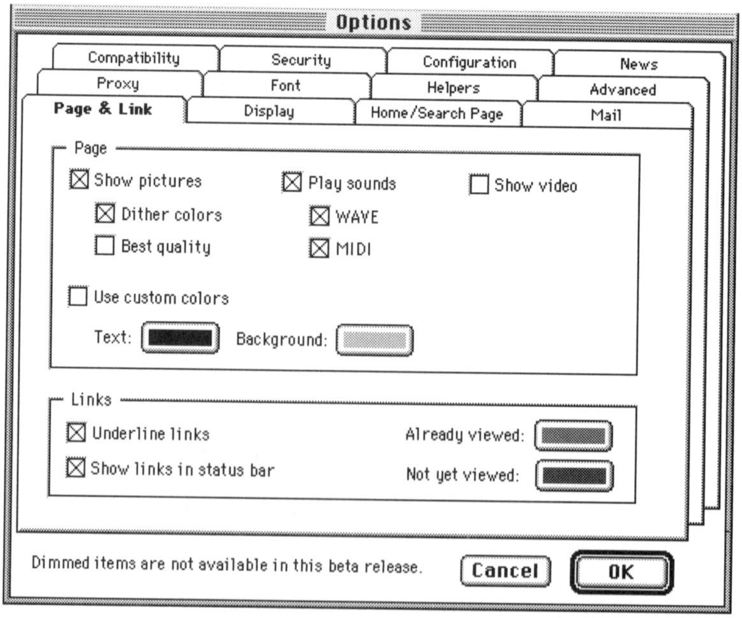

Figure 3.4: Internet Explorer Options window.

3. In the **Page & Link** window select:

   Show Pictures: Dither colors.

   Play Sounds: Both WAVE and MIDI.

   Links: Underline Links

4. Under the **Display** tab choose your reformatting preference based on your connection speed. 14.4K modems and slower should reformat after each image is loaded. In the User Interface section select Show Tool Bar, Show Address Bar, and Show Status Bar.

5. The **Home/Search Page** tab allows you to preconfigure your default homepage and default search page. In the drop-down menu choose Home Page and then click the Use Current button. Click on OK, load the URL of your favorite search site, return to this tab in the Options window, and click the Use Current button.

6. If you plan on using Internet Explorer as your mail program as well (hint: just say no), enter your mail server and personal information under the **Mail** tab.

7. No need to mess with the **Proxy** or **Helpers** tab, doing something wrong in either may only make your life more complicated.

8. The **Font** tab does what it says, so change your display font if you are so inclined.

9. In the **Advanced** tab:

   History: pick a reasonable number between 50 and 500, say 250 or so.

   Cache: select once per session, a full cache can stop you dead in the water.

Size: 5% of your hard disk is plenty.

Connections: definitely support multiple connections, six or so should meet your needs.

10. Don't bother with the **Compatibility, Security, and Configuration** tabs, they're still in the works.

11. If you would like to view Usenet newsgroups with Internet Explorer, you will need to check the top box to activate this tab page. If you do so, you will need to fill in all the information about your NNTP news server.

HOW TO USE IT

Getting Started: Internet Explorer will load the start page you defined in the configuration steps—or the default Microsoft IE homepage—when the browser is opened. Once the page loads, you are ready to surf! You can load new pages by clicking on hyperlinks or using the Open command from the File menu and typing in a URL.

Bookmarks: Microsoft has once again renamed a standard concept: the Internet Explorer bookmark list is called Favorites. Under this menu you can add the current page to the list or jump to the master bookmark/favorite folder to edit or delete saved locations.

HINTS AND TIPS

Go Home: To get to the Microsoft Internet Explorer homepage, all you need to do is hit the home icon on the button bar. However, if in configuring Explorer you changed the start page, you will need to click on the Use Default button in the **Start and Search Pages** tab of the Options window under the View menu to reset the start page. A third way to get home is by accessing the main Microsoft Web site at http:/www.microsoft.com and following the Internet Explorer links.

More Menus: Hold the mouse button down over any part of the browser display window to get a context-sensitive pop-up menu. You can add pages to your list of favorites, view the source, save a links target to disk, grab an image, and even set an image as your desktop wallpaper.

STOP!: The stop button is the page with the red "X" on it. (You'd think they could make something this simple easy to recognize, but, no, Microsoft has to be different.)

Images: One feature that Microsoft got right is displaying all the textual portion of a page before starting to retrieve the graphics or other resources embedded in a Web document. However, if you still want to turn off the auto-load function, go back to the **Appearance** tab in the Options window under the View menu. From this tab page you can turn off the automatic loading of images, sounds, and animations.

Mosaic

Mosaic was the original graphical browser for the World Wide Web developed by NCSA. Over the last three years, it has continued to develop and adapt to changes in the Web landscape (mainly caused by Netscape). Today, Mosaic is still a solid Web browser which has been cloned by over a dozen companies. No list of graphical Web browsers would not be complete without a look at one of the direct descendants of the first-generation Mosaic.

Figure 3.5: Mosaic Web browser.

VERSION AND SYSTEM REQUIREMENTS

The latest release version of Mosaic is 2.0.1, followed by a 3.0.2 beta release that is still buggy. 2.0.1 requires a 68K-based machine or better, system 7 or later, 6MB of RAM, and an unspecified amount of hard disk space, probably 8MB or so to be safe.

WHERE TO FIND IT

The Mosaic for Macintosh page is at http://www.ncsa.uiuc.edu/SDG/Software/MacMosaic/. From this page you can retrieve the release or beta version of the software as well as keep track of the latest Mac-specific goings-on from the Mosaic developers. If you are using an FTP client you can grab the file at ftp://ftp.ncsa.uiuc.edu/ in the /Mac/Mosaic directory.

NIFTY FEATURES

Along with being fully standards-compliant, Mosaic has not been left behind in the race to have more features than a Swiss Army knife. Mosaic's long list of features includes: e-mail, newsgroup and FTP support, hotlist management, auto-surfing, and in window pop-up menus. Mosaic also sports a movable navigation bar, so you can have your forward, back, home, stop, and bookmarks wherever you dang well please on your desktop.

WHY WE LIKE IT

Mosaic is a solid well-featured browser—while it can't do everything, it does what it does very well. The pull down menus are detailed and context sensitive. For example, some of the commands in the pop-up menu are page header and anchor information, saving a background image, and on-the-fly font alterations. There is both local and online help; just select one from the Help command. We also have to say that NCSA's commitment to ensuring there will always be a free browser for education that is comparable to commercial browsers is worth noticing and applauding.

WHAT WE DON'T LIKE

As with Netscape, we have to be picky to list our dislikes of the Mosaic browser. Mosaic does not have a lifetime history list and does not yet have security support. Mosaic also handles FTP transfers internally instead of spawning a separate process, so you cannot continue surfing while downloading a file.

INSTALLATION AND CONFIGURATION

We bet you can't guess how to install Mosaic. Go ahead, give it your best shot. You got it—double click on the installer. Let us all pause for a moment of silence to reflect on the beautiful simplicity of our chosen operating system.

Configuring Mosaic is a little different from configuring Netscape or Internet Explorer but definitely not any harder. We must admit there's very little about this browser you can't alter, so we'll only dwell on the essential features.

1. Run the browser.

2. Resize the browser window to your personal preference.

3. Select Options Preferences.

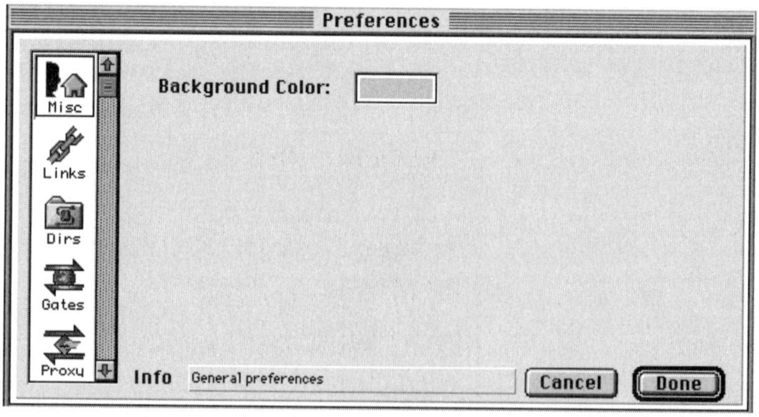

Figure 3.6: Mosaic Preferences window.

4. In the **Misc** window double click on the color sample if you want to change your default background color.

5. Your **Links** preferences are pretty standard:

   Underline Hotlinks

Dim Hotlink colors with age (cool, huh?)

Remove files from Global History somewhere between 10 and 15 days

6. In the **Dirs** window the only change you need to make is to the temporary directory. Click on the Set Temp Directory button and select the downloads or temporary directory we told you to create earlier.

7. The **Gates, Proxy, and Cache** settings are fine as they are.

8. The **IC** window gives you a place to fill in some info about you as well as your e-mail and news server addresses if you intend to run either or both of those services from within the Mosaic browser.

9. Click on Done and open the Styles window under the Options menu.

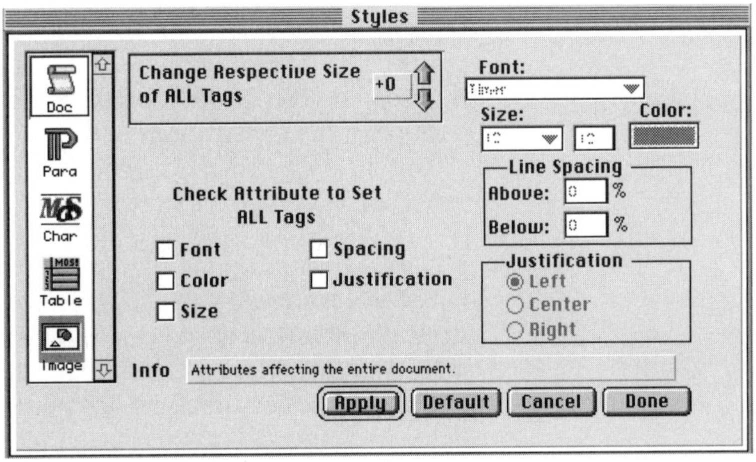

Figure 3.7: Mosaic Styles window.

10. The **Doc, Para, Char,** and **Table** windows are the perfect examples of all you can do with Mosaic. You have the choice to control everything about your fonts, colors, spacing, and justification, or you can leave them all alone. We do recommend increasing the size of all your tags by 1 or 2 if you have a hard time reading text on the screen. Otherwise, have a blast playing with your options.

11. In the **Image** window select:

    Display alternative text for image

    Background images

    Background color

    Colored text

    Paginate around unloaded images

12. Click on Done and you're done.

HOW TO USE IT

Getting Started: Unless you altered the autoload page option, the Mosaic homepage will load when you open Mosaic. You can use this as a starting point or enter another URL with the Open command from the file menu, click on the open folder on the button bar, or click inside the URL list box just below the button bar.

Bookmarks: Mosaic has a great hotlist management utility, which you should take a little time to become familiar with. Basically, select Add Current to Hotlist under the Navigate menu or click on the burning page icon to add a page to the hotlist menu. To access a saved page address, click on the Hotlists command, drag your mouse around until you find the one you want, and click on it. To edit hotlist entries, select Advanced Hotlist Manager from the Navigate menu.

HINTS AND TIPS

Go Home: If you have altered the start page, you can still access the Mosaic homepage from the Hotlist or from the Help Online Resources.

More Menus: Mosaic had the right idea when it added right click on pop-up menus. Try clicking over different areas of a page—images, links, headings, e-mail addresses, etc.—and you'll see dozens of commands you never even thought existed before.

Mail and Print: Mosaic has mail and print. Just click on the File menu command to get to them.

On Screen Text Selection: Netscape is not the only browser to have this feature. Just click on and drag to select any text on the display screen, then <Command-C> to copy it into clipboard.

STOP!: To interrupt loading click on the stop hand sign button, click on the animated Mosaic icon, or select Stop Transfer from the Navigate window.

Images: On the **Document** tab of the Preferences window in the Option menu, you can turn off the Display Inline Images to prevent the automatic loading of graphics. To load graphics again, you will need to turn this option back on.

E-mail

E-mail stands for electronic mail, and it is just what its name says—messages that are transmitted by an electronic medium, i.e., computers. E-mail is the single most important activity on the Internet. More people use e-mail than any other service by an almost two-to-one margin. Think about it. E-mail provides instantaneous, worldwide, free communication. No other means of interaction—telephone, radio, television, or postal service—can provide an easier to use, more powerful, or more universal method to communicate. E-mail can transmit not only written messages but any electronic resource, including audio, video, fax, and entire software packages. And just because you will eventually hear this term, snail mail is any mail that doesn't travel electronically. Aptly named, don't you think?

How Does E-mail Work?

E-mail works by using the TCP/IP network of the Internet to move messages from the author to the recipient. An e-mail message consists of a header, the message body, and any attachments. The header contains information about the origin of the message, the address of the destination mailbox, a time stamp, and routing information. The header is used like the address on an envelope to guide the message to the correct destination. The message body is simply the written text of the message. Attachments are binary files of any type which are "attached" to the message so they are transmitted along with the rest of the e-mail message.

An e-mail mailbox is simply a directory on a host computer. This directory is where e-mail addressed to you is deposited and stored until you transfer it from the ISP's server to your local machine. You have to have an e-mail utility to retrieve the messages from the server, read the messages, and send out your own messages.

There are actually two e-mail protocol types which are very important, POP and SMTP. POP stands for Post Office Protocol. POP is the Internet protocol used to control how a message is transmitted from your incoming mailbox on the ISP mail server to your desktop computer. SMTP stands for Simple Mail Transfer Protocol. This protocol is what is used to transmit e-mail from your e-mail utility across the Internet and into the destination mailbox. You must have an e-mail service utility which is fully compliant with both of these protocols in order to transmit and receive e-mail on the Internet. Both of the utilities we suggest here are fully compliant with all current Internet e-mail standards.

What Is a Signature?

A signature is a short message which is attached to the end of an e-mail message. Generally your signature should contain your name, your e-mail address, Web site URL, and other contact information such as phone, fax, or mailing address. Many people also like to include business information, funny quotations, and ASCII art (pictures made with keyboard characters). There are no rules or requirements, unless defined by your e-mail utility, about the content or length of a signature. However, good netiquette suggests that a signature file of 4 lines is exceptional and up to 10 lines is tolerated. If you do use a signature, keep the information specific, easy to read, and up to date.

E-mail Utilities

Having a reliable e-mail utility is very important. It doesn't take long to accumulate hundreds of important messages.

The two utilities we recommend are both solid products with which you are sure to be pleased.

Eudora

Eudora is one of the most popular e-mail utilities. It is available in both a full-featured commercial version and a free Light version.

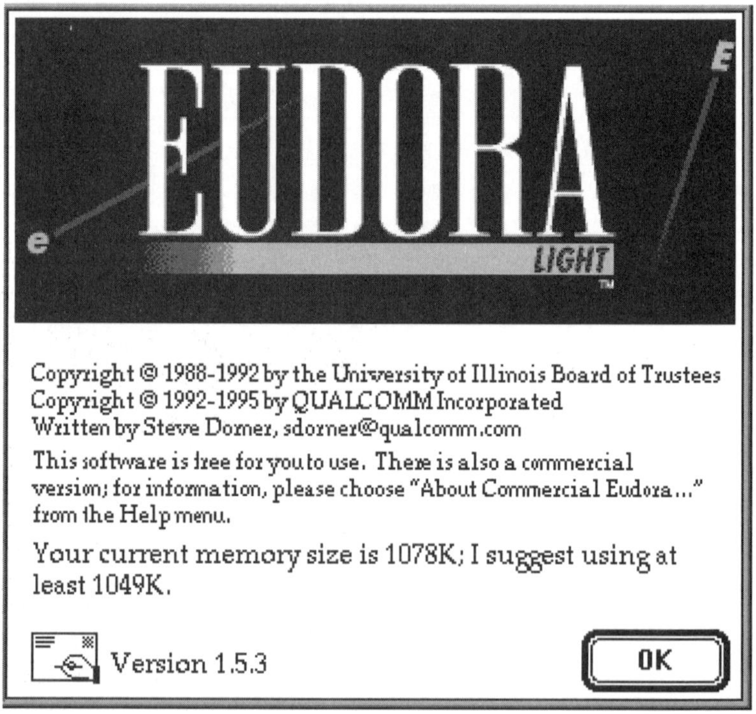

Figure 3.8: Qualcom Eudora Light e-mailer version 1.5.4.

VERSION AND SYSTEM REQUIREMENTS

Eudora's current release version, 1.5.4, requires a 68K-based machine or better, system 7 or later, 340K RAM, and a minimal amount of disk space for the program, although large amounts of saved mail can take up significant space on your hard drive.

WHERE TO FIND IT

You can install Eudora directly from our CD-ROM, download it via your Web browser at http://www.qualcomm.com/ProdTech/quest/light.html (after taking a couple of seconds to fill out their registration form), or FTP it from ftp.qualcomm.com/ in the /Eudora/mac/ directory.

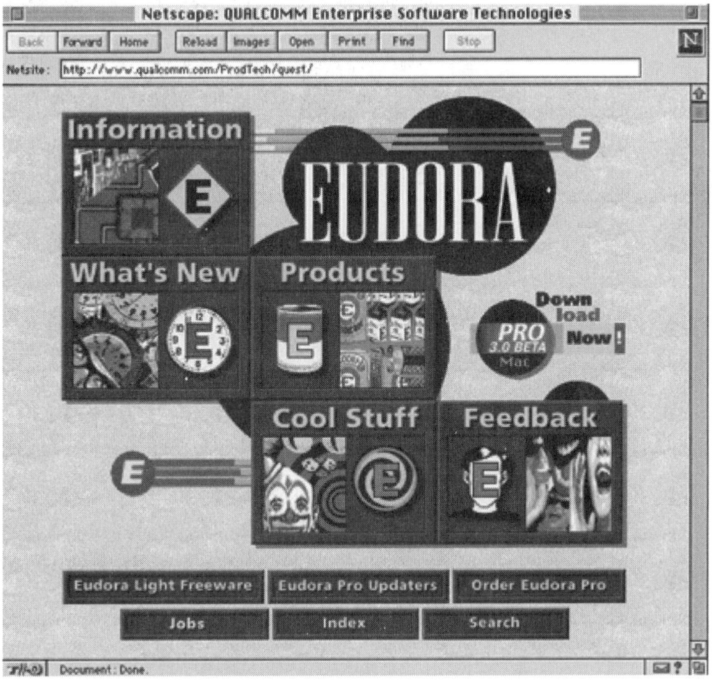

Figure 3.9: Qualcomm's Eudora Web page.

NIFTY FEATURES

Eudora is fully POP and SMTP compliant, with offline reading and writing of messages, find and sort utilities, attachments, hierarchical message filing, and MIME support, and is fully compatible with UNIX mail files. For a complete list of features see: http://www.qualcomm.com/ProdTech/quest/eudora.html.

WHY WE LIKE IT

Eudora is a time-tested utility which has survived and improved under the abuse of its users. Eudora includes almost any type of e-mail function you will ever need. If you have more than one e-mail account (geek) you can create a Eudora settings file for each and access them all from the same program. However, the commercial version packs some extra features that the freeware version lacks, such as message filters and spell checking. If you like the product, spend the cash for the full version.

WHAT WE DON'T LIKE

We don't like it for two reasons. First, the freeware version lacks the ability to spell-check messages. Second, it is a bit cumbersome for the beginning user. If this is your first e-mail utility, take the time to download and read the manual. (Look for it on the Web page or the FTP site.)

INSTALLATION AND CONFIGURATION

Same ol' song and dance, double click on the installer and let it have its way with your computer. It will be gentle, we promise. The configuration can be a bit tricky, but we'll help you through it.

1. Run the application.

2. The Settings window will appear.

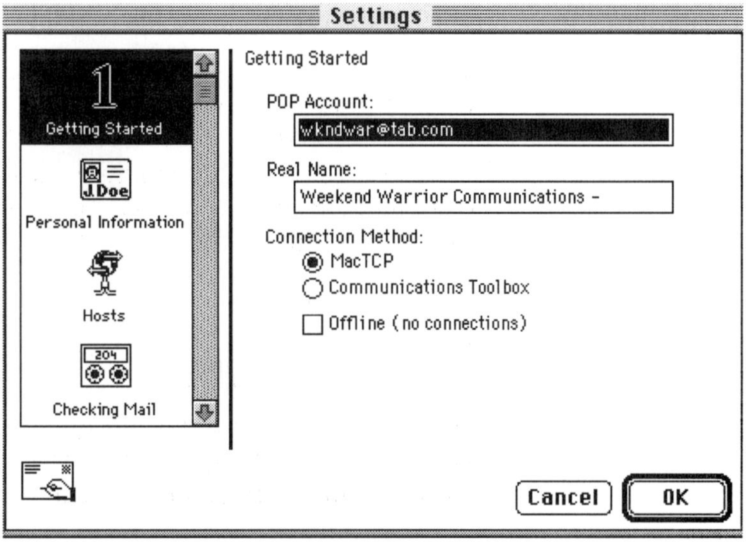

Figure 3.10: Eudora Settings window.

3. In the **Getting Started** window enter your POP account provided by your ISP. If they didn't list one specifically your best bet is to try your username@domain.name. If that doesn't work call their tech support—you paid for 'em, so use 'em. Enter the name, preferably your own, you want to be identified as in your e-mail communications. Choose MacTCP as your Connection Method.

4. Move the **Personal Information** settings. Your POP account and name should have traveled with you from the last window, so all you need to add are your return address, almost always the same as your e-mail address, and your dial-up username.

5. In the **Hosts** window your POP account should magically appear again, and after you enter the SMTP name provided by your ISP you're ready to move on.

6. The **Checking Mail** settings let you customize your mail service. Your POP should still be with you, kind of like a shadow or a piece of gum on your shoe. You can set the utility to check your mail every minute if you want, but that is a little silly and puts more pressure on your ISP's server than is really necessary. Anywhere between 15 minutes and an hour is reasonable. Don't leave your mail on the server, it's only taking up space. Select Send on check and Save Password, and choose the radial button next to Passwords for authentication style, and you've whizzed right through yet another setup window. The first time you connect to your mail server from Eudora it will ask you for a password, but after that it is encrypted and stored in the application's memory.

7. **Sending Mail** is the easiest so far. Now in addition to your POP address you have your SMTP server as a permanent friend. Select all the check boxes, unless you don't want copies of your outgoing mail or have something against curly quotes, and you're almost there.

8. **Attachments** are easy:

   Encoding method: BinHex

   Attachment Folder: Your downloads/temporary folder

   Text files: Whatever editor you chose for your Web browser

9. In the **Fonts and Display** window choose whatever fonts you enjoy reading on the screen and on the printed page and make it so. A good message window width is 80 and a good height is between 40 and 60.

10. Depending on how distracted you are when doing other things at your computer, choose your attention signal in the **Getting Attention** window. Be forewarned, if you choose Use an Alert you can't continue with anything else you are doing until you acknowledge it.

11. The **Reply** window is pretty self-explanatory. Be careful when choosing an automatic reply to all recipients; you could accidentally send e-mail to the wrong person and put the proverbial cyberfoot in your mouth. If you want a copy of your e-mail when you reply to all, then click the box. Don't move recipients from field to field, it gets confusing.

12. **Miscellaneous** is just that, the stuff they couldn't put anywhere else. We suggest you choose Say yes to alerts after 2 minutes and Automatically open next message. All the rest are up to you.

13. Click OK.

Wow, we bet you never thought e-mail could be so complicated. But, one of your key surfboards is smooth as glass and ready to fly across the waves.

HOW TO USE IT

The basics of Eudora can be learned without too much headache. However, the more advanced features such as nicknames, attachments, and signatures will involve you reading through the manual (which you will need to download from the Qualcomm FTP site listed earlier).

To send an e-mail message: Click the new message icon button or select New Message from the Message menu. Enter the address to which you want to send e-mail on the To:

line. Type in a brief subject in the Subject: line. Type your message in the main body area below the line. Once you are finished click on the Send button.

To retrieve e-mail: You can either wait for the timer setting to automatically retrieve your e-mail or select Check Mail from the File menu to do it manually. If you have messages waiting, Eudora will transfer them to your desktop and display the heading information in the "IN" window (if it's not already open, select In from the Window menu).

HINTS AND TIPS

Nicknames: Nicknames aren't just for elementary school anymore. Isn't it easier to remember Bob rather than a bunch-o-numbers@compuserve.com? You can create nicknames in a couple of ways. First, by going to the Nicknames window in the Windows menu and entering the information manually. This is also a great way to create what are called D-lists (distribution lists). If you have a group of people you regularly send common e-mail to, like your friends who enjoy stupid computer humor, you can create a nickname and add all their e-mail addresses to it. When you get the "If computers were beer" e-mail all you have to do is forward it to the nickname Humor, rather than type all those weird e-mail addresses in. The other way to create a nickname is to choose Make Nickname from the Special menu when you get e-mail from someone you'd like to add to your nickname file. Nifty, huh?

Mailboxes: Mailboxes are one of the nicest features of Eudora. After a few months of receiving e-mail you'll have a ton of messages you've saved for some reason or another. If they are all in your inbox you'll have tough time sorting through all of them. Mailboxes are Eudora's answer to e-mail clutter. You simply transfer a message, incoming or outgoing, to mailboxes you've set up in the Mailboxes window under the

Windows menu or to a new mailbox you create on the fly using the New option under the Transfer menu.

Claris E-mailer

The Claris E-mailer, from the same people who bring you ClarisWorks and FileMaker Pro, is a full-featured, robust e-mail management system. Unlike Eudora, Claris E-mailer is available only as a full commercial version.

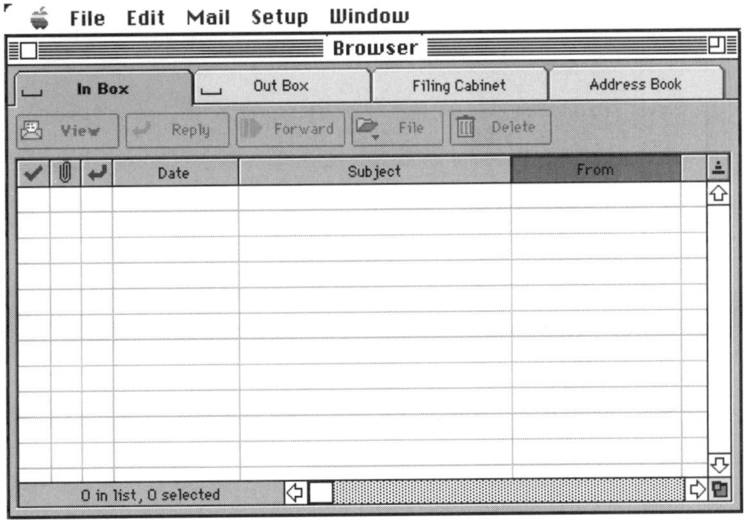

Figure 3.11: Claris E-mailer version 1.0v3.

VERSION AND SYSTEM REQUIREMENTS

Version 1.0v3 requires a 68K-based computer or better, system 7 or later, 1.5MB of RAM required with 4MB recommended, and enough hard disk space to store your e-mail.

WHERE TO FIND IT

Claris E-mailer is available at any software retailer for $49 MSRP. You can also download a trial version that expires after 30 days from the Claris Web site at http://www.claris.com/software/ClarisE-mailer/ClarisE-mailerTrial10v3.hqx or from their FTP site at ftp.claris.com in the /pub/USA-Macintosh/Trial_Software/ folder.

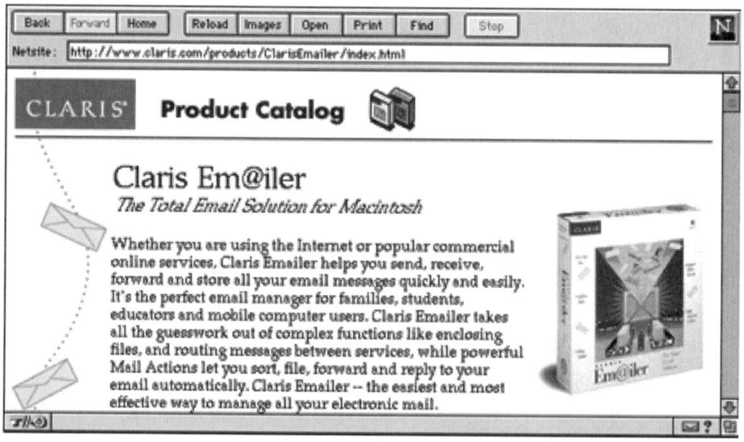

Figure 3.12: Claris E-mailer product information on the Web at http://www.claris.com/products/ClarisE-mailer/index.html.

NIFTY FEATURES

E-mailer has all the standard features you expect in a mail program, including composing and reading mail offline, message sorting, address book, full attachment support, and a scheduling system. What makes E-mailer stand out is its ability to access major online services like America Online, CompuServe, eWorld, and RadioMail. And its total support for Macintosh Drag and Drop.

WHY WE LIKE IT

Claris E-mailer is perfect for managing multiple e-mail accounts from the same program. You feed the application your account information once, and then at any time you can choose which accounts you want to check. With the click of one button all your incoming e-mail is delivered to your desktop. Adding even more functionality is the ability to check your mail up to six times every hour of every day based on a predetermined schedule you set for any or all of your services. If you receive a deluge of mail daily you can sort incoming mail by subject, sender, recipient, and more. Finally, Claris provides near-excellent documentation, so if you're new to the speedy world of e-mail, this may be the product for you.

WHY WE DON'T LIKE IT

Our only gripe with Claris E-mailer is that it doesn't have a spell checker (though it works perfectly with Casady & Greene's SpellCatcher, which is what we use with it).

INSTALLATION AND CONFIGURATION

Even though fully utilizing the functionality of Claris E-mailer may take some reading and experimenting, getting it up and running couldn't be easier. After you grab your beverage of choice while the installer does its job, simply double click on the E-mailer icon and let the program walk you through the setup. Begin with the Easy Setup screen (Figure 3.13) and work your way through to the end.

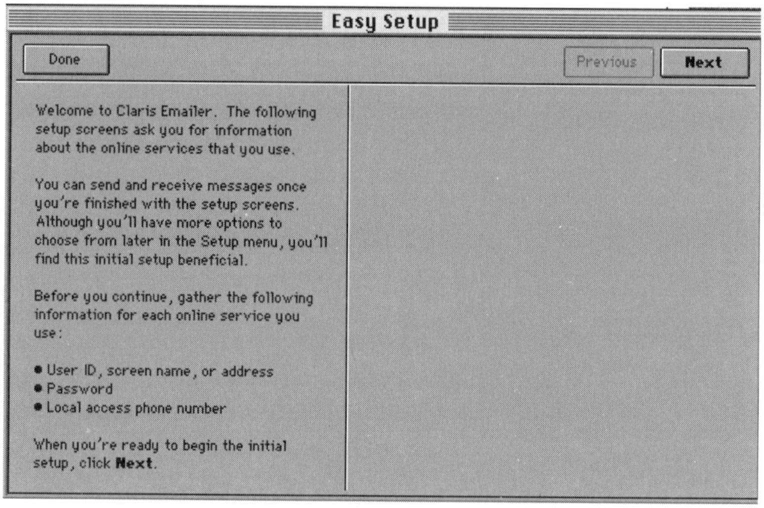

Figure 3.13: Claris E-mailer Easy Setup.

One word of advice to expedite your setup, make sure you have the dial-up, server, and account information for any service you plan to check with Claris. If you have an AOL, CompuServe, Prodigy, or other proprietary online service you may need a little more information than you're accustomed to knowing, such as the POP and SMTP server names. Check with your providers for this information.

HINTS AND TIPS

Scheduling: While it's nice to be able to check your e-mail every ten minutes at all ten of your services, is it really necessary? The scheduling function of Claris E-mailer is a hassle-free way to retrieve your mail without thinking about it, but be realistic in the frequency of your checks, especially if your ISP charges you for connect time. Just because you aren't using the AOL or CompuServe client doesn't mean the time you spend online checking for mail isn't recorded and accordingly charged for.

Destination and Send Via: Just as the application will allow you to check multiple e-mail accounts from the same utility, it will also let you send via multiple e-mail accounts. This can be very helpful in a couple of different ways. To begin with, some services still charge to send and receive Internet or other online services' e-mail. If you have an account like this you can send e-mail to your ISP's other users without incurring those charges. Along the same lines, e-mail among users of the same ISP usually travels faster than from one service to another, so why use your Prodigy account to send to eWorld when you can just as easily choose your eWorld account right from the Claris E-mailer send dialogue?

Mail Actions: When you take the time to set up mail actions correctly they are a godsend when it comes to managing large volumes of e-mail. If you subscribe to several list-servs, have a specific group of people you exchange mail with on a specific topic, or need to be able to get to the message from your Mom ASAP so she doesn't think you've fallen off the face of the earth, then mail actions are for you. You can sort e-mail by any bit of information in the header, assign priorities (do yourself a favor and make Mom priority 1), move messages to a drawer in your file cabinet to read later, automatically forward or reply, or even ignore mail you could care less about. It's your own personal electronic e-mail secretary.

FTP

FTP stands for File Transfer Protocol. FTP is used to transfer files of any type from one Internet machine to another. The Internet has thousands of sites with innumerable files, and to get to them you need an FTP utility. When you access a site, you will be asked to supply a username and a password to gain access to the system. If you have a valid account on the machine, you can enter your personal username and password. If you do not have a valid account, you must try to gain access using anonymous FTP. Anonymous FTP is FTP which offers public access to selected files and directories. To gain access to an anonymous FTP site, you first instruct your FTP utility to access the site by inputting the domain name or IP address. When prompted for your username enter "anonymous" or "guest," then when prompted for a password enter your correct e-mail address in the form: username@domainname. If the site is not full and you did not enter a false e-mail address, you will be given access to all the public file areas.

Fetch

Fetch is the consummate Mac OS FTP program. The interface is easy to use, the commands are intuitive, and there's the cute little dog, running his heart out for you, that makes your whole FTP experience worthwhile. Fetch is a shareware product that is free for educational and nonprofit use and $25 for everyone else. If you fall into the "everyone else" category cough up the cash, you'll get your money's worth in your first session.

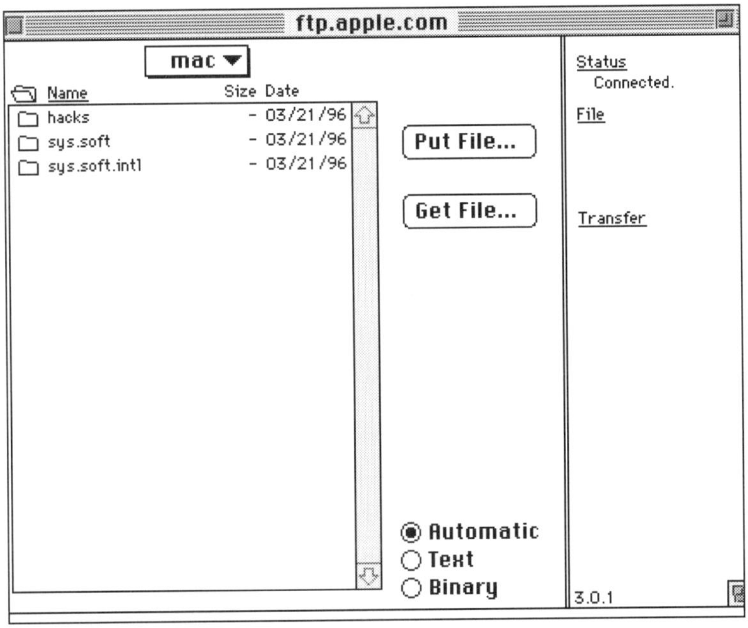

Figure 3.14: Fetch main window.

VERSION AND SYSTEM REQUIREMENTS

Fetch's current release version is 3.0.1. It requires a 68K-based computer or better, system 7 or later, 2MB of RAM, and negligible disk space.

WHERE TO FIND IT

You can retrieve Fetch from any of the big FTP sites at wuarchive.wustl.edu, mirrors.aol.com, mirror.apple.com. Don't forget you can use your Web browser. Also, try searching http://www.shareware.com for other download sites.

NIFTY FEATURES

Fetch has full FTP support, including ASCII and binary file transfers, and is compatible with all major file system types, directory structure transport, and all standard file/directory commands (i.e., rename, move, delete, mkdir, and view). Fetch has many display, notification, action, and function configuration options and supports multiple sessions at one time.

WHY WE LIKE IT

We like Fetch because it is a robust and fast FTP utility. With hundreds of control options this utility is simple and elegant to operate. One great feature that Web authors will appreciate is its ability to transfer a complete directory tree from your desktop to a remote FTP site.

WHY WE DON'T LIKE IT

We honestly have to say there's nothing to dislike about Fetch. That's a rarity in our business, so take advantage of this completely functional program; we definitely do.

INSTALLATION AND CONFIGURATION

Once you've installed the application on your hard disk there is no special configuration required to start using Fetch. There are many different preferences you can tweak to meet your personal needs. Consult the Help file under the Windows menu for detailed instructions.

HOW TO USE IT

When you are ready to begin a new FTP session simply choose New Session from the File menu. A New Connection window, like the one in Figure 3.15, pops up so you can enter the site address, your username and password, and any directory specifications.

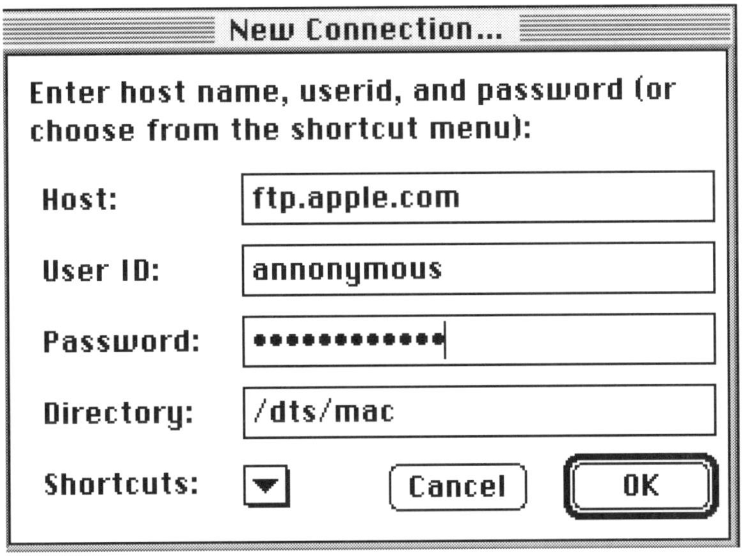

Figure 3.15: Fetch Connection window.

Once you've successfully logged onto a site you simply move through it much like you navigate your hard drive, double clicking on folders to see their contents. When you've found a file you want to download, double click on it and watch the doggie go as it's transferred to your hard drive. After you're done retrieving the information you want from any given site, close the Session window and your connection is shut down. A word about etiquette: many high-traffic sites have a limit to the number of users allowed on at any given time, so once you've got what you came for be courteous and log off to allow others to mine the riches of the Internet as well.

If there are sites you visit frequently you can create bookmarks for them, storing your username and password as well as the specific directory you want to start in, in much the same way as you do with a Web browser. Under the Customize menu choose New Shortcut, which brings up the Bookmark Editor, and fill in the requisite information. Any time you want to visit a bookmarked site you can either double click on it in the Fetch Shortcuts window or choose it from the drop-down menu in the New Connection window.

HINTS AND TIPS

Multiple Files: You can transmit multiple files by selecting more than one file before clicking on the Get button. To select a range, click on the first filename and then hold down <SHIFT> while you click on the second filename. To select multiple single names, click on the first filename, then hold down <Command> and click on each of the other filenames. Once you have selected multiple files by either method, release the hold key and click on the Get button. If you want to upload multiple files from the same or different directories at one time choose Put Folders and Files from the Remote menu and Add each to the list. Click on Done, and they will all be uploaded to the same directory on the site.

Directory Trees: To transfer a directory, simply select the parent directory and click on the Get button. You will be prompted to verify that you want to transfer the directory structures.

Transfer: Fetch keeps a running tally of how much information has been transferred at what rate, and how much is left to go, for each active file in the Session window. This not only is a convenient way to keep track of how much more data needs to be moved but also gives you some idea of your connection speed.

URL Parsing: This has to be one of the coolest features of the latest version of Fetch. Earlier on we talked about the anatomy of a URL and how important it was for you to understand it because some utilities require you to parse it yourself. Not Fetch. If you copy an FTP URL from a browser and then paste it into the New Connection window of Fetch, the application automatically takes the URL apart for you, putting the server URL in the Host box and the file path in the Directory box. You don't even have to think about it.

Archie

Archie is an automatic information-gathering utility designed to create an indexed directory listing for all anonymous FTP sites on the Internet. Archie uses a filename query string to search an Archie server's database to obtain the location of a file. Using an Archie utility may help in locating a file on the Internet if you happen to know part of the filename.

Anarchie

Anarchie, created by Peter Lewis, is a shareware program that combines searching the information on an Archie server with FTP capabilities.

VERSION AND SYSTEM REQUIREMENTS

Anarchie 1.6.0 requires a 68K-based computer or better, less than 1MB of both RAM and hard disk space, and system 7 or later, but it functions best with system 7.5.

WHERE TO FIND IT

You can find both Anarchie information and a list of download sites on the Anarchie Web page at http://www.share.com/peterlewis/anarchie/anarchie.html. It is also available at most of the popular archive sites, such as mirrors.aol.com.

NIFTY FEATURES

Anarchie can search for a file by name as well as browse an entire FTP site. The bookmark function allows you to keep a list of frequently visited sites and places you'd like to revisit when you have more time to dig through their resources.

WHY WE LIKE IT

Anarchie is an absolute gem when it comes to finding a file you wouldn't otherwise know where to begin looking for. If you even know part of the filename you are off and running with Anarchie's help. Once you've found the file you can FTP it directly to your machine without having to run any other application. Anarchie also has great documentation and help files that work with System 7.5's Apple Guide.

WHAT WE DON'T LIKE

Anarchie's FTP capabilities are not as robust as those of a dedicated FTP utility like Fetch, and it should not be relied upon as your only FTP application.

INSTALLATION AND CONFIGURATION

Anarchie is another member of the double click and use family of applications. The .bin file decompresses into a folder you can place anywhere you desire in your application organization scheme. Simply start the program and you're ready to go.

HOW TO USE IT

To search for a particular file choose Archie from the File menu. In the Archie window, like the one in Figure 3.16, enter the filename, or any part of it you know, and choose a server from the drop-down menu to start your search.

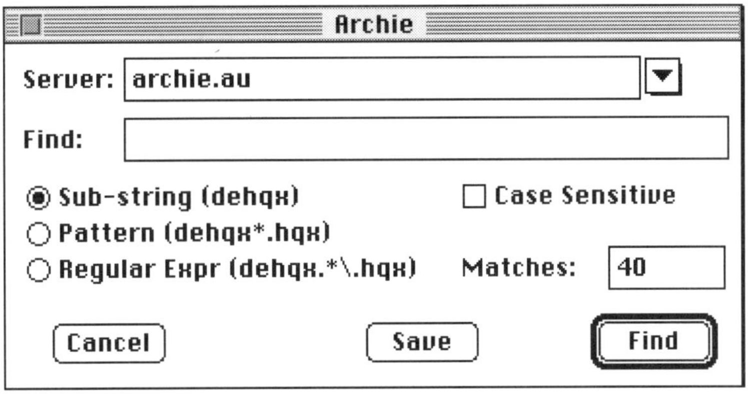

Figure 3.16: Anarchie Archie search window.

When Archie has located the file you want simply double click on the filename and it will be transferred directly to your hard disk. Alternately, if you know the server and pathname of a particular file you want, simply choose Get from the FTP menu and enter the relevant information.

HINTS AND TIPS

Bookmarks: Anarchie comes with an extensive collection of bookmarks, but in case you somehow need more you can easily add to them. When you come to a site or file you would like added, highlight the name and then choose Save Bookmark from the File menu. When you want to see all of your bookmarks choose List Bookmarks from the File menu.

Usenet

Usenet is a worldwide hierarchical message system, where anyone can read and post articles. Usenet is organized into named groups—called newsgroups—organized by topic and focus, with varying degrees of content control from strict moderation to freeform conversation. Almost every newsgroup has a FAQ (frequently asked questions), which is a document containing the focus, purpose, posting limitations, and rules for the specific newsgroup. We strongly suggest (even insist) that you locate and read the FAQ for a newsgroup before you even think about posting. This will save you headaches, frustration, and long lectures or even flaming. Take our word for it—when in doubt about the rules of a newsgroup, DON'T.

There are two acceptable news utilities floating around out there for the Mac OS, Nuntius, and NewsWatcher. Keep in mind that most Web browsers, Netscape and Explorer included, support news now as well. In this case you might want to configure your browser for news and go on.

Nuntius

Nuntius allows you to subscribe, read, post, and reply to Usenet messages.

VERSION AND SYSTEM REQUIREMENTS

The current version of Nuntius, 2.0.4, requires a 68K or better computer, system 7 or later, and 5MB of RAM.

WHERE TO FIND IT

You can find Nuntius on the anonymous FTP site maintained by Peter Speck at ftp://ftp.ruc.dk/pub/nuntius/ as well as on any of the standard software archives. You can also search http://www.shareware.com for other locations.

NIFTY FEATURES

Nuntius gives you almost total control over all aspects of your newsreading environment. You can decide what threads of news to choose based on date and article status (read or unread). Articles can be automatically opened according to any number of criteria, and you can reply to the newsgroup, the author of the article, or both.

WHY WE LIKE IT

Nuntius is so totally customizable that it can make even the most anal-retentive reader happy. The interface is clean and neat, and the commands are relatively intuitive.

WHY WE DON'T LIKE IT

If you ever want to change your news server or personal information you have to delete your Nuntius preferences file and start all over again. This can be a genuine pain. Our biggest complaint is if you need to use a different name and password for your news server than you do for your other Internet services, there is no way to configure that information in Nuntius, and you're basically out of luck.

INSTALLATION AND CONFIGURATION

The first time you run the program you will be prompted for your news server address (Figure 3.17) and it shouldn't ask you again unless you ditch your preferences to switch news servers. Enter the name of your news server and take a break while Nuntius downloads the newsgroup information. In order to post from Nuntius you must enter your name, e-mail address, and organization in the Your Name... window under the Prefs menu.

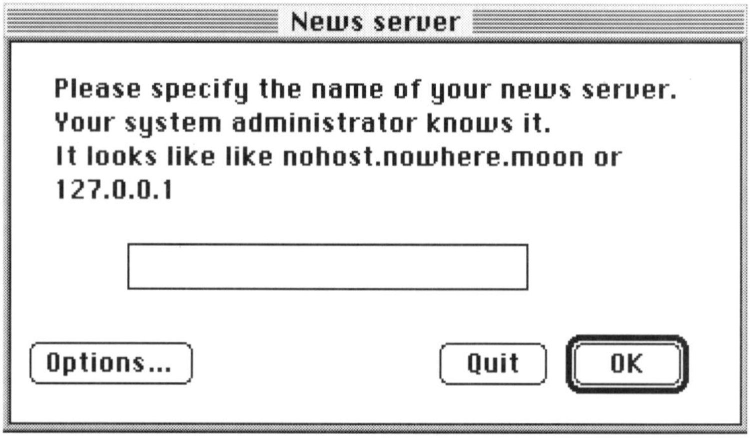

Figure 3.17: Nuntius News Server window.

HOW TO USE IT

Once the database is complete you have a long list of groups to choose from in the All Groups window. Folder icons represent a group of newsgroups and page icons represent actual newsgroups.

To Subscribe: Choose New Group List from the File menu, and when you find a group you want to subscribe to simply drag it to the New Group List window. You can reorder groups in any group window by dragging the icons within the window. Because you can have more than one group list you can sort your newsgroups in any way you want. Figure 3.18 shows the All Groups window as well as a New Group List with a few choice groups.

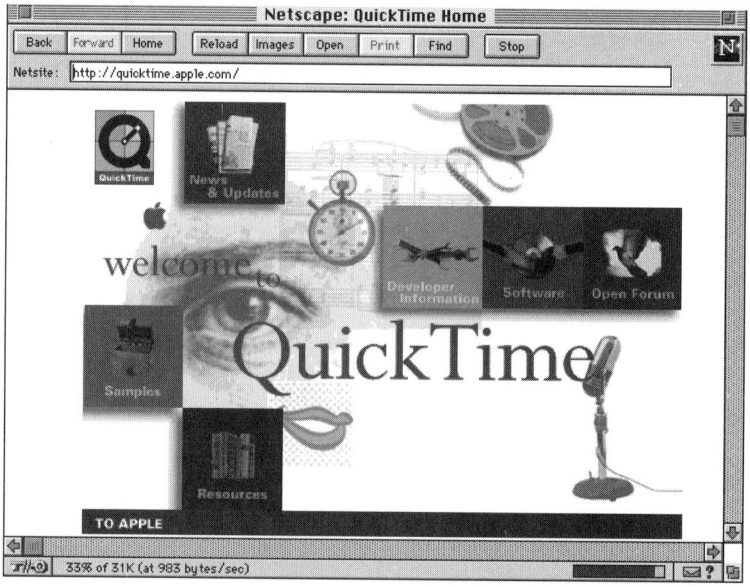

Figure 3.28: QuickTime VR Web site.

On Your Own

You should now have a solid foundation of utilities and additional software on which to build your Internet experience. However, we didn't want to let you go without giving you a little more information about what is out there.

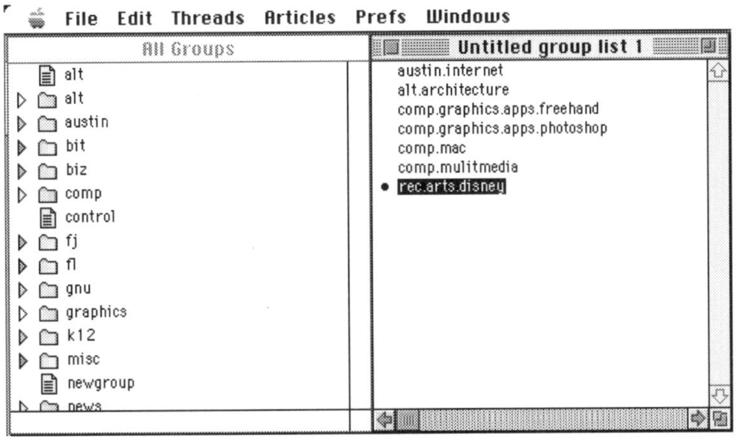

Figure 3.18: Nuntius All Groups and New Group List windows.

T*o Unsubscribe:* Highlight the name of the group you want to unsubscribe from and hit delete. Yes, it's really that simple.

To Read Articles in a Newsgroup: Double click on the page icon to get a list of unread articles and then double click on any article you want to read.

Posting to a Newsgroup: There are several ways to post to a newsgroup using Nuntius. You can choose Post Follow-up Article from the Articles menu to respond to a specific post, or Post Article in New Thread from the Threads menu to begin a new discussion.

HINTS AND TIPS

While Peter Speck has written a pretty useful little utility, he hasn't provided much in the way of documentation and advice to the user. Luckily, faithful users have generated their own. Turn to the Nuntius FAQ at ftp://ftp.cit.cornell.edu/pub/mac/comm/test/Nuntius-archive-mirror/docs/nuntius-faq.txt for general Q&A, the Nuntius Users Guide on the Cornell server at ftp://ftp.cit.cornell.

edu/pub/mac/comm/test/Nuntius-archive-mirror/docs/cornell-nuntius-docs.sit.hqx for advanced information, or Aaron Freimark's Nuntius page at http://www.inch.com/~aaron/nuntius/nuntius.html for the latest Nuntius information.

NEWSWATCHER

Brought to you by John Norstad of Northwestern University, NewsWatcher is the other reliable and robust Usenet utility available for the Mac OS.

Figure 3.19: NewsWatcher masthead.

VERSION AND SYSTEM INFORMATION

Version 2.1.2 requires a 68K-based computer or better, running system 7 or later, with 2.5MB of RAM and minimal hard disk space.

WHERE TO FIND IT

You can get NewsWatcher at ftp://ftp.acns.nwu.edu/pub/newswatcher/ or one of the several archive sites we've mentioned incessantly throughout this chapter. A justification for bookmarks? We think so.

NIFTY FEATURES

NewsWatcher has all you'd expect from a news reader and a little more. Besides providing for reading, posting, and replying by e-mail, NewsWatcher will decode binaries, a must-have for anyone subscribing to graphics-related newsgroups. You can search newsgroups by everything from subject to distribution.

WHY WE LIKE IT

NewsWatcher has a friendly and easy-to-use interface and is also highly customizable by tweaking its many preferences. NewsWatcher supports multiple groups of newsgroups to help you sort and keep track of the news you are interested in. There is also a whole host of NewsWatcher helpers that have been created by netizens to add to the functionality of the utility. Best of all, it's free.

WHAT WE DON'T LIKE

This is another one of the utilities we have a hard time finding fault with. We do admit, though, that the preferences can be a bit overwhelming and confusing to someone new to Usenet and the Internet. Another minor gripe is the groups are not broken down by category (alt., comp., etc.) in the All Groups list but rather listed alphabetically, so you have to literally scan the entire list of newsgroups your provider supports to make your subscription choices—a very time-consuming task in the least, not to mention boring.

INSTALLATION AND CONFIGURATION

Same ol' song and dance here. Just move the NewsWatcher application to whatever folder you're keeping all these little utilities in and double click on the application icon. The first time you use NewsWatcher it will prompt you for your news server and mail server addresses. You can later change the formatting of the Preferences window under the File menu. Almost all of the Preferences windows in News Watcher are designed to set up a newsreading environment tailored to your needs. We recommend you go through each window and choose those options that you want. As you participate in newsgroups more and more you may find you don't want to see every line of every header, or you may want a different signature file. When the time comes, simply change your preferences, quit, and restart the program.

HOW TO USE IT

Once you've entered your server information and the utility has returned a list of newsgroups for you to choose from, open a New Group window under the File menu and you are ready to go (Figure 3.20).

To Subscribe: Drag the group you want to subscribe to from the All Group window to the untitled New Group window, or highlight the group name and choose Subscribe from the Special menu. You can reorder groups in a group window by dragging them up or down.

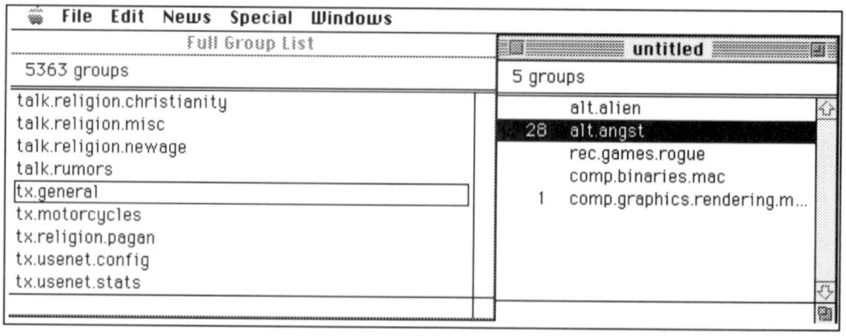

Figure 3.20: NewsWatcher All Group and New Group windows.

To Unsubscribe: Delete a highlighted file from the Group window or choose Unsubscribe from the Special menu.

To Read Articles in a Newsgroup: Double click on the newsgroup to get a listing of the unread articles and then double click on any specific article you want to read.

To Post to a Newsgroup: In the News menu choose New Message to post a new article to the group you are currently reading or Reply to respond to a specific article.

HINTS AND TIPS

NewsWatcher has a very complete Apple Guide help that is part of the program, so look to it first for detailed answers to your questions. Also, keep in mind that while the utility may be fairly straightforward, it's your interactions on the newsgroup that may be tricky. Spend some time lurking to get a feel for the mood of a group, or do a search on netiquette at your favorite search engine to see what tips veteran netizens have for you.

Other Utilities

The list of Internet service utilities gets longer almost daily. You can accomplish 90% of all Internet-related activities with a Web browser, an e-mail utility, an FTP utility, and a newsreader. But if you want to stretch yourself to grab hold of the remaining 10%, we haven't left you completely in the dark. Here are the best supportive utilities which handle online—and some offline—services that you may be interested in.

In this section, we list Web or FTP sites to obtain the utilities. We have listed utilities which are easy to install and provide adequate installation, configuration, and operation instructions. You will need to execute or decompress the original file to locate the utility-specific instructions. Often these are contained in the ReadMe file.

Telnet

Telnet is a Internet utility which allows you to control and operate on a remote system. A Telnet session effectively simulates a VT100 ASCII terminal and will let you log in to any system you have privileges on. The only Telnet application you ever want to use is a public domain utility created by NCSA called, of all things, NCSA Telnet. Version 2.6 is available from any of the standard FTP archives we mentioned when talking about Fetch and installs with a double click of the mouse. To begin a session simply choose Open Connection (Figure 3.21) from the File menu, enter the server name, and a terminal window will prompt you for your login and password.

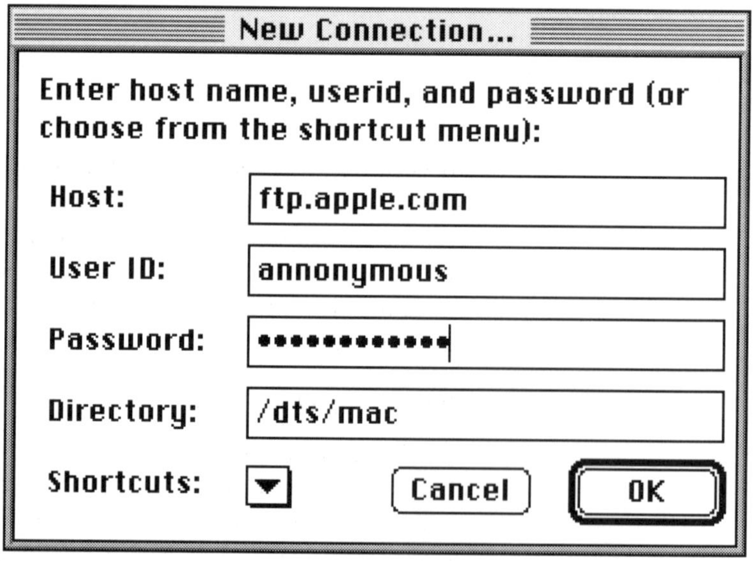

Figure 3.21: NCSA Telnet connection window.

From a Telnet session you can do fun things like IRC, check your e-mail the old-fashioned way, and even browse the

Web with a Lynx browser provided of course your system supports any and all of these functions.

Finger, Whois, and Ping

These three utilities are hard to come by and most of their usefulness is lost outside a UNIX Telnet session. (We recommend using the UNIX command versions in a Telnet session if you have access to a shell account—ask your ISP about that one.) We have not found any utilities we like that add these functions to Windows. However, if you want to search through them on your own, use "finger," "whois," and "ping" as keywords at the shareware library at http://www.shareware.com or http://vsl.cnet.com.

Offline and Other Utilities

The Internet has many, many more services to offer to those who want to explore, and during your exploration you are certain to run across file types, archive methods, and a host of other weird items that you will need help with. Here are the rest of the utilities in our Internet toolbox that we think you should take a look at.

STUFFIT EXPANDER

StuffIt Expander is the one compression utility no Mac OS user should live without. It supports StuffIt (.sit), Zip (.zip), Arj (.arj), Arc (.arc), gzip (.gz, .z), uuencode (.uu, .uue), and BinHex (.hqx), StuffIt, Zip, and Arj self-extracting archives (.exe, .sea), and MacBinary (.bin) format. You can retrieve this utility from the Aladdin System's Web site at http://www.aladdinsys.com/ under Shareware/ Freeware products.

COMPACT PRO:

Compact Pro by Bill Goodman is another excellent compression utility. You can create self-extracting archives (.sea) and then BinHqx them for uploading to FTP sites. This utility is also great for converting .sea, .bin.hqx, and StuffIt archive files. The $25 shareware fee is well worth it. You can download Compact Pro from any of the major archive sites.

Pushing the Envelope

Browsing the World Wide Web has always brought you text and even some graphics. But now full interactive multimedia is available for those with the right browser, a configured helper application, and enough bandwidth. To spice up your Web surfing, take a look at our list of recommended helper applications.

Many of the plug-ins, add-ons, and helpers listed here require Netscape Navigator 2.0 or later. We have focused on this browser and platform; you will need to consult the Web or FTP sites listed to obtain information for other browsers and platforms.

This is a very short list of helper applications and we have highlighted only a few of our favorites. To check out other helper applications, you can use a search engine with keywords "helper applications," "plugins," and "addons," or visit one of these sites:

`http://home.netscape.com/comprod/products/navigator/version_2.0/plugins/index.html`

`http://charlotte.acns.nwu.edu/internet/helper/`

http://wwwhost.cc.utexas.edu/learn/use/helper.html

http://www.ncsa.uiuc.edu/SDG/Software/MacMosaic/Supplementary/Helper.html

RealAudio

In the past, the only sounds available on the Internet were common audio files, like .wav and .au, which the browser passed on to a sound player. However, a new sound technology has surfaced: RealAudio. RealAudio provides live and on-demand real-time audio over 14.4Kbps or faster connections to the Internet. If you have a 28.8 modem and a Power PC, you can use the 2.0 version of the player to hear FM mono quality voice and music. Visit the RealAudio site at http://www.realaudio.com/.

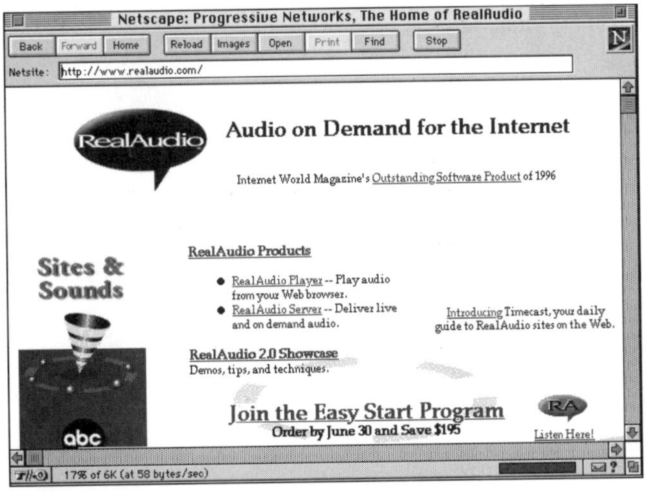

Figure 3.22: RealAudio's Web page.

There are three sites you must visit after you get your RealAudio plug-in installed: C|Net Radio at http://www.cnet.com/Content/Radio/index.html for daily Internet- and computer-related news and information; Net.Radio at http://www.netradio.net for live 24-hour-a-day Internet radio (rock and classical channels); and 1-800-MUSIC-NOW Online at http://www.1800musicnow.mci.com for "You Click, You Listen, You Like, You Buy."

StreamWorks

StreamWorks is an Internet delivery technique developed by Xing Technology Corporation for live and on-demand audio and video. For complete information and to obtain this excellent plug-in, visit the Xing Web site at http://www. xingtech.com/.

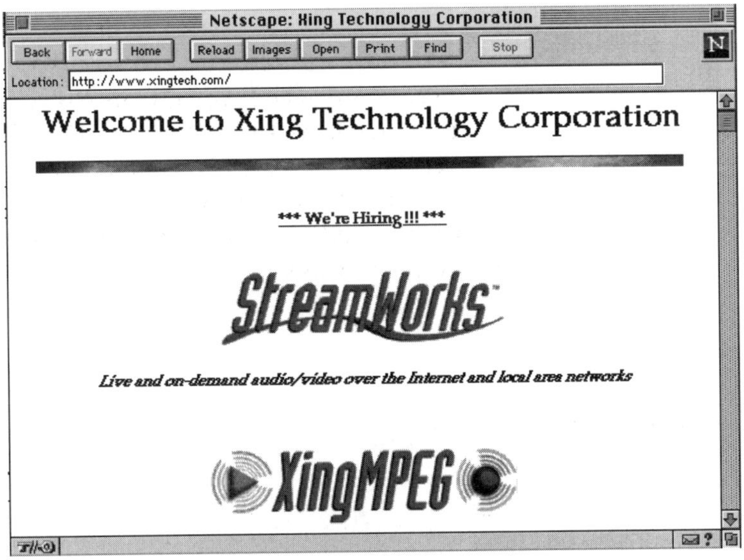

Figure 3.23: Xing's StreamWorks Web page.

Adobe's "Amber" Acrobat

The "Amber" version of the Acrobat Reader lets you view, navigate, and print Portable Document Format (PDF) files right in your Navigator window. PDF files are extremely compact, platform independent, and easy to create. They offer design control, print-ready documents, and an endless array of authoring applications. Many companies are now using the PDF technology to distribute documentation, product information, and other layout-dependent materials. Visit the Adobe Amber Web site at:

`http://www.adobe.com/Amber/Index.html`

One of the best resources on the Net for tax information is the newly updated IRS Web site. You can download PDF files of all the latest tax forms, instruction sheets, and related documentation. Visit the IRS online at http://www.irs.ustreas.gov/prod/cover.html.

Figure 3.24: The IRS's Web site.

Shockwave

The Shockwave plug-in lets you interact with Macromedia Director presentations right in a Netscape Navigator window. Animation, clickable buttons, links to URLs, digital video movies, sound, and more can be integrated within a presentation to deliver a rich multimedia experience. Full interactive multimedia applications created by Director—the industry standard multimedia authoring tool, used to create CD-ROMs—is now available on the Internet. For more information and to get the plug-in, visit http://www.macromedia.com/Tools/Shockwave/sdc/Plugin/index.htm.

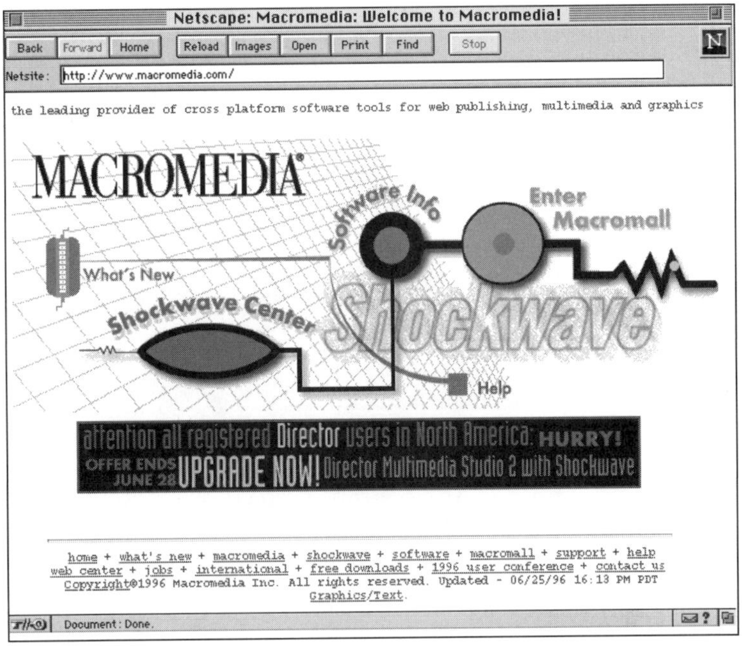

Figure 3.25: The Macromedia main homepage.

Java

Java is a programming language developed by Sun Microsystems to allow client-side execution of applications. Small programs written in Java, called applets, can be quickly transmitted over the Internet and viewed/executed in a Java-compatible browser. Video, sound, interaction, and other special effects are some of the features this revolutionary programming tool can provide. Go for a test drive of the Java beta plug-in available at http://java.sun.com.

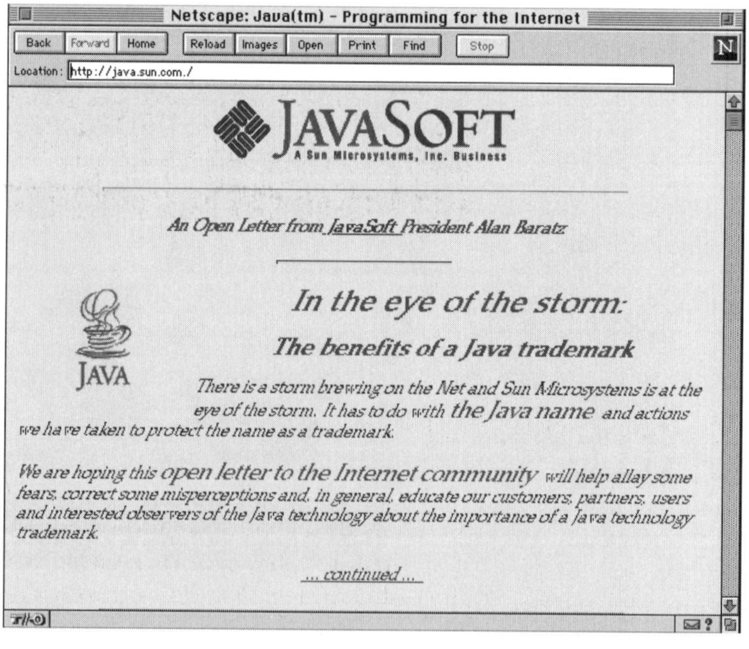

Figure 3.26: Java Web page.

VRML

Virtual Reality Modeling Language is another new tool on the Web scene. VRML allows the creation of three-dimensional worlds that you can travel or walk through using your Web browser. VRML is still in its infancy and it has a long way to go, but the view is amazing even now. For various information regarding VRML, please visit the VRML Web site at http://www.vrml.org/. For one of the popular plug-ins currently available visit http://www.chaco.com for VR Scout VRML; http://www.paperinc.com for WebFX; or http://www.vream.com for WIRL Virtual Reality Browser.

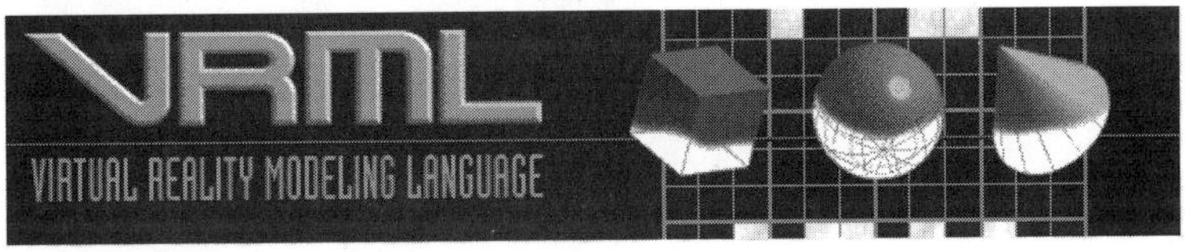

Figure 3.27: VRML logo.

QuickTime VR

QuickTime VR plug-in allows your Web browser to display the virtual reality worlds created using QuickTime movies. The plug-in is still in beta testing; however, it works great. You can find complete information and installation instructions at the QuickTime VR Web site at http://qtvr.quicktime.apple.com/. Get the newest release of the QuickTime Player from http://quicktime.apple.com/.

Tricks of the Trade

The single most important thing you need to keep up with on the Internet and all the rapidly changing, expanding, and emerging technologies is simply to be online. There is no substitute. As hard as we tried to include all the most recent information, this book is already out of date. Completely new software and new versions of the utilities we mentioned are already available. The only way to keep up is to stay acquainted with the hot spots on the Internet and visit them often. Here is a list of the Web sites we visit on a daily basis just to check up on what's new:

C|Net Online: http://www.cnet.com

HotWiReD: http://www.hotwired.com

ZD Net: http://www.zdnet.com

Netscape: http://www.netscape.com

Apple: http://www.apple.com

Search Engines

Search engines are tools to help you locate information on the Internet. There are dozens of search engines, but there are only half a dozen that are really worth taking the time to learn how to use. Each search engine has its own tips, hints, and instructions on how to use its capabilities to the fullest. Take the time to read through the materials the authors placed there for you.

Each of these search engines is designed to access and locate Internet information in different ways.

Yahoo!—http://www.yahoo.com

Excite!—http://www.excite.com

OpenText—http://www.opentext.com

Lycos—http://www.lycos.com

InfoSeek—http://www.infoseek.com

WebCrawler—http://www.webcrawler.com

Betas, Demos, and Other Beasts

Many new and exotic software applications are available on the Internet for you to download and use. However, there are some significant variations between a full commercial application and the beasts lurking on the Internet disguised as software products. Let's take a brief look at the types of animals which are waiting to wreak havoc on your desktop.

Betas

Betas are pre–final release versions of a software product. Usually betas are distributed to a limited testing group for "real-world" stress tests to determine if there are any remaining bugs, glitches, or mistakes in the product's coding. However, with a worldwide audience willing to try anything, software companies are now posting betas on the Internet for anyone to download, hoping to get feedback and testing information for free. When downloading a beta for your personal testing and use, you need to be aware that not every company releases a "safe" version. It is not uncommon for betas to alter startup files, change other application settings, replace applications, corrupt data files, and freeze your system. Always make a backup of your hard drives before installing a beta.

Demos

Demos are small or crippled versions of a software product, often distributed to tease users into purchasing a full commercial product. When retrieving a demo, understand that many of the features you are really interested in may not be active or available in the demo version of the software. There is also another type of demo which you may have encountered—the time-dependent demo. This type of demo is fully functional for a certain length of time or until a specific date, after which it becomes inoperable.

Viruses

"Virus" is one of the few true cuss words on the Internet. Virus protection is a high priority with most computer owners worldwide, both on and off the Internet. But being on the Internet does open your system up to more ways of catching a computer virus. In our years of experience on the Internet, we have encountered only a few viruses on our systems. But just because we have been lucky does not mean we can get lazy about keeping our current virus defenses up. Always check downloaded materials for viruses before using or even before un-archiving them, and run a regular system-wide virus scan on each of your hard drives. If you need information on the latest virus software, perform a search using "virus" as a keyword. Disinfectant is the best known Mac virus whumper, and it's free. Grab a copy today from any of the FTP sites or mirrors mentioned previously.

Trojan Horses

Like the well-known Trojan horse of Greek mythology, there are many false-front software packages appearing on the Internet. Be cautious when retrieving files from non-public or unfamiliar sites, especially when the product is not from a well-known company. You may find that you have been misled into downloading something useless or damaging to your system. Consider every file you retrieve from the Internet as a virus-infected file; don't do anything until you have thoroughly checked and cleaned the file with an up-to-date virus scanner.

Shareware/Freeware

Most of the software which you have legal access to on the Internet is free for the taking. However, there are different categories in the area of "free" that you need to be aware of. Shareware is software which is freely distributed to anyone who wants to try it. If you decide to continue using the software, you are asked to pay a small registration fee, usually less than $45. For this fee you are often entitled to free upgrades, a printed manual, and even technical support. Freeware is software which has no registration fee and no guarantee of technical support or future upgrades. Often the authors simply want to know your opinion of their work and will ask for an e-mail or a postcard (often called postcardware). If you find yourself using a shareware or freeware product consistently, be sure to contact the authors to give feedback, to register, or even to give them a little cash for their efforts. Remember, without them that nifty little software would not exist.

Copyrighted Software

No matter what your personal opinion is about copyrighting computer software, having an unlicensed—and often unpaid for—copy of a software product is illegal in the United States. Even with the strict law enforcement in the United States, there are still hundreds of places to find and download illegal copies of commercial software. Be smart enough to avoid these areas, and when you want to test a commercial product, contact the manufacturer or your local software store—there just might be a demo.

Coming Up!

Well, that should be plenty to get you in way over your head! Don't get overwhelmed by all of this. The main thing is to have fun learning your way around. You can get purposeful later. Remember this advice from the get-go: Try stuff. Experiment. You won't break anything. The best way to learn and get comfortable is to bang around. Read the documentation that comes with everything. We've given you enough to get started, now go have some fun.

In the next chapter we're going to show you some cool places to go on the Net. We've been surfing for a couple of years and know where some great beaches are. Come on. Let's go.

chapter 4

Deals, Steals and Shopping Wheels

And Oh Yeah—Where to Find Everything You've Always Wanted to Know about Everything There Is to Know about Everything That Is…

So now you have everything all set up and ready to rock. It's time to let you in on the best places to go on the Net. Instead of just turning the fire hose on and letting you drown in the sea of information that is the Internet, we're going to pour you a refreshing drink of nectar and turn you on to some of the best places to go.

The Internet can make you feel completely overwhelmed. A little over a year ago you could easily visit every new site in just a few hours of surfing on a Saturday afternoon. Not anymore. We've heard of estimates that there are over 10,000 new WWW sites added every week. In the early days it was fun just to see what everyone was doing with a new site. Nowadays it's more important to know where to go quickly to get what you want—whether it's for fun or for serious research or work.

Yahoo—The Mother of All Sites

Fortunately the nerds of the Net have been doing their part and there are some great "Table of Contents" sites and killer search engines that bring a good measure of orderliness to an extremely dynamic and ever-evolving scene. Let's start with a couple of the best sites on the Net for beginners. These are places that you can go with Netscape and have some fun getting comfortable cruising the Net.

We agree with just about everybody out there that the mother of all sites on the Internet is Yahoo at:

`http://www.yahoo.com`

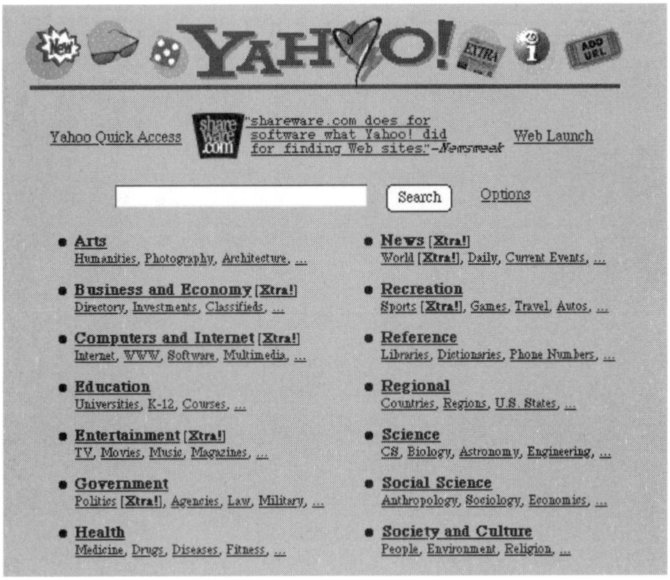

Figure 4.1: Yahoo homepage.

The Yahoo WWW site was started by a couple of Stanford students, David Filo and Jerry Yang. Their brilliance was to build a software "robot" that runs around the Net and categorizes WWW sites based on content. Then they did the Tom Sawyer thing and made it possible for Webmasters (the geeks who build WWW sites) to go to Yahoo and register their own site. With all the people visiting the site, someone there got the bright idea to sell some "banner" space on the Yahoo Web pages to advertisers like IBM, MCI, and others. Pretty soon these guys hit it big and attracted the attention of investors and now have one of the most successful commercial sites on the Net. They've done a tasteful job of it actually.

Yahoo's search page alone gets about 3 million hits a month. So you know that when they charge $20,000 per million hits for an ad, those guys (Filo & Yang) are on their way to the beach. In France. Way to go, guys!

Yahoo has a great search engine that lets you type in keywords and get back a list of links to sites on the Net that match. You can get really sophisticated with search techniques and quickly narrow in on what you're after.

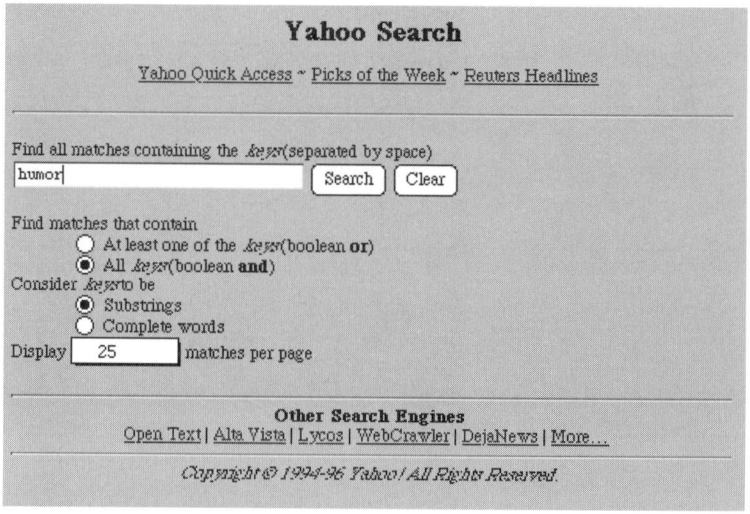

Figure 4.2: Yahoo search engine.

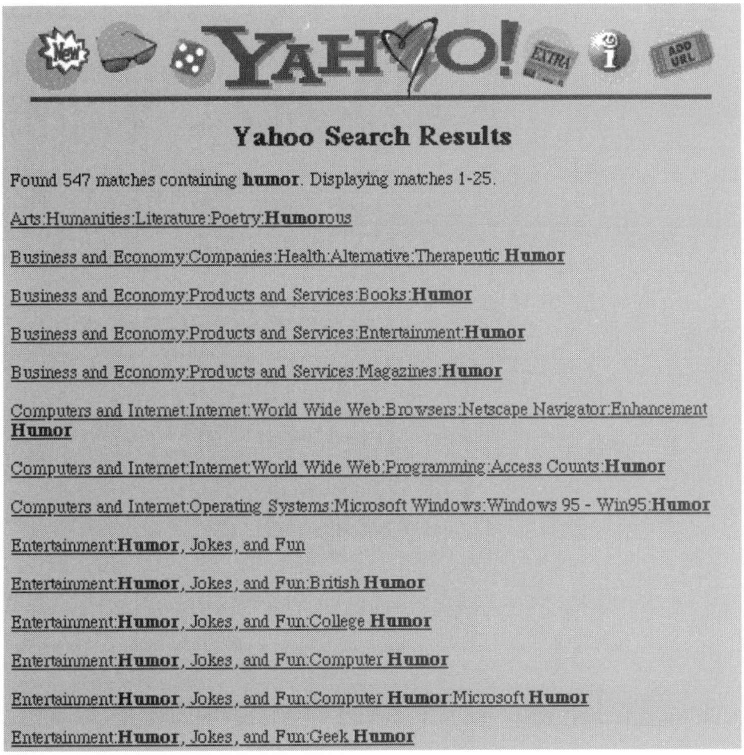

Figure 4.3: Yahoo search results.

There's even a navigation bar (commonly referred to by the big kahuna Net surfers as a "nav bar") at the bottom of a Yahoo search result that points you in the direction of other Internet search engines such as Lycos and AltaVista.

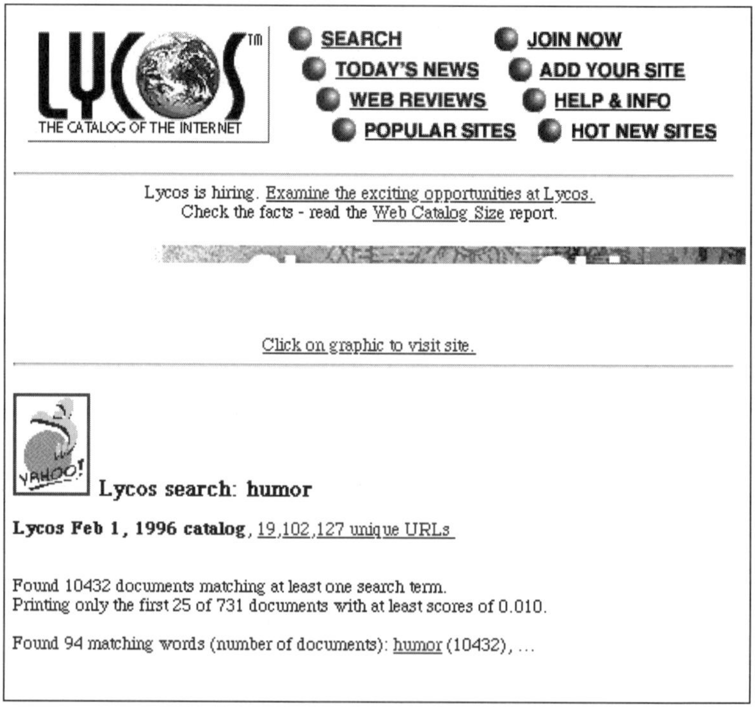

Figure 4.4: Yahoo links to additional WWW site search engines (Lycos in this example).

We visit Yahoo almost every day for something or other. So do a boatload of people. Yahoo is a great site to go for Reuters news, for instance. You can get to it off any Yahoo page right from the news icon on the nav bar at the top of the page.

Figure 4.5: Yahoo nav bar.

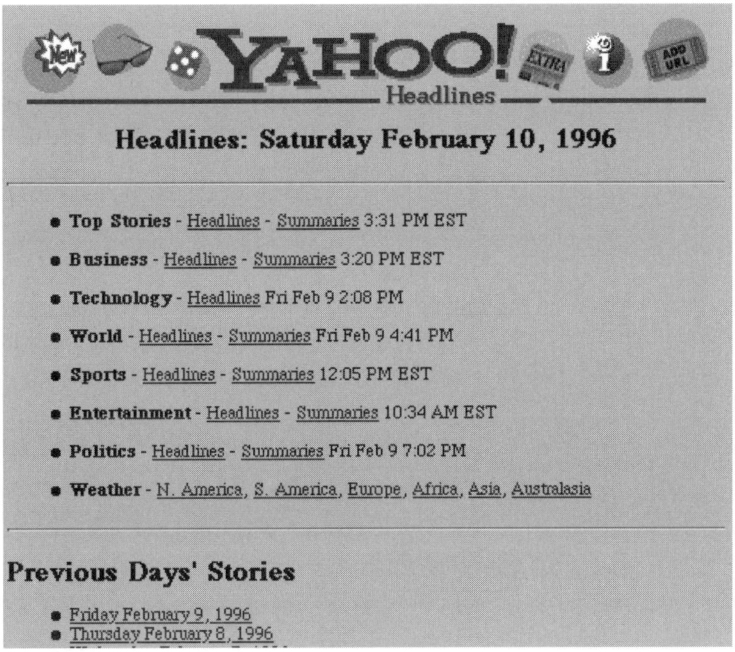

Figure 4.6: Reuters news feed from Yahoo.

With over 100,000 hits a day Yahoo is by far one of the most active sites on the Net. So check it out. Start there. We'd also like to point you to another great Table of Contents site and that's the Galaxy WWW site at:

http://galaxy.tradewave.com

OK, the Galaxy site is based in Austin. So we're partial. It's another great site and definitely one worth checking out. With about 60,000 visits a day it's another of the more popular sites on the Net.

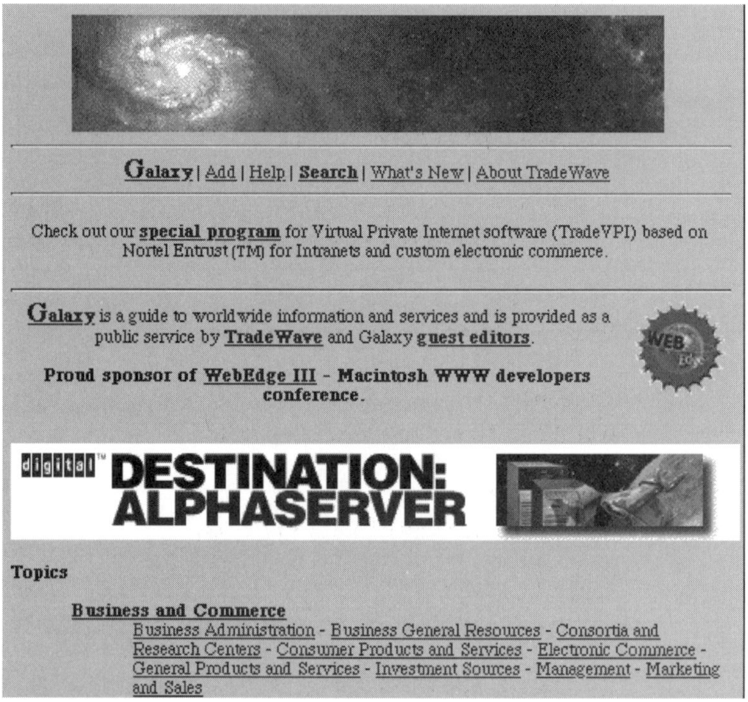

Figure 4.7: Galaxy WWW site homepage.

Most Visited WWW Sites

Here's a list of 10 of the most visited WWW sites on the Internet and their URLs. Check 'em out and see why they are so popular.

CMP Tech Web
http://techweb.cmp.com/

C|Net
http://www.cnet.com

ESPN
http://espnet.sportszone.com/index.text.html

GNN
http://gnn.com

Hot Wired
http://www.hotwired.com/

InfoSeek
http://www.infoseek.com/

Netscape
http://home.netscape.com

Pathfinder
http://www.pathfinder.com

TimesFax
http://nytimesfax.com/cgi-bin/tmp/login

Ziff-Davis/ZD Net
http://www.zdnet.com

Source: *Information Week,* February 1996.

URLs and Domain Name Voodoo Whodo

We're going to pause here for a moment before we surf off to the other most excellent sites in this chapter. But first, there are a couple of mundane things you may be curious about. Like domain names. (If not feel free to skip ahead.)

By now you're probably wondering what the ending ".com" in the address of a WWW site stands for. In fact, what does all the info in an Internet address mean?

The "http://" at the beginning of an Internet address means it's a Web site. The ".com" stands for "commercial." Here are some other common "dot" codes:

- .edu = educational
- .org = nonprofit organization
- .net = Internet providers
- .gov = government
- .mil–millionaires (just kidding: it's military)

(Pronounced "dot edu," "dot org," "dot net," and so on.)

The Net and the Web in particular use URLs to make surfing around easy. URL stands for Uniform Resource Locator. (It's not Uniform Resource Location or Uniform Record Locator. It's Uniform Resource Locator. We've heard and seen all these and worse.)

The Web uses URLs to find files on servers. If you want to cruise to other sites or nab software files off the Net, you need to know how to use URLs.

A URL "address" has the following defined format:

```
scheme://host.domain [:port]/path/filename
```

Yum. It's that UNIX stuff, back to haunt us. You need to understand it, at least a little, if you're going to surf. And since links are what it's all about, take a deep breath and dive in.

Here's what that gobbledygook means.

The *scheme* can be one of the following:

- **file://**
  a file on your local system or on an anonymous FTP server
- **http://**
  a file on a WWW server
- **ftp://**
  a file on an anonymous FTP server
- **gopher://**
  a file on a gopher server
- **WAIS://**
  a file on a WAIS server
- **news://**
  Usenet newsgroup
- **telnet://**
  a connection to a Telnet-based service

The *host.domain* part refers to the machine name (if any) and domain name of the server you want to link to.

The *[:port]* part of the URL syntax is usually not included when you create a link. (The default port for WWW servers is 80, by the way.) But it's part of the official spec, so we had to tell you about it. Unless you see it indicated in the URL of a place you want to link to, leave it out.

The *path/filename* is everything after the domain name (and port if any). It shows what directories or folders you have to work your way down through to get to the file you want to link to. Sometimes all you'll want to link to is the "home-page" of a WWW server, or the top-level directory of an FTP site for instance. In that case you don't have to concern yourself with the path and filename.

Now Blow All That Confusing Stuff Off

Aren't you confused by all this? We were at first. That's why we recommend you just start at Yahoo and cruise from there by clicking on hypertext links. Just be glad you don't have to surf the Net typing in UNIX commands using a command line WWW browser like Lynx. You have no idea how ugly that can get.

Let's march on now, to a bunch of other great sites....

ISP Comparison Shopping

Here's a Catch-22 for you: The best place for extensive information on current Internet service provider pricing is on the Internet itself. Like we said, Catch-22. Hey we just promised to get you started and point you in the right directions. Now that you're jacked in it's time to really nail down who you want to be with for the rest of your Internet connectivity life. We gave you some guidelines. Now it's time for you to do research.

By the way—there's a great article available on the Net on choosing an Internet service provider. It covers a lot of what we've talked about in earlier chapters—and then some. It was written by Rick Adams, the president of UUNet Technologies—one of the best Internet providers going. You can read it by pointing your Web browser to the following URL:

http://web.cnam.fr/Network/Internet-access/how_to_select.html

There are a couple of great sites to go to that have extensive listings of Internet service providers worldwide. Here are the URLs:

http://www.celestin.com/pocia/index.html

http://thelist.com

The List WWW site is particularly useful since it has a searchable database of ISPs. The POCIA list is included in Appendix B of this book.

Figure 4.8: Celestin WWW site—POCIA list.

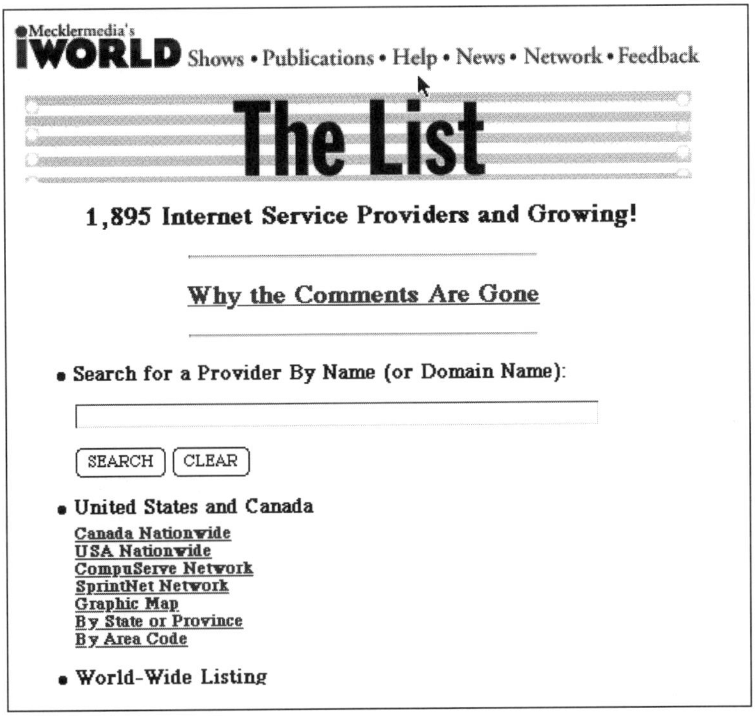

Figure 4.9: The List WWW site homepage.

THE LIST -- Looking for OuterNet

```
OuterNet Connection Strategies
 Area/Country codes: 512
 Automated email:    info@outer.net
 Human email:        support@outer.net
 Phone:              (512) 345-3573
 Fax:                (512) 206-0345
 URL:                http://www.outer.net/
 Services:           dialup+dedicated PPP, SLIP, +ISDN, WWW, consulting
 Fees:               PPP/SLIP: $35/mo(+$50 setup, 60hrs.+$1/hr extra)
                          Dedicated $100/mo(+$150 setup)
                     ISDN : On-Demand $50/mo(60hrs.+$1/hr after)
                     ISDN : Dedicated $195/mo+$350 setup 64K B-Channel
 Notes: Specializing in:ISDN access with a variety of equipment, TCP/IP
        and Internet consulting.
```

Copyright © 1995 by Mecklermedia. All rights reserved.
Maintained by Colossus Inc.

Figure 4.10: Search results on the List WWW site.

So Come On—Where's the Free Access?

Fair enough. We kind of suggest that free Internet access might exist somewhere out there in cyberspace. Well, you can find it. We have.

The thing is you often get scammed by something like a deal where the Internet access is free but you pay big long-distance charges or some gimmick to a company that is in the long-distance business and doing a little Internet on the side.

There is one thing to check out. It's called Free-Net and the "gotcha" catch is a good one. Here's the deal: Free-Nets are a good thing. Their purpose is to help create access to the Internet and the info-superbahn-way to a community at large. That means libraries, schools, rec centers, housing projects, hospitals, public buildings, etc.

Besides offering Internet access, the 100+ Free-Nets that are out there worldwide (mostly in the United States and in varying degrees of development) do content. They often work closely with community groups to get the groups' information repurposed and put up online on a WWW site or bulletin board system.

Here's a picture of the Austin Free-Net's homepage. (We do go on and on about Austin, don't we. We live here and we love it.)

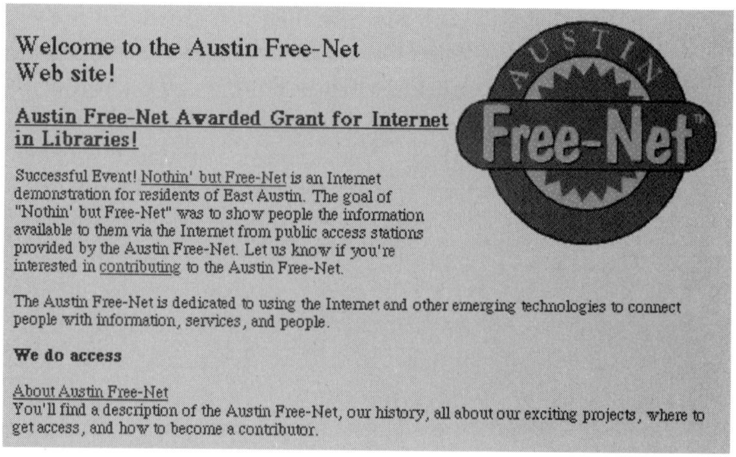
Welcome to the Austin Free-Net Web site!

Austin Free-Net Awarded Grant for Internet in Libraries!

Successful Event! Nothin' but Free-Net is an Internet demonstration for residents of East Austin. The goal of "Nothin' but Free-Net" was to show people the information available to them via the Internet from public access stations provided by the Austin Free-Net. Let us know if you're interested in contributing to the Austin Free-Net.

The Austin Free-Net is dedicated to using the Internet and other emerging technologies to connect people with information, services, and people.

We do access

About Austin Free-Net
You'll find a description of the Austin Free-Net, our history, all about our exciting projects, where to get access, and how to become a contributor.

Figure 4.11: The Austin Free-Net homepage.

So Free-Nets are a good thing. Anything that helps educate people who don't have bucks and helps connect them with others helps everyone in the long run. On all levels. Big time. That's what the Free-Nets are all about.

If you want to hear the doctrine from the source go to the Free-Net home base at the National Public Telecomputing Network (NPTN) WWW site. The URL is:

http://www.nptn.org/

Yeah, yeah. We know. Stop the social commentary already. Get to the point.

OK, OK. Here's the point. Our experience is that you can usually get a free Internet account from a Free-Net with a minimal amount of volunteering. Call one and find out. Helping out a few hours here and there for something worthwhile is a good deal.

Yeah, you're right. That's not exactly free. But what is? That's as close as you're going to get (to free) on the Net, unless you're a student, of course.

You can also try this angle with a commercial provider by the way. Especially a smaller one that is new in the business. Jeff has often gotten free access from different providers by bringing them new accounts with little effort. They're hungry for the business and you just tell your friends or colleagues and bring them along online with you.

Simple. Works too. Try it.

Before we leave the subject, here are the URLs and a brief description for a few more good Free-Net and community computing WWW sites and resources to check out. Most of the Free-Nets are moving to a WWW-based way of organizing community info. A couple are still Telnet sites (that means they're ugly menu-driven UNIX bulletin board systems, basically—an old, complicated, and almost extinct technology and way of organizing content).

FreeNet Newsflash
`http://www.freenet.vancouver.bc.ca/vrfa/newsflash/`
Free-Net news and accomplishments

Beyond our Borders
`http://www.freenet.hamilton.on.ca/Beyond.html`
A list of remote Free-Net sites all over the place

About the Vancouver Regional FreeNet Association
`http://freenet.vancouver.bc.ca/vrfa/`

Community Network guide
`http://http2.sils.umich.edu/~ckummer/community.html`
A WWW guide to community networking

FREEnet INF-0001 General Information
`http://www.free.net/FREEnet/INF/INF-0001.en.html`
A network for research education, and engineering

Some Canadian Free-Nets on the Web
`http://www.synapse.net/~radio/freenet.htm`
Like the title says: some Canadian Free-Nets on the Web

Cleveland Free-Net
`Telnet: freenet-in-a.cwru.edu, freenet-in-b.cwru.edu`
or freenet-in-c.cwru.edu

City.Net

Hey. While we're on the topic of community computing, there are many cities and towns with great WWW sites which organize everything going on in a city from jobs to entertainment. City.Net is "the most comprehensive international guide to communities around the world. City.Net is updated every day to provide easy and timely access to information on travel, entertainment, and local business, plus government and community services for all regions of the world." Check it out—see if a bunch of geeks have organized everything about where you live onto a WWW site. The URL for City.Net is:

`http://www.city.net`

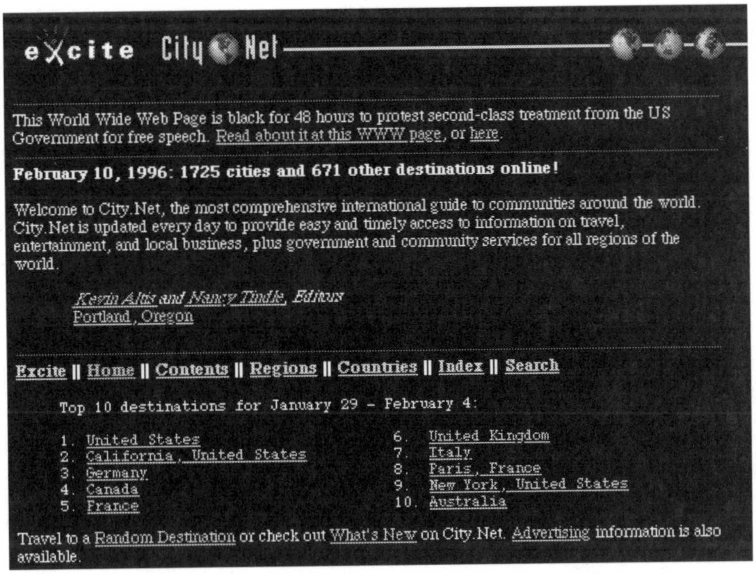

Figure 4.12: City.Net homepage.

So, are we giving you some great places to go or what? Guess what. We made life easy for you. They're all included in Appendix C and as a bookmark file on the CD-ROM that comes with the book, remember? Look for a file named Cheesy.html.

There are a bunch of other great WWW sites we'd like to turn you on to. We're sure to miss some, by the way. Some of those may even turn out to be your favorite. But we want to avoid page after page of boring black-and-white screen shots and instead just get you started. You'll do fine on your own out there.

On the Net there are so many wonderful sites covering every topic you could dream of. Jeff is a weather nut and goes to four to six great weather-related sites regularly. His favorite is the Storm Chaser page and WeatherNet at:

http://taiga.geog.niu.edu/chaser/chaser.html

and

http://cirrus.sprl.umich.edu/wxnet/

But the USA Today and CNN WWW sites also do good weather. Hey it's fun to find and try different ones if weather is all you're into. In fact you could do nothing but weather sites on the Net if that's your trip. You'd be busy for a long, long time.

Here are a few more of our favorite sites. Some are very useful. Others are just fun. We're surfin' here, so don't look for a list that is organized by category. You can get that on the Net itself; we, on the other hand, are ramblin', wandering kinds of guys.

Bob & Jeff Go Surfing

Epicurious

http://www.epicurious.com/

We get hungry just looking at this site. When are they going to have those Star Trek replicators on the Net?

Figure 4.13: Epicurious homepage—yum!

MTV, Music Television

http://www.mtv.com/

Is it just us or is there some retro thing going on? It's like the 60's with no social or political activism all over again.

Figure 4.14: MTV homepage.

Cool Site of the Day

http://www.infi.net/cool.html

Glenn Davis' opinion of what's cool. It's a popular stopping off spot.

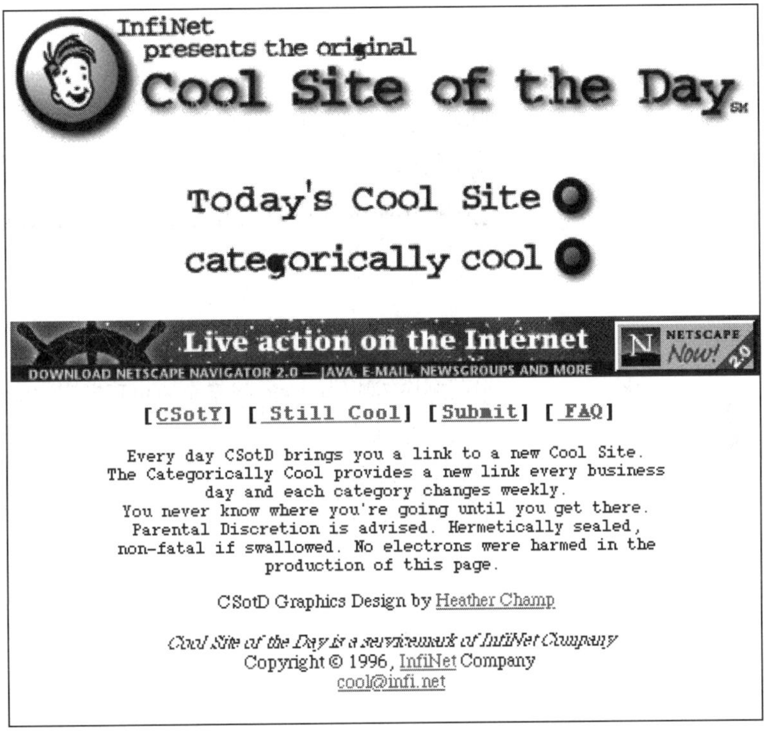

Figure 4.15: Cool site of the Day WWW site.

The Virtual Tourist

`http://www.vtourist.com/webmap/`

So you've got two kids and a job and can't get off your duff and see the world for a few years. Try this.

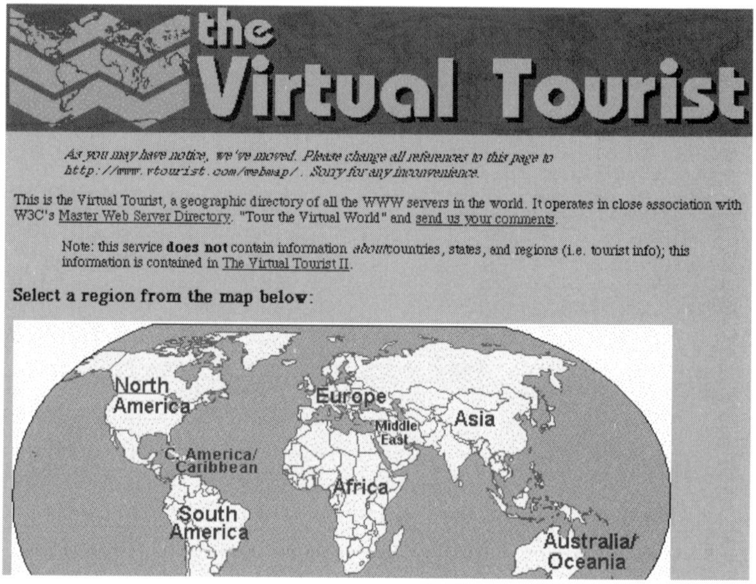

Figure 4.16: Virtual Tourist WWW site.

CBS Eye on the Net

http://www.cbs.com/

You can get to Letterman stuff from here if you don't get enough on the tube.

Figure 4.17: CBS WWW site homepage.

Firehorse

http://www.peg.apc.org/~firehorse/welcome.html

A popular Aussie e-zine.

Figure 4.18: Firehorse WWW site.

Internet Underground Music Archive

http://www.iuma.com/

The Net's great hi-fi music archive.

Figure 4.19: Internet Underground Music WWW site.

Todd Rundgren's Freedom Fighters Home Base

http://www.iglou.com/scm/cgi-bin/todd.pl

Most of the stuff the Rundgren does pushes the envelope, gets you to step back and think a little for a change. Check it out.

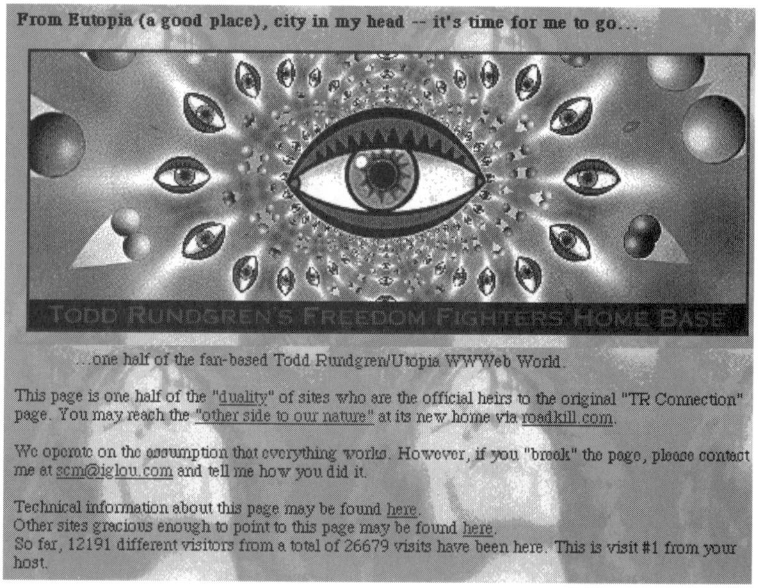

Figure 4.20: Rundgren rocks!

Suck

http://suck.com

"A fish, a barrel, and a smoking gun." Need we say more? Biting social and political satire mixed with unbelievable tales of mirth. Watch it get sucked into the dot on the homepage. You'll get what we mean when you go there. Trust us.

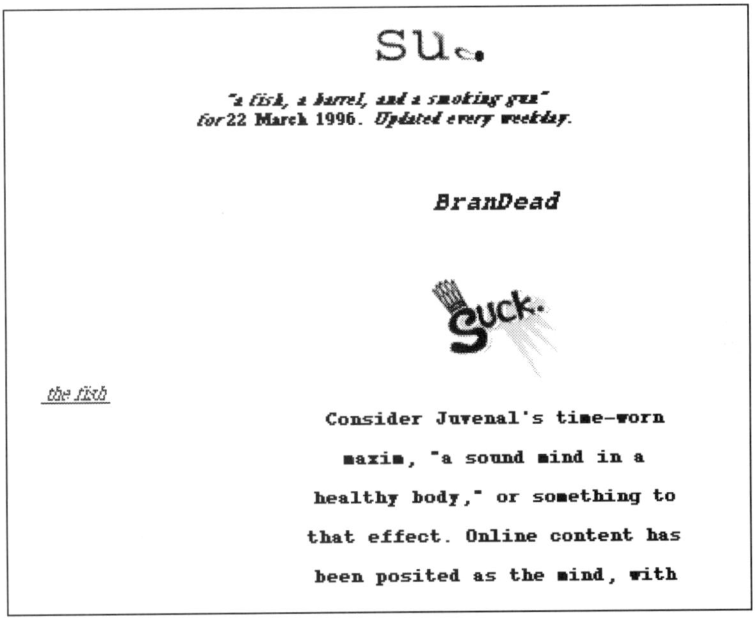

Figure 4.21: Suck.com WWW site.

We were also going to pick out some sites for great jokes and comic strips but that gets to be a real personal thing for some people. Jeff gets tons of e-mail from friends who send him jokes. Most are dumb. He knows who compiles the good ones and uses that Eudora filter we told you about to blow through 'em. So you are on your own for a joke page. (Besides, it's a joke a minute reading this book, isn't it?)

All right, all right. If you insist. Here's a start: Go to Yahoo and follow the Entertainment link on the Yahoo homepage to Comics and you'll be shocked by how much is there. You'll wonder, like we did, "where do all these people find the time to do all this?" In fact there's even a whole collection of over 100 "nothing but useless" pages listed at Yahoo. There are even whole WWW sites that specialize in combining their technological expertise with boredom to give us truly masterful pieces of nothingness.

Figure 4.22: The Useless WWW site.

Bob & Jeff Go Shopping

Has all that got you itching to buy something? Even though lots of people are all flipped out about security and whether or not their credit card is going to get ripped off, electronic commerce is already starting to be a big reality on the Net. Getting ripped off probably happens more often in real life than in cyberspace. Besides, last time we checked the fine print on our credit cards we weren't liable for fraud if we didn't do it.

You can be sure that VISA and MasterCard and Bill Gates and Netscape will figure this all out and give the paranoid on Earth some peace of mind—about the issue of Net security at least. It's going to be a multi-billion-dollar-a-year industry.

We can hardly wait. Besides we can't stand all the junk mail catalogs our wives get. If only we could get them shopping on the Net. It might even get them to chill out on the consumer front for the time it takes them to learn their way around online ordering.

After that we're done for.

Every day there are new places to shop popping up on the Net. Flowers, software, chocolate, collectibles, lawyers, mandolins—you get the idea. If it's not there yet it will be. Try these WWW sites or go to Yahoo and search for online shopping like we did. Keep in mind that sites come and go and that some sites are here today and gone by the time you buy the book.

Shop-the-Net

`http://www.shop-the-net.com/`

Shop 'til you drop. "A family shopping mall. Shop for kids, gifts for your family and products for your home and business."

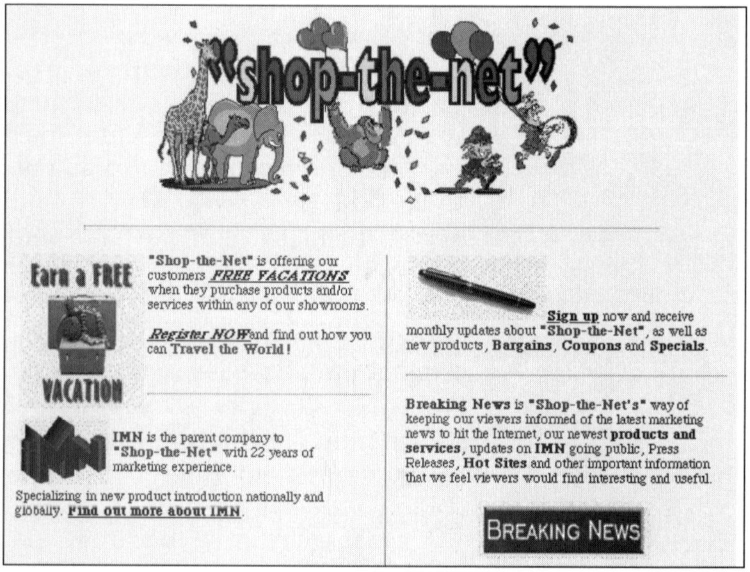

Figure 4.23: Shop-the-net WWW site.

1 World Plaza

http://www2.clever.net/1world/plaza/shop.htm

Even more great shopping: "65 stores full of great, one of a kind quality merchandise and services."

Figure 4.24: 1 World Plaza WWW site.

1 Mall

http://www.1mall.com/

Secure online ordering and a great shopping basket way of buying.

Figure 4.25: 1 Mall WWW site.

1st Shopping Planet

http://www.shoppingplanet.com/

Computers, electronics, software, music, gifts, and then some.

Figure 4.26: 1st Shopping Planet WWW site.

American Internet Mall

`http://www.ammall.com/`

A higher class kind of shopping?

Figure 4.27: The American Internet Mall WWW site.

The INFOMART

http://www.infomartusa.com/

INFOMART is a 1.6 million square foot market center for computer-related products and services located in Dallas, Texas, USA. Its 100 tenants include Andersen Consulting, Apple, AT&T, EDS, Novell, SAS Institute, Toshiba, and Xerox. INFOMART Magazine discusses hot topics for the information systems industry such as client/server, multimedia, ATM, and networking. The INFOMART Directory gives a brief description and telephone number for contacting INFOMART tenants.

Figure 4.28: The INFOMART WWW site.

DreamShop

http://www.dreamshop.com

Eddie Bauer, The Horchow Collections, The Sharper Image, The Bombay Company, Time Warner's Viewer's Edge, Book of the Month Club, Spiegel, and then some.

Figure 4.29: Time Warner's Dream Shop WWW site.

The Front Page

http://www.thefrontpage.com/

Health products, marine products and services, professional services, video, arts, and much much more unrelated to each other stuff.

Figure 4.30: The Front Page WWW homepage.

InterArt

http://www.interart.net/

Nice gifts and artsy artifacts—at least we thought so.

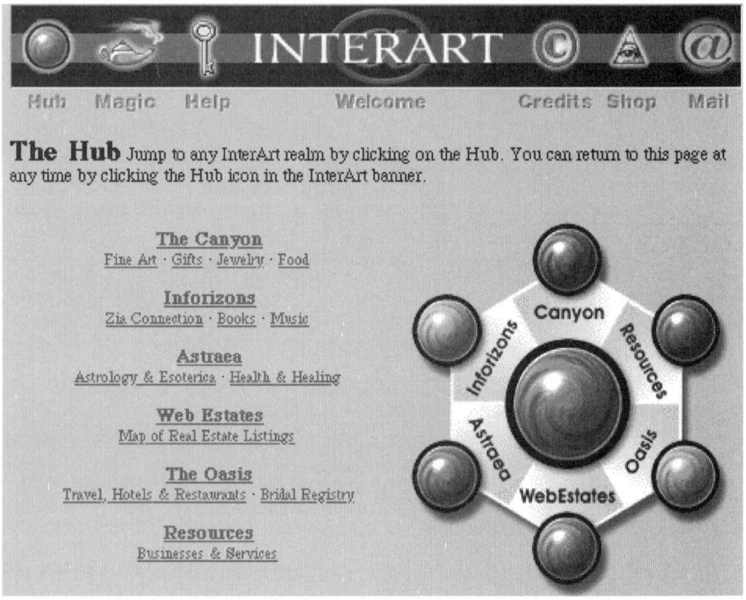

Figure 4.31: Interart's WWW homepage.

MakeMusic.com

http://www.makemusic.com

Instruments, dealers, builders, musicians—the online site for the vintage string instruments. A killer site.

Figure 4.32: MakeMusic.com WWW homepage.

Bob & Jeff Get Real

OK. Settle down. We're not going to keep on giving you list after list of places to go and tons of screen shots to tempt you to visit some of the sites we recommend you check out. We have only a few more of those to do before we're done with you. We don't want to turn this book into some out-of-date book of lists. Let's get back to some useful stuff. There's a ton more of it.

Hey. You're getting the idea, right? Anything you can think of is probably there on the Net. In spades. Just go to the big search engines and search. That's how we all do it.

Did we tell you about the All-in-One Search Site? Holy smokes. You gotta check this one out:

`http://www.albany.net/allinone/`

There are a couple of other types of Internet resources you should know about before we really get out there and show you where the newest things technologically that are happening on the Net can be found. We're saving that for last.

It's useful to know where you can find computer-related resources on the Net. If nothing else, the Net is the quickest way to get a software update for a version of a program you're running that keeps crashing your computer. It's also the best place to get the latest virus killer to deal with the attention deficit disorder creations of the teenage mutants.

Net Bugs, Viruses, and Stupid Toad-Heads

Face it. Viruses are a fact of life if you use a computer. They happen. For the most part they're a stupid nuisance and can be killed easily if they happen to find their way onto your hard drive. They're something you should check for regularly.

There are many good utilities on the Net and commercially that nail viruses. Symantec's Anti-Virus Research Center WWW site at:

http://www.symantec.com/avcenter/avcenter.html

is probably the best place to start looking for the latest info, alerts, and software dealing with viruses. They've got a solid list of associated links to other related sites off that address too.

There are many other computer-related resources on the Net. Just about every hardware and software manufacturer has a site now pitching their products. The sites listed below (yes, another list—but a good one!) are great resources. They're some of the biggies with major Internet presence and are listed alphabetically. Microsoft has an excellent link to Internet resources off its homepage, by the way. They should of course. And they do.

Apple Computer Inc.
http://www.apple.com/

Compaq Computer Corp.
http://www.compaq.com/

David Singer's OS/2 Page of Pointers
http://index.almaden.ibm.com/

Dell Computer Corp.
http://www.us.dell.com

Hewlett-Packard Co.
http://www.hp.com

IBM Corp.
http://www.ibm.com

IBM Personal Software Co.
http://www.austin.ibm.com/pspinfo/

Intel Corp.
http://www.intel.com

Lotus Development Corp.
http://www.lotus.com

Microsoft Corp.
http://www.microsoft.com

NEC Corp.
http://www.nec.com

Netcom Online Communication Services
http://www.netcom.com

Netscape Communications Corp
http://home.netscape.com

Novell Inc.
http://www.novell.com

Performance Systems International Inc.
http://www.psi.net

Power Computing Corp.
http://www.powercc.com

Silicon Graphics Inc.
http://www.sgi.com

Spry Inc.
http://www.spry.com

Sun Microsystems Inc.
http://www.sun.com

UUNET Technologies
http://www.uu.net

Or you can save time and go to the C|Net Vendor Rolodex at:

http://www.cnet.com/Resources/Info/Vendor/index.html

and do all your hunting around from there.

Figure 4.33: Apple WWW site homepage.

You need to know a little about four more ways information on the Net is organized—FTP sites, newsgroups, mailing lists (often referred to as listservs), and Internet BBSs. More important, you need to know where the good ones are, what they have, and how to use them.

FTP Sites

Let's start with FTP sites. You remember that FTP stand for File Transfer Protocol, right?

In addition to all the nonsense that's out there, it's time we turned you on to the spots to go get software, cheaply and easily. Most of the software available on the Internet is freeware or "shareware." Freeware is free. Duh. Shareware is cheap and usually has a nominal fee of 10–20 bucks, sometimes a little more. The trick to nabbing software off the Net is to find a site that isn't swamped with a million other people doing the same thing. Sometimes you have to wait to get into an FTP site—like on the day Netscape Communications Corp. announces a new version of its Netscape Navigator software. Forget it. Wait a day or two or do it at 3 AM when most sane people are sleeping.

Ask your friends. There are lots of hidden FTP sites that aren't publicized that have tons of software. But keep a good thing quiet when you find it. That's what we're going to do.

Keep away from private FTP sites and the pirate Internet bulletin board systems that have Photoshop and Marathon available to download. Don't tell us about them anyway.

Keep it legal. And pay the shareware fees when you're supposed to. Don't be like the majority of online surfers who download shareware, use it regularly, and never send in the $10 it cost them. Don't be lame. It's bogus.

We recommend you just use your favorite Web browser software to search and download stuff. FTP is built into all the good Web browsers. You can use an FTP-specific piece of software like WS-FTP (see Chapter 3 if you forgot about it) and usually increase the speed with which you can download a file—a little. Not enough, though, to notice for a beginner. And it's definitely more complicated than just using one application like Netscape or WinWeb to do everything. Instead of typing **http://** you type **ftp://** at the beginning of the URL address you are after. Here's an example that shows you AOL's .FTP site. There are usually mirror sites for really big FTP sites like AOL's. Try both if you get a message that says the site is swamped with traffic. It help spreads the load.

AOL's master FTP site is at ftp://ftp.aol.com. Their mirror site's URL is ftp://mirror.aol.com. Sometimes the mirror is busier than the master.

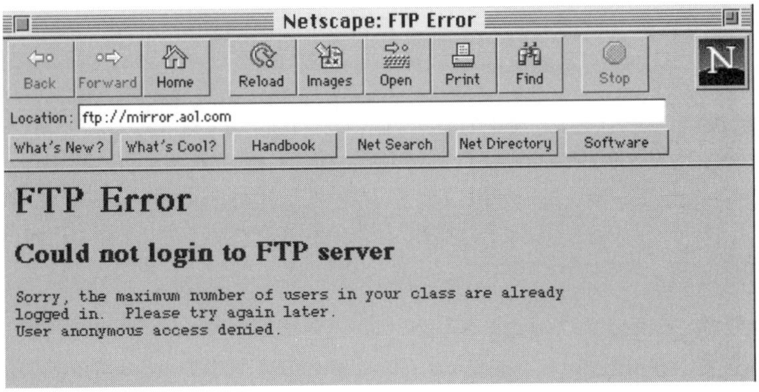

Figure 4.34: AOL FTP server unavailable message.

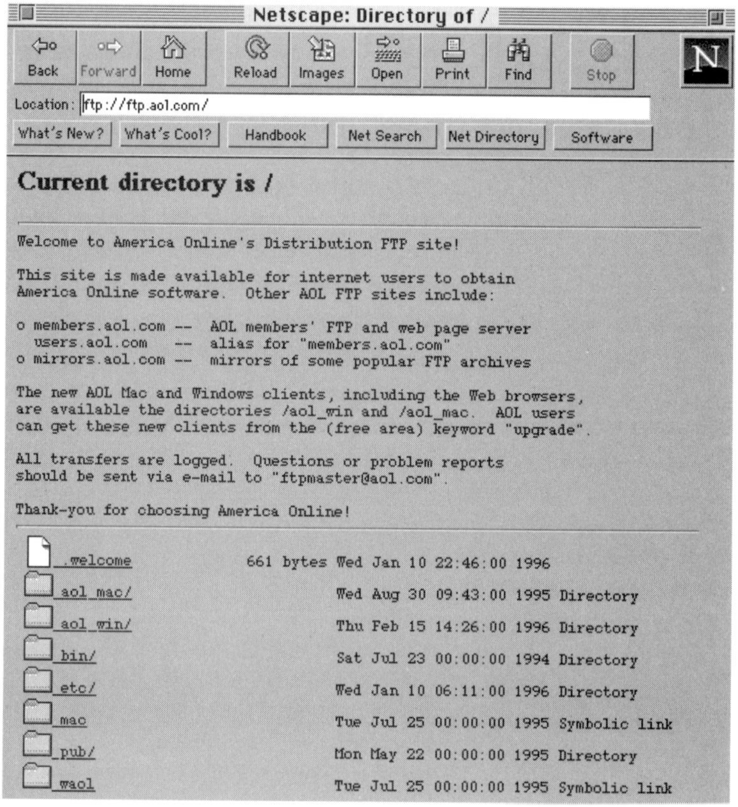

Figure 4.35: AOL FTP site at ftp://ftp.aol.com.

Most public FTP sites just let you log in as an anonymous user with a user ID of "anonymous" and a password of "youremailaddress." It's rare that you have to even deal with entering that info when you're using a WWW browser to do FTP. Here's a quick list of great FTP sites for Mac users on the Net:

UT Mac archive
http://wwwhost.ots.utexas.edu/mac/main.html

Peter Lewis
ftp://ftp:share.com

Info-Mac
ftp://mirror.apple.com

U of Michigan Mac Archives
ftp://grind.iscs.uiowa.edu

C|Net's shareware.com
http://www.shareware.com/

There are lots more. One way to find them—of course—is to do that old search engine thing we've been harping on what must seem like every page. Try a different one this time. Have you been to the Infoseek WWW site yet? Go there. And don't use Yahoo this time. Sometimes it's painfully slow. Come on. Right now, while the iron's hot, get off your duff and go to Infoseek. Here's the URL so you don't have to dig around for it:

http://www.infoseek.com

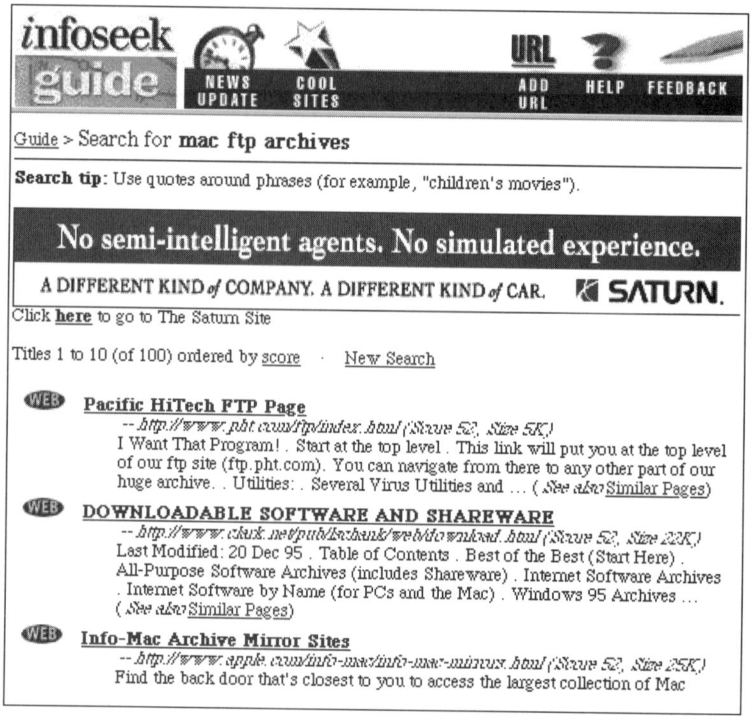

Figure 4.36: Infoseek search results for Mac archives.

Usenet Newsgroups

Usenet is a worldwide hierarchical message system. It was started back in 1980 by four students on the Duke University campus and has grown to become the largest decentralized information repository in existence. A concise definition of what Usenet is and does is difficult to come by, so instead allow the following list of Usenet features help conjure a working definition.

1. Usenet is not controlled or policed by anyone as a whole. No one has authority over Usenet, its users define what does and does not occur. No government owns or controls Usenet, other than standard national security restrictions. The owners of a local server have control over their server, and it is up to them (commonly called "news administrators") to determine what is or isn't transmitted over their site. Individual users and moderators often try to regulate or control the content of specific newsgroups in order to maintain quality for all participants in a group with relative success.

2. Usenet is not an organization, company, or business. Other than the standards required to maintain universal compatibility between news servers, there is no widespread control over how Usenet functions or is used. Usenet is organized, or at least the foundations are organized—the resultant constructs on that basis are not always sound. There are specific organizational measures taken to ensure that Usenet remains an easy-to-use information tool. But as in any activity which involves millions of people, some sloppiness and chaos are fated.

3. Usenet is not fair. Since there are no governing or controlling bodies restricting activities, anyone can post anything anywhere they want. Just another proof for the saying, "Life is not fair." You may be able to get away with a lot but you may also get blamed for something you didn't do.

4. Usenet access is not part of freedom of speech. The owners of the computers which house and transmit Usenet can and do restrict what is transmitted to or from their servers. If you want to have complete control over what you can say and read, buy your own server.

5. Usenet is not a publicly funded entity. It is funded by whatever means necessary to keep existing servers running and to add existing servers as needed. There is no large-scale organized effort to purchase and support equipment for the transmission of Usenet. Each individual or group maintains their servers at their own expense. Even without the direct funding of Usenet, it is carried over much publicly paid for equipment, such as university mainframes, government computers, and public telephone networks.

6. Usenet is not commercial. Even though most hosts are now owned by businesses, blatant widespread commercial advertising is often shunned. Usenet encompasses government agencies, educational facilities, businesses of all sizes, and individual home computers. Sections of Usenet are designated for specific uses based on the needs and desires of the owners and operators of the equipment. However, with proper planning and understanding of the newsgroups involved, personal or corporate gain via advertising can be accomplished successfully without offending the entire Usenet community.

7. Usenet is not the Internet. The Internet is a loose conglomeration of many information exchange, repository, and retrieval systems, only one of which is Usenet. Usenet can and does exist on servers which are not on the Internet. However, the Internet is an indispensable medium which Usenet travels over; if the Internet did not exist, neither would Usenet.

8. Usenet is not only in the United States. Like the Internet, Usenet is worldwide and is limited only by transmission lines and servers. Most of Usenet's

newsgroups can be accessed from all seven continents, including Antarctica!

9. Usenet is the collection of people who post articles to newsgroups. Usenet is not just the bits, the millions and millions of bits transmitted daily, it is the collection of people who care enough to send the very best (or the very worst, or at least what is mediocre and bland). Anyone from anywhere with anything to say about any subject with a connection to any communications network with Usenet access can post and retrieve articles. Usenet is the ultimate equal opportunity employer.

10. Usenet is not just one messaging system, but is many systems tied together which interact with and without human involvement. Most of Usenet exists on the Internet, but other electronic communication entities send and receive articles as well. Usenet can be accessed by e-mail, FTP, gopher, Web, and even Telnet, and that doesn't even cover all the methods possible.

That should just about clear it up. If you still don't have a good grasp of what Usenet is, there is plenty of material online available for you to chew on. First, grab yourself a newsreader (see the previous chapter), then visit one or more of the following newsgroups:

- news.announce.newusers
- news.announce.newgroups
- news.newusers.questions
- news.answers
- news.groups

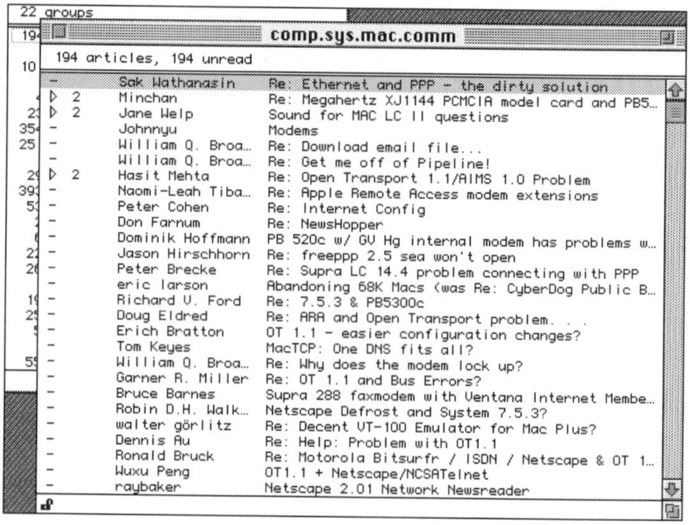

Figure 4.37: NewsWatcher newsreader Showing comp.sys.mac.group.

These newsgroups contain important Usenet-related FAQs and other information postings. If you take the time to read through the materials posted, you will learn more about what Usenet is and the wide range of activities and information which are available to you through Usenet. Some important topics you need to have a good grasp of are: netiquette, posting rules, tone, voice, smileys, group moderation, threads, test groups, signature files, cross-posting, subject lines, and distribution. The simple act of getting online and reading this information from Usenet will not only familiarize you with your newsreader but also give you firsthand experience using Usenet. For a humorous outing on the serious side of Usenet, take a peek at the "101 Ways to be Obnoxious on Usenet" Web site at http://www.indirect.com/user/steiners/usenet.html.

Usenet has over 15,000 newsgroups and more are constantly being added. It would be a daunting task to list every significant group in the confines of this book.

Instead, in the next few paragraphs, we explain how to locate this information in Usenet itself.

Usenet is loosely organized into nine major categories:

- alt — limited distribution groups, often with a wider range of content
- biz — business
- comp — computers, software
- misc — anything that doesn't fit into another category
- news — news and topical subjects
- rec — recreation and entertainment
- sci — science
- soc — social issues and socializing
- talk — debate and discussion

Other categories exist but they are usually limited distribution groups for a specific group of people, such as the TX category, which focuses on Texas-related or -directed subjects. The subsequent portions of a newsgroup's name define its content and focus. Usually broad topics are used for the second name part and more specific and focused topics are included in further parts. Information about main and subcategory groups is often posted to an *.answers group. For information about the comp newsgroups, look in comp.answers.

Almost every newsgroup has a FAQ (frequently asked questions), which is a document containing the focus, purpose, posting limitations, and rules for the specific newsgroup. We strongly suggest (even insist) that you locate and read the FAQ for a newsgroup before you even think about posting. This will save you headaches, frustration, and long lectures or even flaming. Take our word for it—when in doubt about the rules of a newsgroup, DON'T. A newsgroup's FAQ is regularly posted to that group and to alt.answers, news.answers, or the *.answers group of its main category.

A few alternate locations for Usenet FAQs are:

- Usenet Graphics FAQs Web page—this site contains many graphical newsgroup and other related FAQs.
  `http://www.cis.ohio-state.edu/hypertext/faq/usenet/graphics/top.html`

- Oxford's Usenet newsgroup hierarchy with searchable FAQ archive—a large collection of FAQs with search capabilities
  `http://www.lib.ox.ac.uk/internet/news/`

- Usenet newsgroups: Resources
  `http://scwww.ucs.indiana.edu/NetRsc/usenet.html`

- MIT FAQ FTP archive
  `ftp://rtfm.mit.edu/pub/usenet/news.answers/`

Figure 4.38: Oxford's Usenet newsgroup hierarchy with searchable FAQ archive.

If you still feel inadequate to look for meaningful newsgroups on your own, here is a list of Internet topical newsgroups.

- alt.best.of.internet
- alt.internet.services
- comp.infosystems.*
- comp.internet

Welcome to the wild and woolly world of Usenet. BTW (that's "by the way," if you haven't figured it out by now), be sure to tie a rope around your ankle in case someone has to drag you away from your computer. There is so much information in Usenet that is it impossible to read it all, so don't even try.

Mailing Lists

Mailing lists are e-mail–based discussion groups. There are countless thousands of mailing lists, from open discussion to highly moderated. Each mailing list is usually concentrated on a single topic or subject, but a narrow subject definition does not necessarily mean the content will stay focused. Mailing lists can be a regular synopsis of all submitted information or an avalanche of messages. If you are not careful when subscribing to mailing lists, you may find yourself flooded with useless messages. Before you sign up for a list, look for a FAQ or request the help or information file.

Most mailing lists are handled by standardized mailing list protocols. Each protocol has a set of controls or command words which are used to operate within the list. For current detailed information about mailing lists, how to subscribe, and even how to start your own, refer to the following Web URLs:

- Internet Mailing Lists Guides and Resources
  `http://www.nlc-bnc.ca/ifla/I/training/listserv/lists.htm`
- Liszt
  `http://www.liszt.com/`
- Search the List of Lists
  `http://catalog.com/vivian/interest-group-search.html`
- Publicly accessible mailing lists
  `http://www.neosoft.com/internet/paml/index.html`

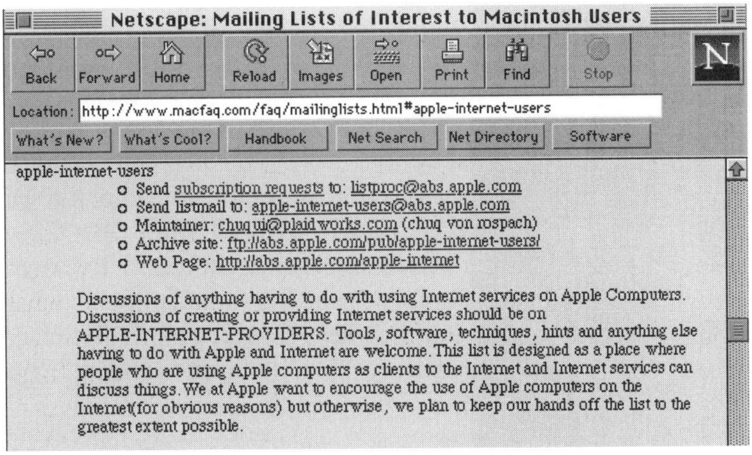

Figure 4.39: Well-connected Mac mailing list example.

There are a few extremely important pieces of mailing list etiquette you should be aware of. First, most mailing lists have two e-mail addresses associated with them. One is the administrative address and the other is the list address. The administrative address is the e-mail address you should use when subscribing, unsubscribing, getting help, requesting information, or altering the status or settings of your subscription. The list address is the e-mail address used to send messages to everyone subscribed to the list. Do not send administrative messages to the list address. The moderator of the list will ban you from his list faster than you can blink if you make that mistake. The second bit of mailing list information you should be aware of is that when you do send a message to the list address, be sure to send valuable content. Valuable content is more than quoting a previous message with one or two short comments added, it is giving quality information in a concise and direct manner. Leave message quoting to Usenet, you wouldn't want a mailbox full of useless replies, so don't send them out.

Most mailing lists use a set of four common commands: subscribe, unsubscribe, help, and info. Sending one of these commands as the body of an e-mail message to the administrative address of a mailing list will cause the action to be performed and usually result in a response message. Always ask for help and info before attempting to subscribe to a list. Usually the help or info message you receive will give detailed instructions and information about the list. The syntax of the subscribe commands varies depending on the type of list protocol used, so be sure to read the help/info messages to determine exactly how to join a list.

The four Web addresses mentioned earlier contain information which is vital to your Internet mailing list survival. If you are reading this paragraph and failed to visit the sites we listed, stop and go online and read the information provided for you. The only way for you to know what to do, what not to do, what you can do, and what you cannot do is to read and find out. Everything you will ever need to know about mailing lists is contained on or through these four Web sites. If you do not go online now and learn about mailing lists, we are going to call your mother.

If you are new to the Internet scene and want to get on a few mailing lists which will boost your Internet knowledge, let us make a few suggestions.

- The C|Net Online weekly newsletter—admin e-mail: subscribe@cnet.com; Subject: SUBSCRIBE DISPATCH; Body: SUBSCRIBE DISPATCH

- newbienewz-digest—admin e-mail: Majordomo@io.com; Body: info newbienewz-digest

- net-guide—admin e-mail: listserv@eff.org; Body: subscribe net-guide

Bob & Jeff Go Surreal and Show You the Really Cool Stuff

You've gotten Internet access, you downloaded a Web browser and have surfed the net—big deal, a bunch of people posting stupid pictures and blathering on about nothing, so what. HA! If that's all you have seen of the Web, you have seen nothing yet baby! Yeah, sure the Web is based in a simple and easy-to-use protocol so anyone with a computer can post whatever they want (notice that having a brain is not a prerequisite). But the Web is also so versatile that interactive live multimedia can and is being transmitted over the Web. Have we piqued your interest? Gaining access to the really cool stuff on the Web is as simple as adding a few extras to your browser and then surfing to the right pages.

The extras you'll need to get the most out of the Web are usually called plug-ins (sometimes plugins), helper applications, or add-ons. No matter what you call them, they all perform one unique function—they add features to your Web browser. There are a few rubs when using Web browser plug-ins. First, most plug-ins are designed for the Windows platforms and then later ported over to Macintosh, if at all. Second, most plug-ins are designed to work with only a limited number of browsers and often only one browser. Usually the one browser a plug-in is compatible with is the Netscape Navigator. And to be even more snobbish, often the only version of Netscape Navigator supported is the Windows 95 32-bit 2.0 version, so there—most Windows users are out of luck. Keeping up with all of the plug-ins is kinda getting out of hand actually. Some of these plug-ins are available for other browsers and other operating systems, so visit the listed Web sites below to find out more information about other browser/OS combinations.

WARNING!!! The Web is a constantly expanding and changing environment. You may encounter some difficulty with plug-ins which are still in beta testing or are not properly configured for your system. The beta version of a software may be fully functional, but it also may be still full of bugs and errors. When you download and install a beta version of a plug-in, you are taking some risk that the software may not work properly or may damage or corrupt your system. Generally, when a beta fails to operate it simply doesn't work. Rarely will a plug-in harm your hard drive or operating system, but there is always that one in a million chance. You should be in the habit of backing up your system regularly, or at least before adding new software. So let's recap: BACKUP, BACKUP, BACKUP, then install.

One more item needs to be discussed before you dive head first into the ocean of the Web with these plug-ins—bandwidth. Bandwidth is the measurement of data that can be transmitted across a communications connection within a given amount of time. You are probably connecting to the Internet using a modem, which means your maximum bandwidth is 14.4 Kbps or 28.8 Kbps. While these are reasonable speeds for most Internet activities, you may find yourself growing impatient as you wait for a "cool" site to load. Many of the data files for the enhancement of Web pages which these plug-ins support are large, usually 500K to 5M each. If you want all the bells and whistles available on the Web, you'll need to wait for the transfer or lay out the cash for a faster Internet connection—such as ISDN. You've been warned, you will be waiting a lot to see some of the cool effects these plug-ins provide; those that support streaming—a continuous flow of data that is processed as it is received—are much more pleasant to use. The longer a data file takes to transfer to your system, the more opportunities there are for the data to be corrupted or interrupted during transfer. So when something doesn't work, try reloading it before giving up.

Oh yeah. Did we mention you need more RAM too?

You do.

About 16 Megs is the minimum. Barely. You really need at least 24 Megs to breath easy.

The deal is, when you start banging around with plug-ins you're heading into the leading-edge stuff. The leading-edge geeks all have plenty of RAM and a big fat pipe of bandwidth.

You need both if you're going to surf with the big boys and girls.

Without further ado then. Check out the brief descriptions that follow for a few of the major plug-ins. Then zip over to Netscape's plug-in page at:

http://home.netscape.com/comprod/products/navigator/version_2.0/plugins/index.html(<—— how's that for an easy-to-remember URL. Not.)

Microsoft should have a plug-in page up by the time you read this too. Their Internet Explorer browser had just been released when we wrote this.

Hey, it was Netscape who did the deal with us for including their browser on the CD-ROM that comes with *Cheap & Easy*. And we didn't want to go back and redo the whole book from another browser's point of view.

Amber

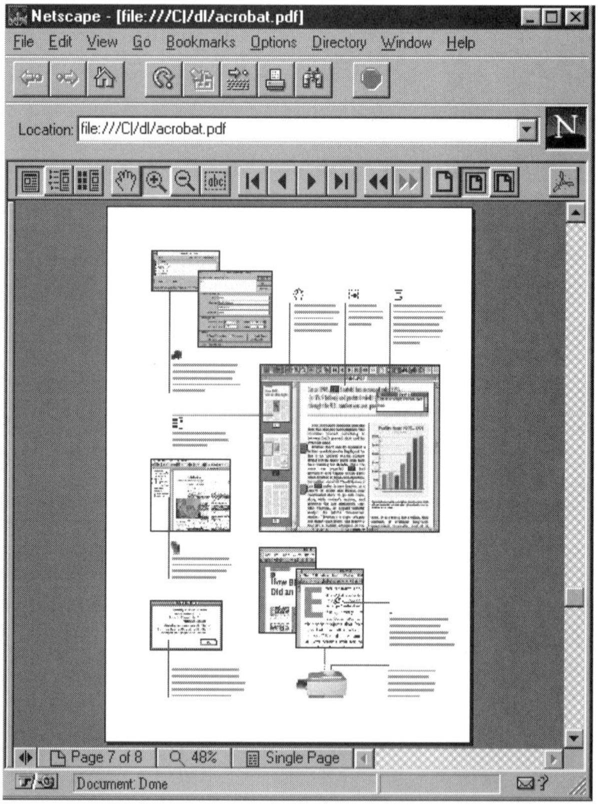

Figure 4.40: Adobe Amber example.

Amber is the Adobe Acrobat Reader plug-in which allows you to view Portable Document Format (PDF) files directly in your Netscape Navigator window. Amber is an browser plug-in adaptation of the free Adobe Acrobat Reader, which can also be configured as an external helper application. A PDF file is a unique cross-platform PostScript-based file format developed by Adobe which contains complete layout, graphic, and font information—on any platform, the document looks exactly like the original. This method of information exchange is quickly becoming a popular way to distribute layout-dependent information, such as manuals and legal forms. To obtain the Amber plug-in, please visit the Adobe Amber Web site at http://w1000.mv.us. adobe.com/Amber/Index.html

Here's an example that will thrill you. Not.

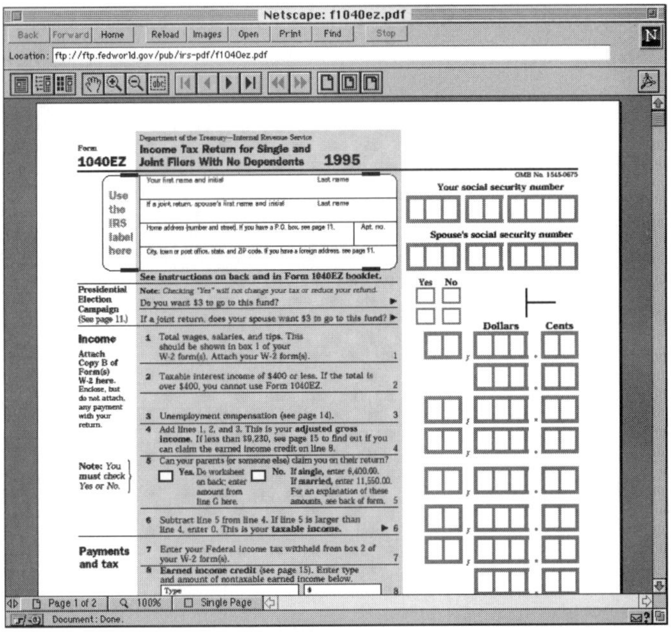

Figure 4.41: Bummer—the IRS does Amber too.

If you are interested in creating PDF files to distribute over the Web, there are a few options you can choose from. If you have a PostScript printer or a least a PostScript printer driver you can print to PDF. For more information about this process, visit http://w1000.mv.us.adobe.com/Amber/makepdf.html. Your second option is to purchase Adobe Exchange, the PDF writer and creation tool. Detailed information about this product is available at http://w 1000.mv.us.adobe.com/Acrobat/Exch.html

Many Web sites have adopted the PDF file format as the dominant method of information exchange. Here are some sites which use PDF:

- Adobe—This one should be obvious; many of the manuals and product brochures are available online in PDF format: `http://www.adobe.com`
- Internal Revenue Service—The guys you love to hate have published most of the tax forms and documentation you'll need in PDF format: `http://www.irs.ustreas.gov/`
- New York Times Fax—A free daily service of highlights from the top news articles from the *New York Times* in PDF format. Once you fill out a simple registration form, you have access to the daily updated eight-page document. `http://nytimesfax.com/`
- Dial-A-Book—An online bookstore where PDF is the print medium. Pay a small fee to get an entire book over the Web: `http://dab.psi.net/DialABook/`
- Centers for Disease Control: Morbidity and Mortality Weekly Report—A lively and informative publication from the people who take notice when you bite the big one: `http://www.cdc.gov/epo/mmwr/mmwr_wk.html`

Shockwave

Shockwave is the technology developed by Macromedia to allow Director multimedia presentations to be transmitted over the Web. Macromedia Director is the industry standard multimedia authoring tool for the creation of CD-ROM-based interactive software. The Shockwave plug-in lets you interact with Director presentations from your Web browser. Now, boring pages come to life with animation, movies, audio, interaction, and much, much more. To obtain the Shockwave plug-in, please visit the Macromedia Shockwave site at http://www.macromedia.com/Tools/Shockwave/sdc/Plugin/index.html.

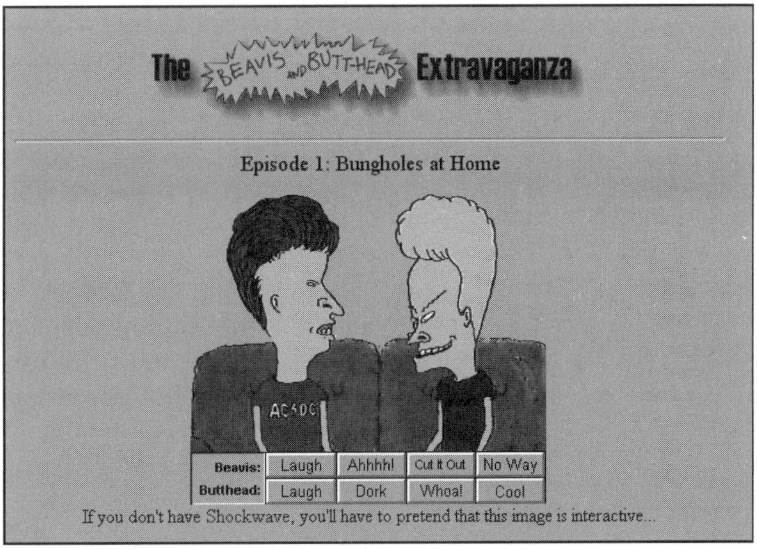

Figure 4.42: ShockWave: our pals do the multimedia thing.

If you are interested in creating your own Macromedia Director presentations for Web distribution, you will need to shell out the $1,000 or so for the full commercial package. To find out more detailed information about the Director authoring tool and other products from Macromedia, please visit http://www.macromedia.com.

Once you have the Shockwave plug-in installed, you will notice Shocked sites everywhere. A Shockwave movie will display the Macromedia background symbol in a box where a movie is being loaded (see Figure 4.43). When you see this type of image, wait for the movie to load and begin playing before you move on.

Figure 4.43: The Macromedia Shockwave background symbol displayed before a movie is played.

There are so many Shockwave-enhanced Web sites that to mention one would be to fail to mention a thousand. So, instead visit the main Shockwave Gallery where all the top Shocked sites are listed: `http://www.macromedia.com/Tools/Shockwave/Gallery/index.html`

Wait a sec, we did find one other Shockwave site collection page that is worth a little print space: ShockeR. ShockeR has a weekly top site and covers many amateur Shockwave sites which the Macromedia gallery overlooks. Take a short tour of the site and the collection of links at http://www.shocker.com/shocker/.

RealAudio

If you have been waiting for live audio on the Internet, then your sojourn is over. RealAudio has brought live FM-mono quality audio to your Web browser. Based on a proprietary compression technology and a streaming data protocol, RealAudio delivers great sound to your ears from across the globe. You need to have a 28.8 modem or faster in order to listen to uninterrupted audio. To obtain the RealAudio plug-in, go visit the RealAudio Web site at http://www.realaudio.com. Here's a screen shot of RealAudio player. Hear it? If so, you're twisted.

Figure 4.44: The RealAudio Player in action.

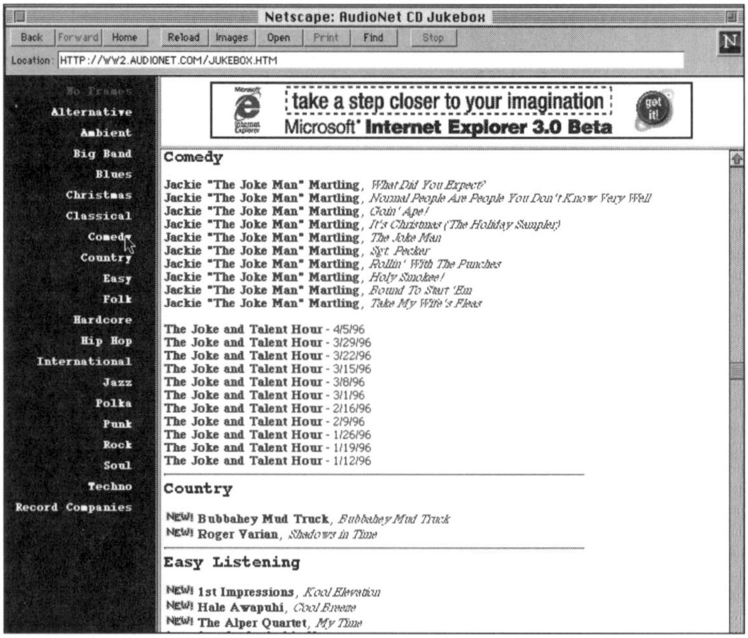

Figure 4.45: The AudioNet Jukebox WWW site.

If you are interested in producing your own RealAudio files for broadcasting over the Web, you will need to read about the RealAudio server and encoder. The encoder can be used free for creating audio-on-demand files. To set up a live audio broadcasting server, you will need to purchase the RealAudio server. All the information about these products is available from the RealAudio homepage http://www.realaudio.com.

Some must-see RealAudio sites are:

- C|Net Radio—a daily Internet- and computer- related news and information broadcast.
  `http://www.cnet.com/Content/Radio/index.html`

- Net.Radio—live 24-hour-a-day Internet radio with rock and classical channels. `http://www.netradio.net`
- 1-800-MUSIC-NOW Online—"You Click, You Listen, You Like, You Buy." `http://www.1800musicnow.mci.com`
- Latest and Greatest RealAudio 2.0 sites—a collection of sites maintained by RealAudio. `http://www.realaudio.com/products/ra2.0/sites/`

Java

Java is a revolutionary programming language developed by Sun Microsystems which allows client-side execution of applications. Java applets can be quickly transmitted over the Internet and viewed in a Java-compatible browser. Video, sound, interaction, and other special effects are only some of the features this unique programming tool can provide. Java is no longer a plug-in but is now embedded into browsers which license Java from Sun. Currently, Netscape Navigator 2.0.1 is the only browser with built-in Java support outside of the HotJava Sun browser. As you may have read in the previous chapter, Netscape far outbrews HotJava, so if you don't already use Netscape, go get it (http://www.netscape.com). For more information about Java, go visit Sun's Java Web site at http://java.sun .com.

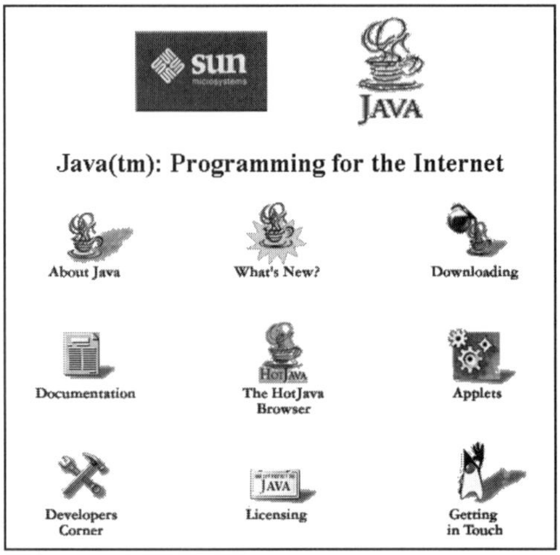

Figure 4.46: Sun's Java Web page.

If you are interested in creating your own Java applets for Web distribution, there are mountains of materials available online. However, you will need to be a fairly good programmer and be familiar with C-based languages in order to write Java code. To get started, visit the Java Web site at http://java.sun.com and follow the About Java and Documentation links.

But why. You're not turning into a geek on us are you?

Java is being incorporated into many Web sites. To take a look at some of the best, visit http://www.gamelan.com/. Gamelan is a highly respected Java directory of Java-enhanced Web sites; however, it lists only those sites with high-impact Java applications. There are a lot of sites on the Web which have Java applets subtly embedded into them, which you may not even notice. Properly designed Java applets become part of the page and do not seem like a separate entity. We are not complaining; seamless integration of multimedia and other Web enhancements is a very good thing. However, the best sites are often unnoticed because their authors did such a wonderful job of designing their presentation.

StreamWorks

Xing Technologies has developed an audio and video streaming delivery method called StreamWorks. Live video and audio are waiting for you on the Web, never watch cable TV again (yeah, right). This technology is extremely dependent on a fast and uninterrupted connection between your browser and the StreamWorks server out on the Internet. Once you get this bad boy configured and establish a good connection, entertainment beyond belief will be transmitted for your senses to bask in. To obtain the StreamWorks plug-in, go visit the Xing Technologies Web site at http://www.xingtech.com/.

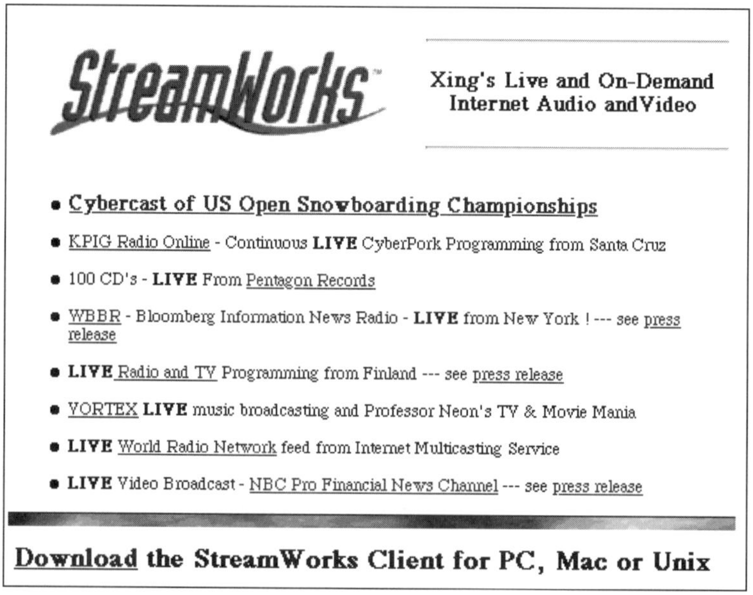

Figure 4.47: Xing's StreamWorks Web page.

If you are interested in producing StreamWork-readable content for Web distribution, read the information available from the Xing Technologies Web site. You should be warned, the server package is extremely expensive, not to mention the hardware and digital camera requirements.

If you download and install the StreamWorks plug-in, you'll have access to many predefined servers with numerous audio and video data streams. To explore other sites, go back to the StreakWorks Web site and visit the servers listed under the "StreamWorks on the Internet—publicly accessible servers" link.

VRML

Virtual Reality Modeling Language or VRML is a programming language that allows Web authors to build three-dimensional worlds which you can walk or fly through and explore inside, upside, and out. From simple box rooms to complete worlds with multimedia (audio, video, text, animation, and more), VRML is a step into the future of virtual reality interaction. It is difficult to describe or define the awe you will experience as you explore VRML worlds; they are simply mind-boggling. Before you get too excited, you need to know that VRML is still under development and is unfortunately a bandwidth hog, but waiting for the data files to transfer is usually rewarded. For information about the VRML language itself and the ongoing development of the technology, go visit the VRML Web site at http://www.vrml.org/.

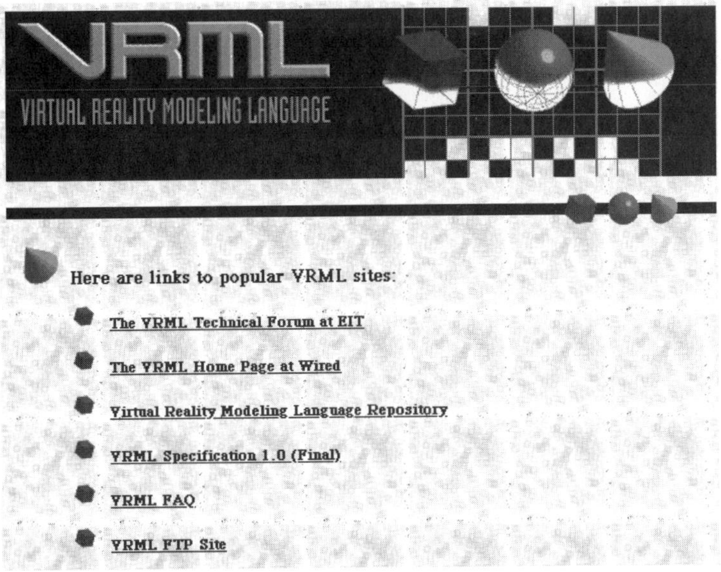

Figure 4.48: VRML Web site.

We've only been able to get the VRML thing happening on the Mac with one app and it wasn't a plug-in yet. It was still a "helper app" that launches in its own separate window from Netscape. It's called Voyager and it's from Virtus Corporation. Cruise over to http://www.virtus.com and check it out. All the instructions on how to configure it for Netscape are there too. Here's a stupid screen shot that doesn't really convey much except to prove that we tried it.

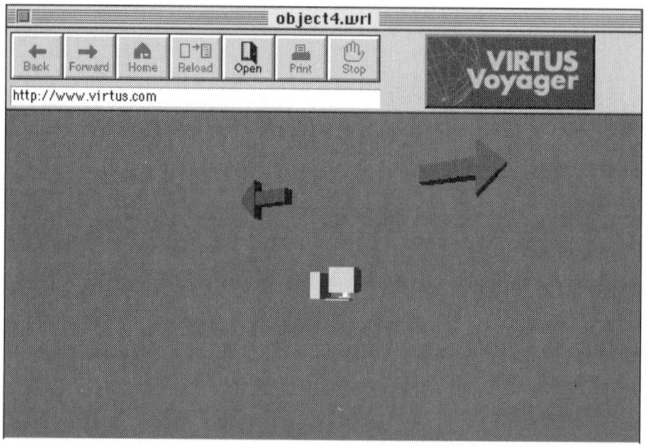

Figure 4.49: Voyager VRML browser showing 3-D model.

There are some great places (or should we say worlds) to get lost in doing the VRML thing. Give 'em a try and let us know if anything works on the Mac. We're going to wait until VRML itself is more developed and is built directly into our browser:

- VRML Site of the Week—A weekly showing of the best VRML world on the Net. `http://www.vir-tus.com/modmonth.html`

- Aerial Search—Search for VRML worlds or look at the Daily VRML site. `http://www.virtpark.com/theme/cgi-bin/serch.html`

- VRML Review—A large collection of links to worlds and other information. `http://www.imaginative.com/Chuck/vrml/`

- Proteinman's Top Ten VRML Worlds— A rotating list of the 10 best worlds. `http://www.virtpark.com/theme/proteinman/`

The problem with writing about VRML is that we can't show you anything really. You have to be there and move your mouse around. It's really pretty primitive, by the way, if you ask us. It's a good start but it sure ain't Metaverse. You're better off staying up all night and reading Neuromancer and Snow Crash. On the Mac the QuickTime VR plug-in is about as close as it gets as of this writing.

QuickTime VR

QuickTime VR allows your Web browser to display the virtual reality worlds created using QuickTime movies. This technology is different from VRML. In VRML, the images you see must be painstakingly drawn or a multimedia image is pasted onto a surface. Thus the world can be a little edgy. With QuickTime VR, movies are made using a video camera of real-world places or using 3-D modeling software to create animation. These movies, once they have been properly processed, give the illusion of reality much better than the current VRML standards. QuickTime VR not only displays great three-dimensional spaces, it also has interactive objects which you can manipulate. To use the plug-in you will need to have Apple QuickTime installed on your system. The plug-in is still in beta testing, but it works great. You can find complete information and installation instructions at the QuickTime VR Web site at `http://qtvr.quicktime.apple.com/`.

Figure 4.50: Apple QuickTime VR Demo.

Internet Telephone

You may have heard the rumor that you can bypass long-distance charges by using your Internet connection as a telephone link to anywhere in the world. Well, the rumor is true, but you can't just dial any phone anywhere, you can only contact other people who have Internet access and the same communications protocol as you. This isn't that difficult of a hurdle to jump over, just send your best pal across the big blue pool a message to buy or download the software with the same protocol that you have and arrange a time to make contact.

For more information about using the Internet for world-wide "free" communications here are some other spots to check out:

- The Internet Telephony Page
  `http://rpcp.mit.edu/~asears/main.html`
- FAQ: "How can I use the Internet as a telephone?"
  `http://www.northcoast.com/savetz/voice-faq.html`

There are many good commercial Internet phone communications packages available, from $35 to $500. The one we like the best is NetPhone. Check out Electric Magic's WWW site at http://www.emagic.com and give it a test run.

Nothing for AT&T to worry about yet on the long-distance front, though. The quality for most of these Internet phone puppies is only fair. It's fun to pretend though.

If you want a broader range of connection sites and want to be able to join an impromptu Internet talk sessions, try using what's probably the most popular shareware package for it: CUSeeMe.

CUSeeMe

CUSeeMe is a project of Cornell University and supports both audio only and videoconferencing over the Internet with up to eight simultaneous connections. To videoconference you will need a digital video camera (such as the Connectix QuickCam). CUSeeMe is currently the only free software which supports real-time two-way videoconferencing over the Internet. This software is available through the CUSeeMe Web site at http://cu-seeme.cornell.edu/

Figure 4.51: CUSeeMe Web site.

Better Late Than Never

If these plug-ins have not satisfied your need for more, more, more on the Web—there are still other places to locate other browser plug-ins. Take a gander at these sights.

- http://home.netscape.com/comprod/products/navigator/version_2.0/plugins/index.html
- http://www2.netscape.com/assist/helper_apps/windowhelper.html
- http://charlotte.acns.nwu.edu/internet/helper/
- http://wwwhost.cc.utexas.edu/learn/use/helper.html

Summary

Hopefully you have figured out by now that no single book or information repository can contain all of the current information about the Internet. You'll need to take the time to explore and search for new materials, enhanced software, and improved information. In this chapter, we tried to give you insight into the amazing world of entertainment, education, and productivity that exists on the Internet. But don't take our word for it, go surfing for yourself.

Appendix A—Glossary

Our friends who do Internet training at LearningCurve, Inc. here in Austin have helped us put together a useful little glossary of Internet terms you come across all the time. Thanks Rachal!

Hey, if you ever make it to Austin and still haven't figured this Internet thing out, be sure to pay them a visit. They'll hold your hand, give you a glass of water, pat you on the back, and help you out. You can check out their WWW site at http://www.learningcurve.com.

ARPANET
Advanced Research Projects Agency Network. TCP/IP-based international network. The precursor to the Internet. Developed in the late 1960s and early 1970s by the U.S. Department of Defense as an experiment in wide-area networking that would survive a nuclear war.

ASCII
American Standard Code for Information Interchange — the de facto worldwide standard for the code numbers used by computers to represent all the uppercase and lowercase Latin letters, numbers, punctuation, etc. There are 128 standard ASCII codes, each of which can be represented by a 7-digit binary number: 0000000 through 1111111.

BACKBONE

High-speed connection within a network which connects shorter (usually slower) branch circuits. A high-speed line or series of connections that forms a major pathway within a network. The term is relative, as a backbone in a small network may be much smaller than many nonbackbone lines in a large network.

BANDWIDTH

The difference, in hertz (Hz), between the highest and lowest frequencies of a transmission channel; the greater the bandwidth, the "faster" the line. Also refers to how much information you can send through a connection. Usually measured in bits per second. A full page of English text is about 16,000 bits. A fast modem can move about 15,000 bits in 1 second. Full-motion, full-screen video would require roughly 10,000,000 bits per second, depending on compression. Also creeping into common usage to indicate time and availability, as in: "I wanted to meet with them, but I didn't have the bandwidth."

BASEBAND

Characteristic of any network like Ethernet that uses a single carrier frequency and requires all stations attached to the network to participate in every transmission.

BAUD

Unit of measure of data transmission speed; usually bits/second. In common usage the "baud rate" of a modem is how many bits it can send or receive per second. Technically, "baud" is the number of times per second that the carrier signal shifts value—so a 2400-bit-per-second modem actually runs at 300 baud, but it moves 4 bits per baud (4 x 300 = 2400 bits per second).

BITNET

Because It's Time Network. TCP/IP-based international network.

BPS

Bits per second. A measure of the rate of data transmission. A 28.8 modem can move 28,800 bits per second.

BROADCAST

A packet delivery system that delivers a copy of a given packet to all hosts that attach to it is said to "broadcast" the packet.

BROWSER

A client program (software) that is used to look at various kinds of Internet resources.

CLIENT

The user of a network service, or a software program that is used to contact and obtain data from a server software program on another computer, often across a great distance. Each client program is designed to work with one or more specific kinds of server programs, and each server requires a specific kind of client.

COAX

Coaxial cable, comprised of a central wire surrounded by dielectric insulator, all encased in a protective sheathing.

COM

One of the top-level domains. Stands for commercial and includes commercial enterprises. For example: info@learningcurve.com

COM PORT

Communications port. Also known as a serial port. On a PC, there are up to four serial ports designated COM1, COM2, COM3, and COM4. Special hardware can allow for more ports. A serial port on a PC has 9 or 25 pins and is generally where an external modem would be connected, using a serial cable. Internal modems also require that a COM port be designated for them, usually selectable on the modem card itself or through software.

CYBERSPACE

The term was originated by author William Gibson in his novel *Neuromancer.* The word cyberspace is currently used to describe the whole range of information resources available through computer networks.

DEFAULT GATEWAY

The first destination for data you wish to send over the Internet, usually the IP address of a router of some kind. Your service provider can tell you what your default gateway will be. Also see "gateway."

DIAL-UP CONNECTION

A connection between machines through a phone line. Modem, ISDN, and other high-speed connections can be loosely defined as dial-up connections if they are not 24-hour-a-day dedicated connections.

DOMAIN

In the Internet, a part of the naming hierarchy. Syntactically, a domain name consists of a sequence of names separated by dots.

DOMAIN NAME

The unique name that identifies an Internet site. Domain names always have two or more parts, separated by dots. The part on the left is the most specific, and the part on the right is the most general. It is possible for a domain name to exist but not be connected to an actual machine. This is often done so that a group or business can have an Internet e-mail address without having to establish a real Internet site. In these cases, one's ISP must handle the mail on behalf of the listed domain name.

EDU

One of the top-level domains. Stands for educational and includes educational institutions. For example: bob@utexas.edu.

E-MAIL

Electronic mail. Messages, usually text, sent from one person to another via computer. E-mail can also be sent automatically to a large number of addresses.

ETHERNET

A very common method of networking computers in a LAN. Ethernet will handle about 10,000,000 bits per second and can be used with almost any kind of computer.

FAQ

Frequently asked questions. FAQs are documents that list and answer the most common questions on a particular subject.

FTP

File Transfer Protocol. A user-level protocol and program that you can use to transfer files over the network. A very common method of moving files between two Internet sites. FTP is a special way to log in to another Internet site for the purpose of retrieving and/or sending files. There are many Internet sites that have established publicly accessible libraries of material that can be obtained using FTP, by logging in using the account name "anonymous"; thus these sites are called "anonymous ftp servers."

GATEWAY

A device that acts as a connector between two logically separate networks. It has interfaces to more than one network and can translate the packets of one network to another, possibly dissimilar, network. For example, Prodigy has a gateway that translates between its internal, proprietary e-mail format and Internet e-mail format. Another, sloppier meaning of gateway is to describe any mechanism for providing access to another system; e.g., AOL might be called a gateway to the Internet.

GOPHER

An older and widely successful method of making menus of material available over the Internet. Gopher is a client and server style program, which requires that the user have a Gopher client program. Although Gopher spread rapidly across the globe in only a couple of years, it is being largely supplanted by Hypertext, also known as WWW (World Wide Web). There are still thousands of Gopher servers on the Internet and we can expect they will remain for a while.

GOV

One of the top-level domains. Stands for government and includes governmental organizations. For example: smith@nssdca.gsfc.nasa.gov.

"HAYES" COMMAND SET

Also known as the "AT" command set. A standard set of modem commands first developed by the Hayes modem company. Most modems have adopted this standard. All commands sent to the modem begin with the characters "AT" for "Attention."

HOST

Any computer on a network that is a repository for services available to other computers on the network. It is quite common to have one host machine provide several services, such as WWW and Usenet.

HTML

HyperText Markup Language. The coding language used create hypertext documents for use on the World Wide Web. HTML looks a lot like old-fashioned typesetting code, where you surround a block of text with instructions that indicate how it should appear. In addition, in HTML you can specify that a block of text, or a word, is "linked" to another file on the Internet. HTML files are meant to be viewed using a World Wide Web client program (browser), such as Mosaic or Netscape.

HTTP

HyperText Transport Protocol. The protocol for moving hypertext files across the Internet. Requires an HTTP client program on one end and an HTTP server program on the other end. HTTP is the primary protocol used in the World Wide Web (WWW).

HYPERTEXT

Generally, any text that contains "links" to other documents—words or phrases in the document that can be chosen by a reader using a browser and which cause another document to be retrieved and displayed.

INTERNET

Physically, a collection of packet-switching networks interconnected by gateways along with protocols that allow them to function logically as a single, large, virtual network. When written in uppercase, Internet refers specifically to the DARPA Internet and the TCP/IP protocols it uses.

INTERNET

The collection of networks and gateways, including the ARPANET, MILNET, and NSFnet, that use the TCP/IP protocol suite and function as a single, cooperative virtual network. The Internet reaches many universities, government research labs, and military installations.

INTERNET ACCESS PROVIDER

See ISP.

INTERNET ADDRESS

The address assigned to hosts that want to participate in the Internet using TCP/IP. This unique number consists of four parts separated by dots, e.g., 165.113.245.2. Every machine that is on the Internet has a unique IP number—if a machine does not have an IP number, it is not really on the Internet.

INTERSLIP/INTERPPP

Macintosh SLIP and PPP shareware packages from InterCon Software.

INTEROPERABILITY

The ability of software and hardware on multiple machines from multiple vendors to communicate meaningfully.

IP

Internet protocol. The Internet standard protocol that defines the Internet datagram as the unit of information passes across the Internet and provides the basis for the Internet connectionless, best-effort packet delivery service.

IP ADDRESS

See "Internet address." Your IP address will either be given to you by your service provider for permanent use or assigned to you dynamically when you connect.

IRQ

Interrupt request. Hardware on a PC uses an interrupt request "channel" to tell the CPU that its normal processing needs to be interrupted to handle a request by the hardware.

Serial ports, printer ports, network cards, and sound cards all use interrupts. The range of IRQs on 386 PCs or better is from 2 to 15. Generally, each piece of hardware will need a unique IRQ associated with it. Many PC problems involving modems and network cards are due to IRQ conflicts.

ISDN

Integrated Services Digital Network. Basically a way to move more data over existing regular phone lines. ISDN is only slowly becoming available in the USA, but where it is available it can provide speeds of 64,000 bits per second over a regular phone line at almost the same cost as a normal phone call.

ISP

Internet service provider (or Internet access provider). A company which provides Internet access and other Internet-related services to businesses or individuals. For example: Netcom and OuterNet.

KERNEL

The level of an operating system or networking system that contains the system-level commands or all of the functions hidden from the user. In a UNIX system, the kernel is a program that contains the device drivers, the memory management routines, the scheduler, and system calls. This program is always running while the system is operating.

LAN

Local area network. A high-speed network connecting machines at one physical site.

LEASED LINE

Refers to a phone line that is rented for exclusive 24-hour, 7-days-a-week use from your location to another location. The highest speed data connections require a leased line.

LISTSERV

The most common kind of mail list. Listservs originated on BITNET, but they are now common on the Internet.

MACSLIP/MACPPP

Macintosh SLIP and PPP shareware packages from Merit Network Inc. and the University of Michigan

MACTTCP

An Apple extension that allows a Mac to speak to TCP/IP. Most SLIP or PPP packages need it as well.

MAIL GATEWAY

A machine that connects to two or more electronic mail systems (especially dissimilar mail systems on two different networks) and transfers mail messages among them.

MAILLIST

A (usually automated) system that allows people to send e-mail to one address, whereupon their message is copied and sent to all of the other subscribers to the maillist. In this way, people who have many different kinds of e-mail access can participate in discussions together.

MIL

One of the top-level domains. Stands for military and includes military organizations. For example: clyde@hqafsc.af.mil.

MODEM

MOdulator, DEModulator. A device that you connect to your computer and to a phone line that allows the computer to talk to other computers through the phone system. Basically, modems do for computers what a telephone does for humans.

MTU

Maximum transmission unit. The size of the packet which can be sent. If you are using TCP/IP on an Ethernet, this will be 1500. If you are using SLIP or PPP, obtain this value from your service provider.

NAME SERVER

A machine which translates Internet host and domain names into IP addresses (e.g., draconis.outer.net→204.96.12.9). Where your connection or network software requests this, enter the IP address of your name server. You can get these numbers from your service provider.

NET

One of the top-level domains. Stands for network and includes network service centers, network information centers, and other organizations that have a hand in network management. For instance: sue@austinfree.net.

NETMASK
A network mask which prevents your system from broadcasting packets to too many other systems. What your netmask is will depend on the size of the network you're on. For example, the netmask for a Class C network (204.96.12.0–204.96.12.255) is 255.255.255.0. Your service provider can tell you what your netmask will be.

NETWORK
A group of machines connected together so they can transmit information to one another. Any time you connect two or more computers together so that they can share resources you have a computer network. Connect two or more networks together and you have an internet.

NETWORK PATH
A series of machine names used to direct electronic mail from one user to another.

NEWSGROUPS
The name for discussion groups on Usenet.

NSFNET
National Science Foundation network. TCP/IP-based network.

ONLINE SERVICE PROVIDER
A company which offers a variety of services on their own private computer network, which customers can dial in to. Most of these companies have connected their private networks to the Internet and now offer some Internet services. For example: America Online and CompuServe.

ORG
One of the top-level domains. Encompasses nonprofit organizations.

PACKET
A unit of data sent across a packet-switching network.

PACKET DRIVER
A network software driver which allows data to be sent to and from a networked DOS or Windows machine in the form of packets. Most network cards for PCs will include packet driver software. When used in conjunction with TCP/IP stack software, such as Trumpet Winsock, a packet driver allows a PC to communicate using TCP/IP over a network.

PACKET SWITCHING

Data transmission technique in which data is segmented and routed in packets. The method used to move data around on the Internet. In packet switching, all the data coming out of a machine is broken up into chunks; each chunk has the address of where it came from and where it is going. This enables chunks of data from many different sources to move on the same lines and be sorted and directed to different routes by special machines along the way. This way many people can use the same lines at the same time.

PPP

Point to Point Protocol. Most well known as a protocol that allows a computer to use a regular telephone line and a modem to make a TCP/IP connection and thus be really and truly on the Internet. PPP is gradually replacing SLIP for this purpose.

PROTOCOL

A formal set of rules governing the format, timing, and error control of transmissions on a network or the protocol that networks use to communicate with each other.

ROUTE

The path that network traffic takes from its source to its destination.

ROUTER

A hardware and software device that connects hosts on different networks. A special-purpose computer (or software package) that handles the connection between two or more networks. Routers spend all their time looking at the destination addresses of the packets passing through them and deciding which route to send them on.

ROUTING

The process of selecting the correct path (circuit) for a transmission over a network.

SERVER

A computer, or a software package, that provides a specific kind of service to client software running on other computers. The term can refer to a particular piece of software, such as a WWW server, or to the machine on which the software is running, e.g., "Our mail server is down today, that's why e-mail isn't getting out." A single server machine could have several different server software packages running on it, thus providing many different services to clients on the network.

SLIP
Serial Line Internet Protocol. A standard for using a regular telephone line (a "serial line") and a modem to connect a computer as a real Internet site. SLIP is gradually being replaced by PPP.

SMTP
Simple Mail Transfer Protocol. The Internet standard protocol for transferring electronic mail messages from one machine to another.

T1
AT&T term for digital circuit carrying transmissions at a rate of 1,544,000 bits/second. At maximum theoretical capacity, a T1 line could move a megabyte in less than 10 seconds.

T3
Transmission rate on this type of circuit is 45,000,000 bits per second. This is more than enough to do full-screen, full-motion video.

TCP
Transmission Control Protocol. The Internet standard transport level protocol that provides the reliable, full duplex, stream service on which many application protocols depend.

TRUMPET WINSOCK
A shareware program developed by Peter Tattam of Trumpet Software International. It provides a winsock library, an internal SLIP and PPP driver, a Windows packet driver, and a convenient dialer. It's available from ftp.trumpet.com.au.

UNIX
A computer operating system (the basic software running on a computer, underneath things like word processors and spreadsheets). UNIX is designed to be used by many people at the same time (it is "multiuser") and has TCP/IP built in. It is the most common operating system for servers on the Internet.

URL
Uniform (or Universal) Resource Locator. The standard way to define the address of any resource on the Internet that is part of the World Wide Web (WWW).

USENET

A worldwide system of discussion groups, with comments passed among hundreds of thousands of machines. Not all Usenet machines are on the Internet. Usenet is completely decentralized, with over 15,000 discussion areas, called newsgroups.

USER-LEVEL PROTOCOLS

Protocols, such as Telnet, SMTP, and FTP, which allow you to perform operations via client-side applications on the network.

UUCP

UNIX to UNIX Copy Program.

VIRTUAL CIRCUIT

A network service that allows two processes to communicate as if they were directly connected to each other. A virtual circuit is similar to a UNIX pipe.

VJ COMPRESSION

Van Jacobson compression. A technique used to compress data going through a SLIP or PPP connection. Ask your service provider if they support VJ compression.

WAN

Wide-area network.

WINSOCK

Winsock is the general name for a software specification which provides a standard TCP/IP networking layer for Windows systems. The official name for this specification is Windows Sockets, and the software routines for TCP/IP networking are generally found in a Windows library file called WINSOCK.DLL. Winsocks are available from Microsoft, IBM, Internet in a Box, Chameleon, Trumpet, and other Internet packages.

WWW

World Wide Web. Two meanings. First, loosely used, the whole constellation of resources that can be accessed using a variety of tools and protocols. Second, the universe of hypertext servers, which are the servers that allow text, graphics, and sound files to be mixed together and linked using hypertext markup language to define addresses.

Appendix B—Internet Service Providers

Here's the latest list of Internet Service Providers courtesy of Paul Celestin. The most current version is available by sending an e-mail to info@celestin.com with the words SEND POCIA.TXT in the subject line of the message. There's another good source for Internet Service Providers available on the WWW at http://thelist.com—it's searchable by all sorts of categories and is very well organized. Check it out too if you're ISP shopping.

All of the information in this directory was supplied to Celestin Company directly by the service providers and is subject to change without notice. Celestin Company does not endorse any of the providers in this directory. If you do not see a provider listed for your area, please do not ask them or us about it, as we both only know about providers in this directory. This directory is brought to you as a public service. Celestin

Company does not receive any compensation from the providers listed here, and neither do we. Since Internet service providers come and go and frequently change their offers, we strongly urge you to contact them for additional information and/or restrictions.

The latest version of this document is available at the following location:

ftp://ftp.celestin.com/biz/celestin/pocia/pocia.txt

If you have Web access, try http://www.celestin.com/pocia/ for the hypertext version of this list, which includes addresses, telephone numbers, fax numbers, e-mail addresses, and pricing.

DOMESTIC

A listing of Internet service providers in the U.S. and Canada, sorted by area code. Fields are area code, service provider name, voice phone number, and e-mail address for more information.

Free Service Providers

For the cost of a long-distance phone call, you can dial any of these Internet providers and give the Internet a try.

Free.org (shell,slip,ppp) modem ->	715 743 1600 info@free.org
Free.I.Net (must dial via AT&T) modem ->	801 471 2266 info@free.i.net
SLIPNET (shell,slip,ppp) modem ->	217 792 2777 info@slip.net

Nationwide Service Providers

The following access providers provide service to more than just one part of the United States/Canada. Many of them provide service regardless of your geographic location, but may charge a higher price than local service providers.

AGIS (Apex Global Information Services)	313 730 1130 info@agis.net
ANS	703 758 7700 info@ans.net
BBN Planet	617 873 2905 net-info@bbnplanet.com
Concentric Research Corp.	800 745 2747 info@cris.com
CRL Network Services	415 837 5300 sales@crl.com
DataXchange Network, Inc.	800 863 1550 info@dx.net
Delphi Internet Services Corp.	800 695 4005 info@delphi.com
EarthLink Network, Inc.	213 644 9500 sales@earthlink.net
Exodus Communications, Inc.	408 522 8450 info@exodus.net
4GL Corp.	713 589 8077 info@4gl.com
Global Connect, Inc.	804 229 4484 info@gc.net
Information Access Technologies (Holonet)	510 704 0160 info@holonet.net
Institute for Global Communications	415 442 0220 igc-info@igc.apc.org
Liberty Information Network	800 218 5157 info@liberty.com
MIDnet	800 682 5550 info@mid.net
Moran Communications	716 639 1254 info@moran.com
NETCOM On-Line Communications Services	408 554 8649 info@netcom.com
Netrex, Inc.	800 3 NETREX info@netrex.com
Network 99, Inc.	800 NET 99IP net99@cluster.mcs.net
Performance Systems International	800 827 7482 all-info@psi.com
Portal Information Network	408 973 9111 info@portal.com
SprintLink - Nationwide 56K - 45M access	800 817 7755 info@sprint.net
The ThoughtPort Authority, Inc.	800 ISP 6870 info@thoughtport.com
WareNet	714 348 3295 info@ware.net
Zocalo Engineering	510 540 8000 info@zocalo.net

Toll-Free Service Providers

These access providers allow you to dial a toll-free 800 number to connect to the Internet. Most of them charge for this privilege, but it may save you money over long-distance charges if you do not have local Internet access.

Allied Access Inc.	618 684 2255 sales@intrnet.net
ARInternet Corp.	301 459 7171 info@ari.net
American Information Systems, Inc.	708 413 8400 info@ais.net
Association for Computing Machinery	817 776 6876 account-info@acm.org
CICNet, Inc.	313 998 6103 info@cic.net
Cogent Software, Inc.	818 585 2788 info@cogsoft.com
Cyberius Online, Inc.	613 233 1215 info@cyberus.ca
Colorado SuperNet, Inc.	303 296 8202 info@csn.org
EarthLink Network, Inc.	213 644 9500 sales@earthlink.net
Global Connect, Inc.	804 229 4484 info@gc.net
Internet Express	719 592 1240 info@usa.net
Iowa Network Services	800 546 6587 service@netins.net
Mnematics, Inc.	914 359 4546 service@mne.com
Msen, Inc.	313 998 4562 info@msen.com
NeoSoft, Inc.	713 684 5969 info@neosoft.com
NETCOM On-Line Communications Services	408 554 8649 info@netcom.com
New Mexico Technet, Inc.	505 345 6555 granoff@technet.nm.org
Pacific Rim Network, Inc.	360 650 0442 info@pacificrim.net
Rocky Mountain Internet	800 900 7644 info@rmii.com
Synergy Communications, Inc.	800 345 9669 info@synergy.net
VivaNET, Inc.	800 836 UNIX info@vivanet.com
VoiceNet	800 835 5710 info@voicenet.com
WLN	800 342 5956 info@wln.com

Regional Service Providers

These access providers specialize in particular regions, some as small as a town of a thousand people, others as large as the San Francisco Bay Area.

201 Carroll-Net, Inc.	201 488 1332 info@carroll.com
201 Crystal Palace Networking, Inc.	201 300 0881 info@crystal.palace.net
201 Digital Express Group	301 847 5000 info@digex.net
201 Eclipse Internet Access	800 483 1223 info@eclipse.net
201 Galaxy Networks	201 825 2310 info@galaxy.net
201 GBN InternetAccess	201 343 6427 gbninfo@gbn.net
201 I-2000, Inc.	800 464 3820 info@i-2000.com
201 INTAC Access Corp.	800 504 6822 info@intac.com
201 Interactive Networks, Inc.	201 881 1878 info@interactive.net
201 Intercall, Inc.	800 758 7329 sales@intercall.com
201 InterCom Online	212 714 7183 info@intercom.com
201 The Internet Connection Corp.	201 435 4414 info@cnct.com
201 Internet Online Services	x226 -> 201 928 1000 help@ios.com
201 Lightning Internet Services, LLC	516 248 8400 sales@lightning.net
201 Mordor International BBS	201 433 4222 ritz@mordor.com
201 New York Net	718 776 6811 sales@new-york.net
201 NIC - Neighborhood Internet Connection	201 934 1445 info@nic.com
201 Openix - Open Internet Exchange	201 443 0400 info@openix.com
201 Planet Access Networks	201 691 4704 info@planet.net
201 ZONE One Network Exchange	212 824 4000 info@zone.net
202 American Information Network	410 855 2353 info@ai.net
202 ARInternet Corp.	301 459 7171 info@ari.net
202 CAPCON Library Network	202 331 5771 info@capcon.net
202 Charm.Net	410 558 3900 info@charm.net
202 Cyber Services, Inc.	703 749 9590 info@cs.com
202 Digital Express Group	301 847 5000 info@digex.net
202 Genuine Computing Resources	703 878 4680 info@gcr.com
202 I-Link, Ltd.	800 ILINK 99 info@i-link.net
202 Internet Online, Inc.	301 652 4468 info@intr.net
202 Interpath	800 849 6305 info@interpath.net
202 LaserNet	703 591 4232 info@laser.net
202 Quantum Networking Solutions, Inc.	805 538 2028 info@qnet.com
202 RadixNet Internet Services	301 567 9831 info@radix.net
202 Smartnet Internet Services, LLC	301 470 3400 info@smart.net
202 SONNETS, Inc.	703 502 8589 office@sonnets.net
202 UltraPlex Information Providers	301 598 6UPX info@upx.net
202 Universal Telecomm Corp.	703 758 0550 root@utc.net

202 US Net, Inc.	301 572 5926 info@us.net
202 World Web Limited	703 838 2000 info@worldweb.net
202 Xpress Internet Services	301 601 5050 info@xis.com
203 Computerized Horizons	203 335 7431 sysop@fcc.com
203 Connix: Connecticut Internet Exchange	860 349 7059 office@connix.com
203 Continuum Communications, Inc.	203 885 3576 gph@q.continuum.net
203 Futuris Networks, Inc.	203 359 8868 info@futuris.net
203 I-2000, Inc.	800 464 3820 info@i-2000.com
203 imagine.com	860 527 9245 Postmaster@imagine.com
203 Lightning Internet Services, LLC	516 248 8400 sales@lightning.net
203 MCIX, Inc.	860 572 8720 info@mcix.com
203 Mindport Internet Services, Inc.	860 892 2081 staff@mindport.net
203 NETPLEX	203 233 1111 info@ntplx.net
203 North American Internet Company	800 952 INET info@nai.net
203 Paradigm Communications, Inc.	203 250 7397 info@pcnet.com
203 ZONE One Network Exchange	212 824 4000 info@zone.net
204 Cycor Communications, Inc.	902 892 7354 signup@cycor.ca
204 Gate West Communications	204 663 2931 info@gatewest.net
205 AIRnet Internet Services, Inc.	800 247 6388 efelton@AIRnet.net
205 Community Internet Connect, Inc.	205 722 0199 info@cici.com
205 HiWAAY Information Services	205 533 3131 info@HiWAAY.net
205 Hub City Area Access	601 268 6156 info@hub1.hubcity.com
205 interQuest, Inc.	205 464 8280 info@iquest.com
205 MindSpring Enterprises, Inc.	800 719 4332 info@mindspring.com
205 Renaissance Internet Services	205 535 2113 info@ro.com
205 Scott Network Services, Inc.	205 987 5889 info@scott.net
206 Blarg! Online Services	206 782 6578 info@blarg.net
206 Cyberspace	206 281 5397 info@cyberspace.com
206 Digital Forest	206 487 6414 info@forest.net
206 Eskimo North	206 367 7457 nanook@eskimo.com
206 I-Link, Ltd.	800 ILINK 99 info@i-link.net
206 InEx Net	206 670 1131 info@inex.com
206 Interconnected Associates, Inc. (IXA)	206 622 7337 mike@ixa.com
206 Internet Express	719 592 1240 info@usa.net

206 ISOMEDIA.COM	206 881 8769 info@isomedia.com
206 Northwest Nexus, Inc.	206 455 3505 info@nwnexus.wa.com
206 NorthWestNet	206 562 3000 info@nwnet.net
206 Olympic Computing Solutions	206 989 6698 ocs@oz.net
206 Oregon Information Technology Centeres	503 469 6699 hmaster@harborside.com
206 Pacific Rim Network, Inc.	x11 -> 360 650 0442 info@pacificrim.net
206 Seanet Online Services	206 343 7828 info@seanet.com
206 SenseMedia	408 335 9400 sm@picosof.com
206 Structured Network Systems, Inc.	503 656 3530 info@structured.net
206 Teleport, Inc.	503 223 4245 info@teleport.com
206 Transport Logic	503 243 1940 sales@transport.com
206 WLN	800 342 5956 info@wln.com
207 Agate Internet Services	207 947 8248 ais@agate.net
207 Internet Maine	207 780 0416 info@mainelink.net
207 MaineStreet Communications	207 657 5078 rainmaker@maine.com
207 Midcoast Internet Solutions	207 594 8277 accounts@midcoast.com
207 MV Communications, Inc.	603 429 2223 info@mv.mv.com
207 Northern Lights Internet Services	207 773 4941 jkilday@nlbbs.com
208 Micron Internet Services	208 368 5400 sales@micron.net
208 Minnesota Regional Network	612 342 2570 info@mr.net
208 NICOH Net	208 233 5802 info@nicoh.com
208 NorthWestNet	206 562 3000 info@nwnet.net
208 Primenet	602 870 1010 info@primenet.com
208 SRVnet	208 524 6237 nlp@srv.net
208 Structured Network Systems, Inc.	503 656 3530 info@structured.net
208 Transport Logic	503 243 1940 sales@transport.com
209 The Computer Depot	209 223 5043 admin@cdepot.net
209 Cybergate Information Services	209 486 4283 cis@cybergate.com
209 Infonet Communications, Inc.	209 446 2360 mikeb@icinet.net
209 InReach Internet Communications	800 446 7324 info@inreach.com
209 InterNex Tiara	408 496 5466 info@internex.net
209 Primenet	602 870 1010 info@primenet.com
209 ValleyNet Communications	209 486 8638 info@valleynet.com
209 West Coast Online	707 586 3060 info@calon.com

210 Connect International, Inc.	210 341 2599 info@connecti.com
210 Delta Design and Development, Inc.	800 763 8265 sales@deltaweb.com
210 The Eden Matrix	512 478 9900 info@eden.com
210 I-Link, Ltd.	800 ILINK 99 info@i-link.net
210 Phoenix DataNet, Inc.	713 486 8337 info@phoenix.net
212 Advanced Standards, Inc advn.com	212 302 3366 kolian@advn.com
212 Alternet (UUNET Technologies, Inc.)	703 204 8000 info@alter.net
212 Blythe Systems	212 226 7171 infodesk@blythe.org
212 BrainLINK	718 805 6559 info@beast.brainlink.com
212 bway.net / Outernet, Inc.	212 982 9800 info@bway.net
212 Calyx Internet Access	212 475 5051 info@calyx.net
212 Creative Data Consultants (SILLY.COM)	718 229 0489 info@silly.com
212 Digital Express Group	301 847 5000 info@digex.net
212 Echo Communications Group	212 255 3839 info@echonyc.com
212 escape.com - Kazan Corp	212 888 8780 info@escape.com
212 I-2000, Inc.	800 464 3820 info@i-2000.com
212 I-Link, Ltd.	800 ILINK 99 info@i-link.net
212 Ingress Communications, Inc.	212 679 2838 info@ingress.com
212 INTAC Access Corp.	800 504 6822 info@intac.com
212 Intellitech Walrus	212 406 5000 info@walrus.com
212 Interactive Networks, Inc.	201 881 1878 info@interactive.net
212 Intercall, Inc.	800 758 7329 sales@intercall.com
212 InterCom Online	212 714 7183 info@intercom.com
212 The Internet Connection Corp.	201 435 4414 info@cnct.com
212 Internet Online Services	x226 -> 201 928 1000 help@ios.com
212 Internet QuickLink Corp.	212 307 1669 info@quicklink.com
212 Interport Communications Corp.	212 989 1128 info@interport.net
212 Lightning Internet Services, LLC	516 248 8400 sales@lightning.net
212 Long Island Internet HeadQuarters	516 439 7800 support@pb.net
212 Mordor International BBS	201 433 4222 ritz@mordor.com
212 Mnematics, Inc.	914 359 4546 service@mne.com
212 New World Data	718 962 1725 dmk@nwdc.com
212 New York Net	718 776 6811 sales@new-york.net
212 NY WEBB, Inc.	800 458 4660 wayne@webb.com
212 NYSERNet	800 493 4367 sales@nysernet.org
212 Panix (Public Access uNIX)	212 741 4400 info@panix.com
212 Phantom Access Technologies, Inc.	212 989 2418 bruce@phantom.com

212 Pipeline New York	212 267 3636 info@pipeline.com
212 Real Life Pictures RealNet	212 366 4434 reallife@walrus.com
212 Spacelab.Net	212 966 8844 mike@mxol.com
212 The ThoughtPort Authority, Inc.	800 ISP 6870 info@thoughtport.com
212 ThoughtPort of New York City	212 645 7970 info@precipice.com
212 tunanet/InfoHouse	212 229 8224 info@tunanet.com
212 ZONE One Network Exchange	212 824 4000 info@zone.net
213 ArtNetwork	800 395 0692 info@artnet.net
213 BeachNet Internet Access	310 823 3308 info@beachnet.com
213 Cogent Software, Inc.	818 585 2788 info@cogsoft.com
213 Cyberverse Online	310 643 3783 info@cyberverse.com
213 Delta Internet Services	714 778 0370 info@deltanet.com
213 DigiLink Network Services	310 542 7421 info@digilink.net
213 DirectNet	213 383 3144 info@directnet.com
213 Electriciti	619 338 9000 info@powergrid.electriciti.com
213 Exodus Communications, Inc.	408 522 8450 info@exodus.net
213 Flamingo Communications, Inc.	310 532 3533 sales@fcom.com
213 I-Link, Ltd.	800 ILINK 99 info@i-link.net
213 Instant Internet Corp. (InstaNet)	818 772 0097 charlyg@instanet.com
213 InterWorld Communications, Inc.	310 726 0500 sales@interworld.net
213 The Loop Internet Switch Co.	213 465 1311 info@loop.com
213 KAIWAN Internet	714 638 2139 info@kaiwan.com
213 KTB Internet Online	818 240 6600 info@ktb.net
213 Leonardo Internet	310 395 5500 jimp@leonardo.net
213 Liberty Information Network	800 218 5157 info@liberty.com
213 Network Intensive	714 450 8400 info@ni.net
213 Online-LA	310 967 8000 sales@online-la.com
213 OutWest Network Services	818 545 1996 info@outwest.net
213 Primenet	602 870 1010 info@primenet.com
213 QuickCom Internet Communcations	213 634 7735 info@quickcom.net
213 Saigon Enterprises	818 246 0689 info@saigon.net
213 ViaNet Communications	415 903 2242 info@via.net
214 Alternet (UUNET Technologies, Inc.)	703 204 8000 info@alter.net
214 CompuTek	214 994 0190 info@computek.net
214 Connection Technologies - ConnectNet	214 490 7100 sales@connect.net
214 Delta Design and Development, Inc.	800 763 8265 sales@deltaweb.com

214	DFW Internet Services, Inc.	817 332 5116 info@dfw.net
214	I-Link, Ltd.	800 ILINK 99 info@i-link.net
214	OnRamp Technologies, Inc.	214 746 4710 info@onramp.net
214	Texas Metronet, Inc.	214 705 2900 info@metronet.com
215	Cheap Net	302 993 8420 sammy@ravenet.com
215	Digital Express Group	301 847 5000 info@digex.net
215	epix	800 374 9669 karndt@epix.net
215	FishNet	610 337 9994 info@pond.com
215	GlobalQUEST, Inc.	610 696 8111 info@globalquest.net
215	I-2000, Inc.	800 464 3820 info@i-2000.com
215	Internet Tidal Wave	610 770 6187 steve@itw.com
215	InterNetworking Technologies	302 398 4369 itnt.com@itnt.com
215	The Magnetic Page	302 651 9753 info@magpage.com
215	Microserve Information Systems	717 779 4430 info@microserve.com
215	Net Access	215 576 8669 support@netaxs.com
215	NetReach, Inc.	215 283 2300 info@netreach.net
215	Network Analysis Group	800 624 9240 nag@good.freedom.net
215	OpNet	610 520 2880 info@op.net
215	RaveNet Systems, Inc.	302 993 8420 waltemus@ravenet.com
215	VivaNET, Inc.	800 836 UNIX info@vivanet.com
215	VoiceNet	800 835 5710 info@voicenet.com
215	You Tools Corp. / FASTNET	610 954 5910 info@fast.net
216	APK Public Access UNI Site	216 481 9436 info@wariat.org
216	Branch Information Services	313 741 4442 branch-info@branch.com
216	CanNet Internet Services	216 484 2260 info@cannet.com
216	CommercePark Interactive, Ltd.	216 523 2240 info@commercepark.com
216	ExchangeNet	216 261 4593 info@en.com
216	Gateway to Internet Services	216 656 5511 ytc@gwis.com
216	Multiverse, Inc.	216 344 3080 multiverse.com
216	New Age Consulting Service	216 524 3162 damin@nacs.net
216	OARnet (corporate clients only)	614 728 8100 info@oar.net
217	Allied Access, Inc.	618 684 2255 sales@intrnet.net
217	Net66	217 328 0066 sales@net66.com
217	Shouting Ground Technologies, Inc.	217 351 7921 admin@shout.net
217	Sol Tec, Inc.	317 920 1SOL info@soltec.com

218 Minnesota OnLine	612 225 1110 info@mn.state.net
218 Red River Net	701 232 2227 info@rrnet.com
218 Protocol Communications, Inc.	612 541 9900 info@protocom.com
219 Custom Logic Systems	219 255 5201 info@cl-sys.com
219 Wink Communications Group, Inc.	708 310 9465 sales@winkcomm.com
301 ABSnet Internet Services	410 361 8160 info@abs.net
301 American Information Network	410 855 2353 info@ai.net
301 ARInternet Corp.	301 459 7171 info@ari.net
301 Charm.Net	410 558 3900 info@charm.net
301 Clark Internet Services, Inc. ClarkNet	410 995 0691 info@clark.net
301 Cyber Services, Inc.	703 749 9590 info@cs.com
301 Digital Express Group	301 847 5000 info@digex.net
301 FredNet	301 631 5300 info@fred.net
301 Genuine Computing Resources	703 878 4680 info@gcr.com
301 Internet Online, Inc.	301 652 4468 info@intr.net
301 Kompleat Internet Services LLC	301 293 4333 netadmin@kis.net
301 LaserNet	703 591 4232 info@laser.net
301 Quantum Networking Solutions, Inc.	805 538 2028 info@qnet.com
301 RadixNet Internet Services	301 567 9831 info@radix.net
301 Smartnet Internet Services, LLC	301 470 3400 info@smart.net
301 SONNETS, Inc.	703 502 8589 office@sonnets.net
301 SURAnet	301 982 4600 marketing@sura.net
301 UltraPlex Information Providers	301 598 6UPX info@upx.net
301 Universal Telecomm Corp.	703 758 0550 root@utc.net
301 US Net, Inc.	301 572 5926 info@us.net
301 World Web Limited	703 838 2000 info@worldweb.net
301 Xpress Internet Services	301 601 5050 info@xis.com
302 Cheap Net	302 993 8420 sammy@ravenet.com
302 Delaware Common Access Network	302 654 1019 info@dca.net
302 First State Web, Inc.	302 234 0721 info@wittnet.com
302 InterNetworking Technologies	302 398 4369 itnt.com@itnt.com
302 The Magnetic Page	302 651 9753 info@magpage.com
302 RaveNet Systems, Inc.	302 993 8420 waltemus@ravenet.com
302 SSNet, Inc.	302 378 1386 info@ssnet.com
302 VoiceNet	800 835 5710 info@voicenet.com

303 ABWAM, Inc.	303 730 6050 info@entertain.com
303 Colorado SuperNet, Inc.	303 296 8202 info@csn.org
303 CSDC, Inc.	303 665 8053 support@ares.csd.net
303 The Denver Exchange, Inc.	303 455 4252 info@tde.com
303 ENVISIONET, Inc.	303 770 2408 info@envisionet.net
303 EZLink Internet Access	970 482 0807 ezadmin@ezlink.com
303 I-Link, Ltd.	800 ILINK 99 info@i-link.net
303 Indra's Net, Inc.	303 546 9151 info@indra.com
303 Internet Express	719 592 1240 info@usa.net
303 NETConnect	800 689 8001 office@tcd.net
303 NetWay 2001, Inc.	303 794 1000 info@netway.net
303 New Mexico Technet, Inc.	505 345 6555 granoff@technet.nm.org
303 Online Network Enterprises, Inc.	303 444 2522 info@netONE.com
303 Rocky Mountain Internet	800 900 7644 info@rmii.com
303 Shaman Exchange, Inc.	303 674 9784 info@dash.com
303 Stonehenge Internet Communications	800 RUN INET info@henge.com
304 RAM Technologies, Inc.	800 950 1726 info@ramlink.net
305 Acquired Knowledge Systems, Inc.	305 525 2574 info@aksi.net
305 CyberGate, Inc.	305 428 4283 sales@gate.net
305 Electronic Link	305 378 1128 info@elink.net
305 The EmiNet Domain	407 731 0222 info@emi.net
305 ICANECT	305 621 9200 sales@icanect.net
305 InteleCom Data Systems, Inc.	401 885 6855 info@ids.net
305 Internet Providers of Florida, Inc.	305 273 7978 office@ipof.fla.net
305 Internet World Information Network	305 535 3090 webmaster@winnet.net
305 Magg Information Services, Inc.	407 642 9841 help@magg.net
305 NetMiami Internet Corp.	305 554 4463 picard@netmiami.com
305 Netpoint Communications, Inc.	305 891 1955 info@netpoint.net
305 Paradise Communications, Inc.	404 980 0078 info@paradise.net
305 PSS InterNet Services	800 463 8499 support@america.com
305 SatelNET Communications, Inc.	305 434 8738 admin@satelnet.org
305 Shadow Information Services, Inc.	305 594 2450 admin@shadow.net
305 WebIMAGE, an internet presence provider	407 723 0001 info@webimage.com
305 Zimmerman Communications	954 584 0199 bob@zim.com
306 Cycor Communications, Inc.	902 892 7354 signup@cycor.ca

307 CoffeyNet	307 234 5443 web@coffey.com
307 NETConnect	800 689 8001 office@tcd.net
307 wyoming.com	307 332 3030 info@wyoming.com
308 Synergy Communications, Inc.	800 345 9669 info@synergy.net
309 CICNet, Inc.	313 998 6103 info@cic.net
309 Driscoll Communications	309 367 2006 info@dris.com
309 Interactive Communications & Explorations	309 454 4638 icenet@ice.net
310 ArtNetwork	800 395 0692 info@artnet.net
310 BeachNet Internet Access	310 823 3308 info@beachnet.com
310 Business Access Technologies	714 577 8978 Techs@batech.com
310 Cloverleaf Communications	714 895 3075 sales@cloverleaf.com
310 Cogent Software, Inc.	818 585 2788 info@cogsoft.com
310 CruzNet	714 680 6600 info@cruznet.net
310 Cyberverse Online	310 643 3783 info@cyberverse.com
310 Delta Internet Services	714 778 0370 info@deltanet.com
310 DigiLink Network Services	310 542 7421 info@digilink.net
310 Exodus Communications, Inc.	408 522 8450 info@exodus.net
310 Flamingo Communications, Inc.	310 532 3533 sales@fcom.com
310 Instant Internet Corp. (InstaNet)	818 772 0097 charlyg@instanet.com
310 InterWorld Communications, Inc.	310 726 0500 sales@interworld.net
310 KAIWAN Internet	714 638 2139 info@kaiwan.com
310 KTB Internet Online	818 240 6600 info@ktb.net
310 Leonardo Internet	310 395 5500 jimp@leonardo.net
310 Liberty Information Network	800 218 5157 info@liberty.com
310 Lightside, Inc.	818 858 9261 Lightside@Lightside.Com
310 The Loop Internet Switch Co.	213 465 1311 info@loop.com
310 Network Intensive	714 450 8400 info@ni.net
310 Online-LA	310 967 8000 sales@online-la.com
310 OutWest Network Services	818 545 1996 info@outwest.net
310 QuickCom Internet Communcations	213 634 7735 info@quickcom.net
310 QuickNet, Inc.	714 969 1091 sales@quick.net
310 Saigon Enterprises	818 246 0689 info@saigon.net
310 SoftAware	310 305 0275 info@softaware.com
310 ViaNet Communications	415 903 2242 info@via.net

312 American Information Systems, Inc.	708 413 8400	info@ais.net
312 CICNet, Inc.	313 998 6103	info@cic.net
312 CIN.net Computerese Information Network	708 310 1188	info@cin.net
312 Compunet Technology Consultants	708 355 XNET	webmaster@ms.com-punet.com
312 InterAccess Co.	708 498 2542	info@interaccess.com
312 Interactive Network Systems, Inc.	312 881 3039	info@insnet.com
312 MCSNet	312 803 6271	info@mcs.net
312 Ripco Communications, Inc.	312 477 6210	info@ripco.com
312 Tezcatlipoca, Inc.	312 850 0181	info@tezcat.com
312 The ThoughtPort Authority, Inc.	800 ISP 6870	info@thoughtport.com
312 Wink Communications Group, Inc.	708 310 9465	sales@winkcomm.com
312 WorldWide Access	708 367 1870	info@wwa.com
312 XNet Information Systems	708 983 6064	info@xnet.com
313 Branch Information Services	313 741 4442	branch-info@branch.com
313 CICNet, Inc.	313 998 6103	info@cic.net
313 Great Lakes Information Systems	810 786 0454	info@glis.net
313 ICNET / Innovative Concepts	313 998 0090	info@ic.net
313 Isthmus Corp.	313 973 2100	info@izzy.net
313 Michigan Internet Cooperative Assn	810 355 1438	info@coop.mica.net
313 Mich.com, Inc.	810 478 4300	info@mich.com
313 Msen, Inc.	313 998 4562	info@msen.com
313 RustNet, Inc.	810 650 6812	info@rust.net
313 Voyager Information Networks, Inc.	517 485 9068	help@voyager.net
314 accessU.S., Inc.	800 638 6373	info@accessus.net
314 Allied Access, Inc.	618 684 2255	sales@intrnet.net
314 Inlink	314 432 0935	support@inlink.com
314 NeoSoft, Inc.	713 684 5969	info@neosoft.com
314 Online Information Access Network	618 692 9813	info@oia.net
314 MVP-Net, Inc.	314 731 2252	info@MO.NET
314 SOCKET Internet Services Corp.	314 499 9131	office@socketis.net
314 Tetranet Communications, Inc.	314 256 4495	info@tetranet.net
314 The ThoughtPort Authority, Inc.	800 ISP 6870	info@thoughtport.com
315 NYSERNet	800 493 4367	sales@nysernet.org
315 ServiceTech, Inc.	716 263 3360	info@servtech.com
315 Spectra.net	607 798 7300	info@spectra.net

315 Syracuse Internet	315 233 1948 info@vcomm.net
315 VivaNET, Inc.	800 836 UNIX info@vivanet.com
316 Elysian Fields, Inc.	316 267 2636 info@elysian.net
316 Future Net, Inc.	316 652 0070 rgmann@fn.net
316 SouthWind Internet Access, Inc.	316 263 7963 info@southwind.net
317 HolliCom Internet Services	317 883 4500 cale@holli.com
317 IQuest Internet, Inc.	317 259 5050 info@iquest.net
317 Metropolitan Data Networks Limited	317 449 0539 info@mdn.com
317 Net Direct	317 251 5252 kat@inetdirect.net
317 Sol Tec, Inc.	317 920 1SOL info@soltec.com
318 Linknet Internet Services	318 442 5465 rdalton@linknet.net
318 Net-Connect, Ltd.	318 234 4396 services@net-connect.net
319 Freese-Notis Weather.Net	515 282 9310 hfreese@weather.net
319 ia.net	319 393 1095 info@ia.net
319 INTERLINK L.C.	319 524 2895 postmaster@interl.net
319 Iowa Network Services	800 546 6587 service@netins.net
334 Datasync Internet Services	601 872 0001 info@datasync.com
334 Gulf Coast Internet Company	904 438 5700 info@gulf.net
334 OnLine Montgomery	334 271 9576 rverble@bbs.olm.com
334 MindSpring Enterprises, Inc.	800 719 4332 info@mindspring.com
334 Scott Network Services, Inc.	205 987 5889 info@scott.net
334 WSNetwork Communications Services, Inc.	334 263 5505 custserv@wsnet.com
360 The Bellingham Internet Cafe	360 650 0442 tonys@inet-cafe.com
360 Interconnected Associates, Inc. (IXA)	206 622 7337 mike@ixa.com
360 NorthWest CommLink	360 336 0103 info@nwcl.net
360 NorthWestNet	206 562 3000 info@nwnet.net
360 Olympia Networking Services	360 753 3636 info@olywa.net
360 Olympic Net	360 692 0651 info@olympic.net
360 Olympus	360 385 0464 info@olympus.net
360 Pacifier Computers	360 693 2116 info@pacifier.com
360 Pacific Rim Network, Inc.	x11 -> 360 650 0442 info@pacificrim.net
360 Premier1 Internet Services	360 793 3658 info@premier1.net

360 Skagit On-Line Services	360 755 0190 info@sos.net
360 Structured Network Systems, Inc.	503 656 3530 info@structured.net
360 Teleport, Inc.	503 223 4245 info@teleport.com
360 Transport Logic	503 243 1940 sales@transport.com
360 TSCNet, Inc.	360 613 0708 info@tscnet.com
360 Whidbey Connections, Inc.	360 678 1070 info@whidbey.net
360 WLN	800 342 5956 info@wln.com
401 brainiac services, Inc.	401 539 9050 info@brainiac.com
401 CompUtopia	401 732 5588 allan@computopia.com
401 InteleCom Data Systems, Inc.	401 885 6855 info@ids.net
401 The Internet Connection, Inc.	508 261 0383 info@ici.net
401 MCIX, Inc.	860 572 8720 info@mcix.com
401 Plymouth Commercial Internet Exchange	617 741 5900 info@pcix.com
401 Saturn Internet Corp.	617 451 9121 info@saturn.net
402 Greater Omaha Public Access Unix Corp.	402 558 5030 info@gonix.com
402 Internet Nebraska	402 434 8680 info@inetnebr.com
402 Iowa Network Services	800 546 6587 service@netins.net
402 The Online Pitstop	402 291 1542 bob@top.net
402 Pioneer Internet	712 271 0101 info@pionet.net
402 ProLinx Communications, Inc.	402 551 3036 techsupport@nfinity.nfinity.com
402 Synergy Communications, Inc.	800 345 9669 info@synergy.net
402 Zelcom International, Inc.	402 333 2441 administration-dept@zelcom.com
403 AGT Limited	800 608 1155 info@agt.net
403 Alberta SuperNet, Inc.	403 441 3663 info@supernet.ab.ca
403 CCI Networks	403 450 6787 info@ccinet.ab.ca
403 Cycor Communications, Inc.	902 892 7354 signup@cycor.ca
403 Debug Computer Services	403 248 5798 root@debug.cuc.ab.ca
403 TST Consulting	403 529 1560 sales@TST-MedHat.com
403 UUNET Canada, Inc.	416 368 6621 info@uunet.ca
404 CyberNet Communications Corp.	404 518 5711 sfeingold@atlwin.com
404 Digital Service Consultants, Inc.	770 455 9022 info@dscga.com
404 First Internet Resources	800 577 5969 jcarter@1stresource.com
404 I-Link, Ltd.	800 ILINK 99 info@i-link.net
404 Internet Atlanta	404 410 9000 info@atlanta.com

404 MindSpring Enterprises, Inc.	800 719 4332 info@mindspring.com
404 NetDepot, Inc.	770 434 5595 info@netdepot.com
404 Paradise Communications, Inc.	404 980 0078 info@paradise.net
404 Random Access, Inc.	404 804 1190 sales@randomc.com
404 vividnet	770 933 0999 webadmin@vivid.net
405 Internet Oklahoma	405 721 1580 info@ionet.net
405 Questar Network Services	405 848 3228 info@qns.net
406 CyberPort Montana	406 863 3221 skippy@cyberport.net
406 Internet Montana	406 255 9699 support@comp-unltd.com
406 Montana Internet Cooperative	406 443 3347 admin@mt.net
406 Montana Online	406 721 4952 info@montana.com
406 NorthWestNet	206 562 3000 info@nwnet.net
407 Acquired Knowledge Systems, Inc.	305 525 2574 info@aksi.net
407 CyberGate, Inc.	305 428 4283 sales@gate.net
407 The EmiNet Domain	407 731 0222 info@emi.net
407 Florida Online	407 635 8888 info@digital.net
407 GS-Link Systems, Inc.	407 671 8682 info@gslink.net
407 I-Link, Ltd.	800 ILINK 99 info@i-link.net
407 ICANECT	305 621 9200 sales@icanect.net
407 InteleCom Data Systems, Inc.	401 885 6855 info@ids.net
407 Internet Providers of Florida, Inc.	305 273 7978 office@ipof.fla.net
407 InternetU	407 952 8487 info@iu.net
407 Magg Information Services, Inc.	407 642 9841 help@magg.net
407 MagicNet, Inc.	407 657 2202 info@magicnet.net
407 MetroLink Internet Services	407 726 6707 jtaylor@metrolink.net
407 PSS InterNet Services	800 463 8499 support@america.com
407 Shadow Information Services, Inc.	305 594 2450 admin@shadow.net
407 WAM / NetRunner	407 392 9422 wam@wamsyst.com
407 WebIMAGE, an internet presence provider	407 723 0001 info@webimage.com
408 A-Link Network Services, Inc.	408 720 6161 info@alink.net
408 Aimnet Information Services	408 257 0900 info@aimnet.com
408 Alternet (UUNET Technologies, Inc.)	703 204 8000 info@alter.net
408 Bay Area Internet Solutions	408 447 8690 tjw00@bayarea.net
408 Brainstorm's Internet Power Connection	415 473-6411 info@brainstorm.net

408 BTR Communications Company	415 966 1429 support@btr.com
408 Click.Net	415 579 2535 info@click.net
408 Cruzio	408 423 1162 office@cruzio.com
408 Direct Network Access	510 649 6110 support@dnai.com
408 The Duck Pond Public Unix	modem -> 408 249 9630 postmaster@kfu.com
408 Electriciti	619 338 9000 info@powergrid.electriciti.com
408 Exodus Communications, Inc.	408 522 8450 info@exodus.net
408 GST Net	510 792 0768 info@gst.net
408 ICOnetworks	408 461 4638 info@ico.net
408 Infoserv Connections	408 335 5600 root@infoserv.com
408 Internet Avenue	408 727 0777 sales@ave.net
408 InterNex Tiara	408 496 5466 info@internex.net
408 ISP Networks	408 653 0100 info@isp.net
408 Liberty Information Network	800 218 5157 info@liberty.com
408 meernet	415 428 7111 info@meer.net
408 Monterey Bay Internet	408 642 6100 info@mbay.net
408 NetGate Communications	408 565 9601 sales@netgate.net
408 Network Solutions	408 946 6895 info@inow.com
408 San Jose Co-op	408 978 3958 sales@sj-coop.net
408 Scruz-Net	408 457 5050 info@scruz.net
408 SenseMedia	408 335 9400 sm@picosof.com
408 South Valley Internet	408 683 4533 info@garlic.com
408 Silicon Valley Public Access Link	408 448 3071 abem@svpal.org
408 West Coast Online	707 586 3060 info@calon.com
408 zNET	619 755 7772 info@znet.com
408 Zocalo Engineering	510 540 8000 info@zocalo.net

409 Brazos Information Highway Services	409 693 9336 info@bihs.net
409 CVTV - Internet	800 247 8885 cyndyz@cvtv.net
409 Cybercom Corp.	409 268 0771 www@cy-net.net
409 Delta Design and Development Inc.	800 763 8265 sales@deltaweb.com
409 Fayette Area Internet Services	409 968 3999 mcooper@fais.net
409 Internet Connect Services, Inc.	512 572 9987 info@icsi.net
409 PERnet Communications, Inc.	409 729 4638 info@mail.pernet.net
409 Phoenix DataNet, Inc.	713 486 8337 info@phoenix.net

410 ABSnet Internet Services	410 361 8160 info@abs.net
410 American Information Network	410 855 2353 info@ai.net

410 ARInternet Corp.	301 459 7171 info@ari.net
410 BayServe Technologies, Inc.	410 360 2216 sales@bayserve.net
410 CAPCON Library Network	202 331 5771 info@capcon.net
410 Charm.Net	410 558 3900 info@charm.net
410 Clark Internet Services, Inc. ClarkNet	410 995 0691 info@clark.net
410 Cyber Services, Inc.	703 749 9590 info@cs.com
410 Digital Express Group	301 847 5000 info@digex.net
410 jaguNET Access Services	410 931 3157 info@jagunet.com
410 Smartnet Internet Services, LLC	410 792 4555 info@smart.net
410 Softaid Internet Services Inc.	410 290 7763 sales@softaid.net
410 UltraPlex Information Providers	410 880 4604 info@upx.net
410 US Net, Inc.	301 572 5926 info@us.net
412 CityNet, Inc.	412 481 5406 info@city-net.com
412 epix	800 374 9669 karndt@epix.net
412 FYI Networks	412 898 2323 info@fyi.net
412 Pittsburgh OnLine, Inc.	412 681 6130 sales@pgh.net
412 Stargate Industries, Inc.	412 942 4218 info@sgi.net
412 Telerama Public Access Internet	412 481 3505 info@telerama.lm.com
412 The ThoughtPort Authority, Inc.	800 ISP 6870 info@thoughtport.com
412 USA OnRamp	412 391 4382 info@usaor.com
412 Westmoreland Online Inc.	412 830 4900 sales@westol.com
413 Mallard Electronics, Inc.	413 732 0214 gheacock@map.com
413 ShaysNet.COM	413 772 3774 staff@shaysnet.com
413 SoVerNet, Inc.	802 463 2111 info@sover.net
413 the spa!, inc.	413 539 9818 info@the-spa.com
414 Excel.Net, Inc.	414 452 0455 manager@excel.net
414 Exec-PC, Inc.	414 789 4200 info@execpc.com
414 FullFeed Communications	608 246 4239 info@fullfeed.com
414 Internet Access LLC	414 648 3837 info@intaccess.com
414 MIX Communications	414 351 1868 info@mixcom.com
414 NetNet, Inc.	414 499 1339 info@netnet.net
414 The Peoples Telephone Company	414 326 3151 info@peoples.net
414 TRC Access	414 827 9111 info@trcaccess.net
414 Wink Communications Group, Inc.	708 310 9465 sales@winkcomm.com

415	A-Link Network Services, Inc.	408 720 6161 info@alink.net
415	Aimnet Information Services	408 257 0900 info@aimnet.com
415	Alternet (UUNET Technologies, Inc.)	703 204 8000 info@alter.net
415	APlatform	415 941 2647 support@aplatform.com
415	Bay Area Internet Solutions	408 447 8690 tjw00@bayarea.net
415	Beckemeyer Development	510 530 9637 info@bdt.com
415	Brainstorm's Internet Power Connection	415 473-6411 info@brainstorm.net
415	BTR Communications Company	415 966 1429 support@btr.com
415	Click.Net	415 579 2535 info@click.net
415	Community ConneXion - NEXUS-Berkeley	510 549 1383 info@c2.org
415	Datatamers	415 367 7919 info@datatamers.com
415	Direct Network Access	510 649 6110 support@dnai.com
415	emf.net	510 704 2929 sales@emf.net
415	Exodus Communications, Inc.	408 522 8450 info@exodus.net
415	GST Net	510 792 0768 info@gst.net
415	I-Link, Ltd.	800 ILINK 99 info@i-link.net
415	Idiom Consulting	510 644 0441 info@idiom.com
415	InReach Internet Communications	800 446 7324 info@inreach.com
415	InterNex Tiara	408 496 5466 info@internex.net
415	ISP Networks	408 653 0100 info@isp.net
415	LanMinds, Inc.	510 843 6389 info@lanminds.com
415	Liberty Information Network	800 218 5157 info@liberty.com
415	LineX Communications	415 455 1650 info@linex.com
415	meernet	415 428 7111 info@meer.net
415	MobiusNet	415 821 0600 info@mobius.net
415	NetGate Communications	408 565 9601 sales@netgate.net
415	Network Solutions	408 946 6895 info@inow.com
415	QuakeNet	415 655 6607 info@quake.net
415	San Francisco Online (Televolve, Inc.)	415 861 7712 info@sfo.com
415	Sirius	415 284 4700 info@sirius.com
415	SLIPNET	415 281 3132 info@slip.net
415	Silicon Valley Public Access Link	408 448 3071 abem@svpal.org
415	Ultima Tool	415 775 8960 info@ultima.org
415	Value Net Internetwork Services	510 943 5769 info@value.net
415	ViaNet Communications	415 903 2242 info@via.net
415	The WELL	415 332 4335 info@well.com
415	22 Solutions	415 431 9903 info@catch22.com
415	West Coast Online	707 586 3060 info@calon.com

415 zNET	619 755 7772 info@znet.com
415 Zocalo Engineering	510 540 8000 info@zocalo.net
416 ComputerLink/Internet Direct	416 233 7150 info@idirect.com
416 Cycor Communications, Inc.	902 892 7354 signup@cycor.ca
416 HookUp Communications	905 847 8000 info@hookup.net
416 Internex Online, Inc.	416 363 8676 support@io.org
416 InterLog Internet Services	416 975 2655 internet@interlog.com
416 Internet Light and Power	416 502 1512 staff@ilap.com
416 Magic Online Services International, Inc.	416 591 6490 info@magic.ca
416 Neptune Internet Services	905 895 0898 info@neptune.on.ca
416 UUNET Canada, Inc.	416 368 6621 info@uunet.ca
417 DialNet (Digital Internet Access Link)	417 873 3425 sales@dialnet.net
417 Panther Creek Information Services	417 767 2126 info@pcis.net
417 Woodtech Information Systems, Inc.	417 886 0234 info@woodtech.com
418 autoroute.net	514 333 3145 info@autoroute.net
418 UUNET Canada, Inc.	416 368 6621 info@uunet.ca
419 Branch Information Services	313 741 4442 branch-info@branch.com
419 GlassNet Communications, LTD.	419 382 6800 info@glasscity.net
419 OARnet (corporate clients only)	614 728 8100 info@oar.net
419 Primenet	602 870 1010 info@primenet.com
423 accessU.S., Inc.	800 638 6373 info@accessus.net
423 MindSpring Enterprises, Inc.	800 719 4332 info@mindspring.com
423 Preferred Internet, Inc.	615 323 1142 info@preferred.com
423 Virtual Interactive Center	423 544 7902 info@vic.com
501 A2ZNET	901 854 1871 webmaster@a2znet.com
501 Aristotle Internet Access	501 374 4638 info@aristotle.net
501 Cloverleaf Technologies	903 832 1367 helpdesk@clover.cleaf.com
501 IntelliNet ISP	501 376 7676 info@intellinet.com
502 accessU.S., Inc.	800 638 6373 info@accessus.net
502 IgLou Internet Services	800 436 4456 info@iglou.com
502 Mikrotec Internet Services, Inc.	606 225 1488 info@mis.net

503 Alternet (UUNET Technologies, Inc.)	703 204 8000 info@alter.net
503 aracnet.com	503 626 8696 info@aracnet.com
503 aVastNet	503 263 0912 info@vastnet.com
503 Cascade Connection	503 282 8303 info@casconn.com
503 Cenornet	503 557 9047 info@cenornet.com
503 Colossus, Inc.	x19 -> 312 528 1000 colossus@romney.mtjeff.com
503 Data Research Group, Inc.	503 465 3282 info@ordata.com
503 Gorge Networks	503 386 8300 postmaster@gorge.net
503 Europa	503 222 9508 info@europa.com
503 Hevanet Communications	503 228 3520 info@hevanet.com
503 I-Link, Ltd.	800 ILINK 99 info@i-link.net
503 Interconnected Associates, Inc. (IXA)	206 622 7337 mike@ixa.com
503 Internet Communications	503 848 8139 info@iccom.com
503 NorthWestNet	206 562 3000 info@nwnet.net
503 Open Door Networks, Inc.	503 488 4127 info@opendoor.com
503 Oregon Information Technology Centeres	503 469 6699 hmaster@harborside.com
503 Pacifier Computers	360 693 2116 info@pacifier.com
503 RainDrop Laboraties/Agora	503 293 1772 info@agora.rdrop.com
503 Structured Network Systems, Inc.	503 656 3530 info@structured.net
503 Teleport, Inc.	503 223 4245 info@teleport.com
503 Transport Logic	503 243 1940 sales@transport.com
503 WLN	800 342 5956 info@wln.com
504 AccessCom Internet Services	504 887 0022 info@accesscom.net
504 Communique, Inc.	504 527 6200 info@communique.net
504 Cyberlink	504 277 4186 cladmin@eayor.cyberlink-no.com
504 Hollingsworth Information Services, Inc.	504 769 2156 webmaster@rouge.net
504 Hub City Area Access	601 268 6156 info@hub1.hubcity.com
504 I-Link, Ltd.	800 ILINK 99 info@i-link.net
504 InterSurf Online, Inc.	504 755 0500 info@intersurf.net
504 JAMNet Internet Services, Inc.	504 361 3492 info@jis.net
504 NeoSoft, Inc.	713 684 5969 info@neosoft.com
505 Computer Systems Consulting	505 984 0085 info@spy.org
505 Internet Direct, Inc.	800 879 3624 info@direct.net
505 Internet Express	719 592 1240 info@usa.net
505 Network Intensive	714 450 8400 info@ni.net
505 New Mexico Internet Access	505 877 0617 info@nmia.com

505 New Mexico Technet, Inc.	505 345 6555 granoff@technet.nm.org
505 Southwest Cyberport	505 271 0009 info@swcp.com
505 WhiteHorse Communications, Inc.	915 584 6630 whc.net.html
505 ZyNet SouthWest	505 343 8846 zycor@zynet.com
506 Agate Internet Services	207 947 8248 ais@agate.net
506 Cycor Communications, Inc.	902 892 7354 signup@cycor.ca
507 Desktop Media	507 373 2155 isp@dm.deskmedia.com
507 Internet Connections, Inc.	507 625 7320 info@ic.mankato.mn.us
507 Millennium Communications, Inc.	612 338 5509 info@millcomm.com
507 Minnesota OnLine	612 225 1110 info@mn.state.net
507 Minnesota Regional Network	612 342 2570 info@mr.net
507 Protocol Communications, Inc.	612 541 9900 info@protocom.com
508 Argo Communications	508 261 6121 info@argo.net
508 Channel 1	617 864 0100 support@channel1.com
508 CompUtopia	401 732 5588 allan@computopia.com
508 The Destek Group, Inc.	603 635 3857 inquire@destek.net
508 Empire.Net, Inc.	603 889 1220 info@empire.net
508 FOURnet Information Network	508 291 2900 info@four.net
508 The Internet Access Company (TIAC)	617 276 7200 info@tiac.net
508 The Internet Connection, Inc.	508 261 0383 info@ici.net
508 Intuitive Information, Inc.	508 342 1100 info@iii.net
508 Kersur Technologies, Inc.	508 384 1404 info@kerser.net
508 MV Communications, Inc.	603 429 2223 info@mv.mv.com
508 PICTAC	508 999 1565 sales@pictac.com
508 Pioneer Global Telecommunications, Inc.	617 375 0200 info@pn.com
508 Plymouth Commercial Internet Exchange	617 741 5900 info@pcix.com
508 Saturn Internet Corp.	617 451 9121 info@saturn.net
508 Shore.Net	617 593 3110 info@shore.net
508 StarNet	508 922 8238 info@venus.star.net
508 TerraNet, Inc.	617 450 9000 info@terra.net
508 UltraNet Communications, Inc.	508 229 8400 info@ultranet.com
508 USAinternet, Inc.	800 236 9737 info@usa1.com
508 The World	617 739 0202 info@world.std.com
508 Wilder Systems, Inc.	617 933 8810 info@id.wing.net

509 Cascade Connections, Inc.	509 663 4259 carrie@cascade.net
509 Interconnected Associates, Inc. (IXA)	206 622 7337 mike@ixa.com
509 Internet On-Ramp, Inc.	509 624 RAMP info@on-ramp.ior.com
509 NorthWestNet	206 562 3000 info@nwnet.net
509 Structured Network Systems, Inc.	503 656 3530 info@structured.net
509 Transport Logic	503 243 1940 sales@transport.com
509 WLN	800 342 5956 info@wln.com
510 A-Link Network Services, Inc.	408 720 6161 info@alink.net
510 Aimnet Information Services	408 257 0900 info@aimnet.com
510 Alternet (UUNET Technologies, Inc.)	703 204 8000 info@alter.net
510 Beckemeyer Development	510 530 9637 info@bdt.com
510 BTR Communications Company	415 966 1429 support@btr.com
510 Community ConneXion - NEXUS-Berkeley	510 549 1383 info@c2.org
510 Direct Network Access	510 649 6110 support@dnai.com
510 emf.net	510 704 2929 sales@emf.net
510 Exodus Communications, Inc.	408 522 8450 info@exodus.net
510 GST Net	510 792 0768 info@gst.net
510 Idiom Consulting	510 644 0441 info@idiom.com
510 InterNex Tiara	408 496 5466 info@internex.net
510 LanMinds, Inc.	510 843 6389 info@lanminds.com
510 Liberty Information Network	800 218 5157 info@liberty.com
510 LineX Communications	415 455 1650 info@linex.com
510 MobiusNet	415 821 0600 info@mobius.net
510 Network Solutions	408 946 6895 info@inow.com
510 San Francisco Online (Televolve, Inc.)	415 861 7712 info@sfo.com
510 Sirius	415 284 4700 info@sirius.com
510 SLIPNET	415 281 3132 info@slip.net
510 22 Solutions	415 431 9903 info@catch22.com
510 Ultima Tool	415 775 8960 info@ultima.org
510 Value Net Internetwork Services	510 943 5769 info@value.net
510 West Coast Online	707 586 3060 info@calon.com
510 Zocalo Engineering	510 540 8000 info@zocalo.net
512 @sig.net	512 306 0700 sales@aus.sig.net
512 CVTV - Internet	800 247 8885 cyndyz@cvtv.net
512 Delta Design and Development Inc.	800 763 8265 sales@deltaweb.com
512 The Eden Matrix	512 478 9900 info@eden.com

512 I-Link, Ltd.	800 ILINK 99 info@i-link.net
512 Illuminati Online	512 462 0999 info@io.com
512 Internet Connect Services, Inc.	512 572 9987 info@icsi.net
512 Onramp Access, Inc.	512 322 9200 info@onr.com
512 OuterNet Connection Strategies	512 345 3573 question@outer.net
512 Phoenix DataNet, Inc.	713 486 8337 info@phoenix.net
512 Real/Time Communications	512 451 0046 info@realtime.net
512 Turning Point Information Services, Inc.	512 499 8400 info@tpoint.net
512 Zilker Internet Park, Inc.	512 206 3850 info@zilker.net
513 The Dayton Network Access Company	513 237 6868 info@dnaco.net
513 IgLou Internet Services	800 436 4456 info@iglou.com
513 Internet Access Cincinnati	513 887 8877 info@iac.net
513 Local Internet Gateway Co.	510 503 9227 sdw@lig.net
513 OARnet (corporate clients only)	614 728 8100 info@oar.net
513 Premier Internet Cincinnati, Inc.	513 561 6245 pic@cinti.net
514 Accent Internet	514 737 6077 admin@accent.net
514 autoroute.net	514 333 3145 info@autoroute.net
514 CiteNet Telecom, Inc.	514 721 1351 info@citenet.net
514 Communication Accessibles Montreal	514 288 2581 info@cam.org
514 Communications Inter-Acces	514 367 0002 info@interax.net
514 Cycor Communications, Inc.	902 892 7354 signup@cycor.ca
514 Odyssee Internet	514 861 3432 info@odyssee.net
514 UUNET Canada, Inc.	416 368 6621 info@uunet.ca
515 Freese-Notis Weather.Net	515 282 9310 hfreese@weather.net
515 ia.net	319 393 1095 info@ia.net
515 Iowa Network Services	800 546 6587 service@netins.net
515 JTM MultiMedia, Inc.	515 277 1990 jtm@ecity.net
515 Minnesota OnLine	612 225 1110 info@mn.state.net
515 Synergy Communications, Inc.	800 345 9669 info@synergy.net
516 ASB Internet Services	516 981 1953 info@asb.com
516 bway.net / Outernet, Inc.	212 982 9800 info@bway.net
516 Creative Data Consultants (SILLY.COM)	718 229 0489 info@silly.com
516 Echo Communications Group	212 255 3839 info@echonyc.com
516 I-2000, Inc.	800 464 3820 info@i-2000.com

516 INTAC Access Corp.	800 504 6822 info@intac.com
516 LI Net, Inc.	516 476 1168 info@li.net
516 Lightning Internet Services, LLC	516 248 8400 sales@lightning.net
516 Long Island Information, Inc.	516 294 0124 info@liii.com
516 Long Island Internet HeadQuarters	516 439 7800 support@pb.net
516 Network Internet Services	516 543 0234 info@netusa.net
516 New World Data	718 962 1725 dmk@nwdc.com
516 NYSERNet	800 493 4367 sales@nysernet.org
516 Panix (Public Access uNIX)	212 741 4400 info@panix.com
516 Pipeline New York	212 267 3636 info@pipeline.com
516 Real Life Pictures RealNet	212 366 4434 reallife@walrus.com
516 ZONE One Network Exchange	212 824 4000 info@zone.net
517 Branch Information Services	313 741 4442 branch-info@branch.com
517 Freeway, Inc. (tm)	616 347 2400 info@freeway.net
517 The Internet Ramp	800 502 0620 newaccts@tir.com
517 Mich.com, Inc.	810 478 4300 info@mich.com
517 Msen, Inc.	313 998 4562 info@msen.com
517 Voyager Information Networks, Inc.	517 485 9068 help@voyager.net
518 AlbanyNet	518 462 6262 info@albany.net
518 epix	800 374 9669 karndt@epix.net
518 Global One, Inc.	518 452 1465 lorin@global1.net
518 Klink Net Communications	518 725 3000 admin@klink.net
518 NetHeaven	800 910 6671 info@netheaven.com
518 NYSERNet	800 493 4367 sales@nysernet.org
518 SoVerNet, Inc.	802 463 2111 info@sover.net
518 Wizvax Communications	518 273 4325 info@wizvax.com
519 Electro-Byte Technologies	519 332 8235 info@ebtech.net
519 Execulink Internet Services Corp.	519 451 4288 info@execulink.com
519 FastLane.Net Ltd.	519 679 0908 info@fastlane.ca
519 headwaters network	519 940 9252 sales@headwaters.com
519 HookUp Communications	905 847 8000 info@hookup.net
519 HyperNet	519 652 3790 Admin@L2.lonet.ca
519 Information Gateway Services	519 884 7200 info@kw.igs.net
519 Inter•Com Information Services	519 679 1620 info@icis.on.ca
519 Magic Online Services International, Inc.	416 591 6490 info@magic.ca

519 MGL Systems Computer Technologies, Inc.	519 836 1295 info@mgl.ca
519 Network Enterprise Technology, Inc.	905 525 4555 info@netinc.ca
519 UUNET Canada, Inc.	416 368 6621 info@uunet.ca
519 Windsor Infromation Network Company	519 945 9462 kim@wincom.net
520 InfoMagic, Inc.	520 526 9565 info@infomagic.com
520 Internet Direct, Inc.	800 879 3624 info@direct.net
520 Opus One	602 324 0494 sales@opus1.com
520 Primenet	602 870 1010 info@primenet.com
520 RTD Systems & Networking, Inc.	602 318 0696 info@rtd.com
520 Sedona Internet Services, Inc.	520 204 2247 info@sedona.net
540 Cyber Services, Inc.	703 749 9590 info@cs.com
541 aVastNet	503 263 0912 info@vastnet.com
601 A2ZNET	901 854 1871 webmaster@a2znet.com
601 Datasync Internet Services	601 872 0001 info@datasync.com
601 Gulfcoast On-Line Development, Inc.	601 864 2423 info@goldinc.com
601 Hub City Area Access	601 268 6156 info@hub1.hubcity.com
602 Crossroads Communications	602 813 9040 crossroads@xroads.com
602 I-Link, Ltd.	800 ILINK 99 info@i-link.net
602 InfoMagic, Inc.	520 526 9565 info@infomagic.com
602 Internet Direct, Inc.	800 879 3624 info@direct.net
602 Internet Express	719 592 1240 info@usa.net
602 New Mexico Technet, Inc.	505 345 6555 granoff@technet.nm.org
602 Opus One	602 324 0494 sales@opus1.com
602 Phoenix Computer Specialists	602 265 9188 info@pcslink.com
602 Primenet	602 870 1010 info@primenet.com
602 RTD Systems & Networking, Inc.	602 318 0696 info@rtd.com
602 StarLink Internet Services	602 878 7001 sysop@starlink.com
602 Systems Solutions, Inc.	602 955 5566 support@syspac.com
603 Agate Internet Services	207 947 8248 ais@agate.net
603 Empire.Net, Inc.	603 889 1220 info@empire.net
603 The Destek Group, Inc.	603 635 3857 inquire@destek.net
603 MV Communications, Inc.	603 429 2223 info@mv.mv.com

603 NETIS Public Access Internet	603 437 1811 epoole@leotech.mv.com
603 Rocket Science Computer Services, Inc.	603 334 6444 info@rscs.com
603 SoVerNet, Inc.	802 463 2111 info@sover.net
603 StarNet	508 922 8238 info@venus.star.net
603 UltraNet Communications, Inc.	508 229 8400 info@ultranet.com
604 AMT Solutions Group, Inc. Island Net	604 727 6030 info@islandnet.com
604 auroraNET, Inc.	604 294 4357 sales@aurora.net
604 Cycor Communications, Inc.	902 892 7354 signup@cycor.ca
604 Fairview Technology Centre, Ltd.	604 498 4316 bwklatt@ftcnet.com
604 The InterNet Shop, Inc.	604 376 3719 info@netshop.net
604 Mind Link!	604 534 5663 info@mindlink.bc.ca
604 Okanagan Internet Junction	604 549 1036 info@junction.net
604 Sunshine Net, Inc.	604 886 4120 admin@sunshine.net
604 UUNET Canada, Inc.	416 368 6621 info@uunet.ca
605 Internet Services of the Black Hills	605 642 2244 postmaster@blackhills.com
605 Pioneer Internet	712 271 0101 info@pionet.net
606 IgLou Internet Services	800 436 4456 info@iglou.com
606 Internet Access Cincinnati	513 887 8877 info@iac.net
606 Mikrotec Internet Services, Inc.	606 225 1488 info@mis.net
606 RAM Technologies, Inc.	800 950 1726 info@ramlink.net
607 Art Matrix - Lightlink	607 277 0959 info@lightlink.com
607 Clarity Connect, Inc.	607 257 2070 chuck@baka.com
607 epix	800 374 9669 karndt@epix.net
607 NYSERNet	800 493 4367 sales@nysernet.org
607 ServiceTech, Inc.	716 263 3360 info@servtech.com
607 Spectra.net	607 798 7300 info@spectra.net
608 BOSSNet Internet Services	608 362 1340 mbusam@bossnt.com
608 Exec-PC, Inc.	414 789 4200 info@execpc.com
608 FullFeed Communications	608 246 4239 info@fullfeed.com
609 CyberComm Online Services	908 506 6651 info@cybercomm.net
609 Cyberenet (Kaps, Inc.)	609 753 9840 access-sales@cyberenet.net

609 Digital Express Group	301 847 5000 info@digex.net
609 Eclipse Internet Access	800 483 1223 info@eclipse.net
609 InterActive Network Services	609 227 6380 info@jersey.net
609 K2NE Software	609 893 0673 vince-q@k2nesoft.com
609 Net Access	215 576 8669 support@netaxs.com
609 NetReach, Inc.	215 283 2300 info@netreach.net
609 New Jersey Computer Connection	609 896 2799 info@pluto.njcc.com
609 Texel International	908 297 0290 info@texel.com
609 VoiceNet	800 835 5710 info@voicenet.com
610 Cheap Net	302 993 8420 sammy@ravenet.com
610 Digital Express Group	301 847 5000 info@digex.net
610 ENTER.Net	610 366 1300 info@enter.net
610 epix	800 374 9669 karndt@epix.net
610 FishNet	610 337 9994 info@pond.com
610 GlobalQUEST, Inc.	610 696 8111 info@globalquest.net
610 Internet Tidal Wave	610 770 6187 steve@itw.com
610 InterNetworking Technologies	302 398 4369 itnt.com@itnt.com
610 The Magnetic Page	302 651 9753 info@magpage.com
610 Microserve Information Systems	717 779 4430 info@microserve.com
610 Net Access	215 576 8669 support@netaxs.com
610 NetReach, Inc.	215 283 2300 info@netreach.net
610 Network Analysis Group	800 624 9240 nag@good.freedom.net
610 Night Vision	610 366 9767 info@n-vision.com
610 SSNet, Inc.	302 378 1386 info@ssnet.com
610 Oasis Telecommunications, Inc.	610 439 8560 staff@oasis.ot.com
610 OpNet	610 520 2880 info@op.net
610 RaveNet Systems Inc.	302 993 8420 waltemus@ravenet.com
610 VivaNET, Inc.	800 836 UNIX info@vivanet.com
610 VoiceNet	800 835 5710 info@voicenet.com
610 You Tools Corp. / FASTNET	610 954 5910 info@fast.net
612 Cloudnet	612 240 8243 info@cloudnet.com
612 DCC, Inc.	612 378 4000 kgastony@dcc.com
612 Freese-Notis Weather.Net	515 282 9310 hfreese@weather.net
612 GlobalCom	612 920 9920 info@globalc.com
612 James River Group, Inc.	612 339 2521 jriver@jriver.jriver.COM
612 Millennium Communications, Inc.	612 338 5509 info@millcomm.com

612 Minnesota OnLine	612 225 1110 info@mn.state.net
612 Minnesota Regional Network	612 342 2570 info@mr.net
612 Orbis Internet Services, Inc.	612 645 9663 info@orbis.net
612 pclink.com	612 541 5656 infomatic@pclink.com
612 Primenet	602 870 1010 info@primenet.com
612 Protocol Communications, Inc.	612 541 9900 info@protocom.com
612 Sihope Communications	612 829 9667 info@sihope.com
612 Sound Communications Internet	612 722 8470 root@scc.net
612 StarNet Communications, Inc.	612 941 9177 info@winternet.com
612 Synergy Communications, Inc.	800 345 9669 info@synergy.net
612 Vector Internet Services, Inc.	612 288 0880 info@visi.com
613 autoroute.net	514 333 3145 info@autoroute.net
613 Cyberius Online, Inc.	613 233 1215 info@cyberus.ca
613 Cycor Communications, Inc.	902 892 7354 signup@cycor.ca
613 Information Gateway Services (Ottawa)	613 592 5619 info@igs.net
613 Interactive Telecom, Inc.	613 727 5258 info@intertel.net
613 HookUp Communications	905 847 8000 info@hookup.net
613 Magma Communications, Ltd.	613 228 3565 info@magmacom.com
613 o://info.web	613 225 3354 kevin@magi.com
613 UUNET Canada, Inc.	416 368 6621 info@uunet.ca
614 ASCInet (Columbus)	614 798 5321 info@ascinet.com
614 Branch Information Services	313 741 4442 branch-info@branch.com
614 Internet Access Cincinnati	513 887 8877 info@iac.net
614 OARnet (corporate clients only)	614 728 8100 info@oar.net
614 RAM Technologies, Inc.	800 950 1726 info@ramlink.net
615 accessU.S., Inc.	800 638 6373 info@accessus.net
615 ERC, Inc. / The Edge	615 455 9915 staff@edge.ercnet.com
615 First Internet Resources	800 577 5969 jcarter@1stresource.com
615 GoldSword Systems	615 691 6498 info@goldsword.com
615 ISDN-Net, Inc.	615 377 7672 jdunlap@rex.isdn.net
615 MindSpring Enterprises, Inc.	800 719 4332 info@mindspring.com
615 Preferred Internet, Inc.	615 323 1142 info@preferred.com
615 The Telalink Corp.	615 321 9100 sales@telalink.net
615 The Tri-Cities Connection	615 378 5355 info@tricon.net
615 U.S. Internet	615 522 6788 info@usit.net

615 Virtual Interactive Center	423 544 7902 info@vic.com
616 Branch Information Services	313 741 4442 branch-info@branch.com
616 Freeway, Inc. (tm)	616 347 2400 info@freeway.net
616 The iserv Co.	616 281 5254 info@iserv.net
616 Mich.com, Inc.	810 478 4300 info@mich.com
616 Msen, Inc.	313 998 4562 info@msen.com
616 NetLink Systems L.L.C.	616 345 LINK info@serv01.net-link.net
616 Novagate Communications Corp.	616 847 0910 info@novagate.com
616 RustNet, Inc.	810 650 6812 info@rust.net
616 Traverse Communication Company	616 935 1705 info@traverse.com
616 Voyager Information Networks, Inc.	517 485 9068 help@voyager.net
617 Alternet (UUNET Technologies, Inc.)	703 204 8000 info@alter.net
617 Argo Communications	508 261 6121 info@argo.net
617 Channel 1	617 864 0100 support@channel1.com
617 CompUtopia	401 732 5588 allan@computopia.com
617 COWZ Technologies	617 497 0058 system@cow.net
617 Cyber Access Internet Communications, Inc.	617 396 0491 info@cybercom.net
617 FOURnet Information Network	508 291 2900 info@four.net
617 The Internet Access Company (TIAC)	617 276 7200 info@tiac.net
617 The Internet Connection, Inc.	508 261 0383 info@ici.net
617 Intuitive Information, Inc.	508 342 1100 info@iii.net
617 Pioneer Global Telecommunications, Inc.	617 375 0200 info@pn.com
617 Plymouth Commercial Internet Exchange	617 741 5900 info@pcix.com
617 Saturn Internet Corp.	617 451 9121 info@saturn.net
617 Shore.Net	617 593 3110 info@shore.net
617 TerraNet, Inc.	617 450 9000 info@terra.net
617 UltraNet Communications, Inc.	508 229 8400 info@ultranet.com
617 USAinternet, Inc.	800 236 9737 info@usa1.com
617 The World	617 739 0202 info@world.std.com
617 Wilder Systems, Inc.	617 933 8810 info@id.wing.net
617 The Xensei Corp.	617 376 6342 info@xensei.com
618 accessU.S., Inc.	800 638 6373 info@accessus.net
618 Allied Access, Inc.	618 684 2255 sales@intrnet.net
618 Applied Personal Computing, Inc.	618 632 7282 spider@apci.net
618 Online Information Access Network	618 692 9813 info@oia.net

618 MVP-Net, Inc.	314 731 2252	info@MO.NET
619 CONNECTnet Internet Network Services	619 450 0254	info@connectnet.com
619 CTS Network Services	619 637 3637	info@cts.com
619 Cyberg8t Internet Services	909 398 4638	sales@cyberg8t.com
619 Delta Internet Services	714 778 0370	info@deltanet.com
619 The Cyberspace Station	619 634 2894	info@cyber.net
619 Electriciti	619 338 9000	info@powergrid.electriciti.com
619 I-Link, Ltd.	800 ILINK 99	info@i-link.net
619 Liberty Information Network	800 218 5157	info@liberty.com
619 Primenet	602 870 1010	info@primenet.com
619 RidgeNET	619 371 3501	saic@owens.ridgecrest.ca.us
619 Sierra-Net	702 831 3353	giles@sierra.net
619 WANet, Software Design Associates, Inc.	619 679 5900	info@WANet.net
701 NorthWestNet	206 562 3000	info@nwnet.net
701 Red River Net	701 232 2227	info@rrnet.com
702 @wizard.com	702 871 4461	info@wizard.com
702 Connectus, Inc.	702 323 2008	info@connectus.com
702 Great Basin Internet Services	702 829 2244	info@greatbasin.com
702 InterMind	702 878 6111	support@terminus.intermind.net
702 NETConnect	800 689 8001	office@tcd.net
702 Sierra-Net	702 831 3353	giles@sierra.net
702 Skylink Networks, Inc.	702 368 0700	sales@skylink.net
703 Alternet (UUNET Technologies, Inc.)	703 204 8000	info@alter.net
703 ARInternet Corp.	301 459 7171	info@ari.net
703 CAPCON Library Network	202 331 5771	info@capcon.net
703 Charm.Net	410 558 3900	info@charm.net
703 Clark Internet Services, Inc. ClarkNet	410 995 0691	info@clark.net
703 Cyber Services, Inc.	703 749 9590	info@cs.com
703 Digital Express Group	301 847 5000	info@digex.net
703 Genuine Computing Resources	703 878 4680	info@gcr.com
703 Internet Online, Inc.	301 652 4468	info@intr.net
703 Interpath	800 849 6305	info@interpath.net
703 LaserNet	703 591 4232	info@laser.net
703 Preferred Internet, Inc.	615 323 1142	info@preferred.com

703 Quantum Networking Solutions, Inc.	805 538 2028 info@qnet.com
703 RadixNet Internet Services	301 567 9831 info@radix.net
703 Smartnet Internet Services, LLC	410 792 4555 info@smart.net
703 SONNETS, Inc.	703 502 8589 office@sonnets.net
703 UltraPlex Information Providers	410 880 4604 info@upx.net
703 Universal Telecomm Corp.	703 758 0550 root@utc.net
703 US Net, Inc.	301 572 5926 info@us.net
703 World Web Limited	703 838 2000 info@worldweb.net
703 Xpress Internet Services	301 601 5050 info@xis.com
704 Interpath	800 849 6305 info@interpath.net
704 SunBelt.Net	803 328 1500 info@sunbelt.net
704 Vnet Internet Access	704 334 3282 info@vnet.net
705 Barrie Connex, Inc.	705 725 0819 info@bconnex.net
705 Magic Online Services International Inc.	416 591 6490 info@magic.ca
705 Mindemoya Computing	705 523 0243 info@mcd.on.ca
705 Neptune Internet Services	905 895 0898 info@neptune.on.ca
705 SooNet Corp.	705 253 4700 service@soonet.ca
706 Athens' ISP, Inc.	706 613 0611 info@athens.net
706 InteliNet	803 279 9775 administrator@intelinet.net
706 internet@Dalton	706 673 4715 support@dalton.net
706 Internet Atlanta	404 410 9000 info@atlanta.com
706 MindSpring Enterprises, Inc.	800 719 4332 info@mindspring.com
707 Beckemeyer Development	510 530 9637 info@bdt.com
707 CASTLES Information Network	707 422 7311 info@castles.com
707 Datatamers	415 367 7919 info@datatamers.com
707 InReach Internet Communications	800 446 7324 info@inreach.com
707 Liberty Information Network	800 218 5157 info@liberty.com
707 Value Net Internetwork Services	510 943 5769 info@value.net
707 West Coast Online	707 586 3060 info@calon.com
707 Zocalo Engineering	510 540 8000 info@zocalo.net
708 American Information Systems, Inc.	708 413 8400 info@ais.net
708 CICNet, Inc.	313 998 6103 info@cic.net
708 CIN.net Computerese Information Network	708 310 1188 info@cin.net

708 Compunet Technology Consultants	708 355 XNET	webmaster@ms.com-punet.com
708 I Connection, Inc.	708 662 0877	info@iconnect.net
708 InterAccess Co.	708 498 2542	info@interaccess.com
708 Interactive Network Systems, Inc.	312 881 3039	info@insnet.com
708 MCSNet	312 803 6271	info@mcs.net
708 Ripco Communications, Inc.	312 477 6210	info@ripco.com
708 TensorNet Co.	708 665 3637	info@tensornet.com
708 Tezcatlipoca, Inc.	312 850 0181	info@tezcat.com
708 Wink Communications Group, Inc.	708 310 9465	sales@winkcomm.com
708 WorldWide Access	708 367 1870	info@wwa.com
708 XNet Information Systems	708 983 6064	info@xnet.com
709 InterActions Limited	709 745 4638	connect@nfld.com
712 Freese-Notis Weather.Net	515 282 9310	hfreese@weather.net
712 Greater Omaha Public Access Unix Corp	402 558 5030	info@gonix.com
712 ia.net	319 393 1095	info@ia.net
712 Iowa Network Services	800 546 6587	service@netins.net
712 The Online Pitstop	402 291 1542	bob@top.net
712 Pioneer Internet	712 271 0101	info@pionet.net
712 ProLinx Communications, Inc.	402 551 3036	techsupport@nfinity.nfinity.com
712 Synergy Communications, Inc.	800 345 9669	info@synergy.net
712 Zelcom International, Inc.	402 333 2441	administration-dept@zelcom.com
713 Alternet (UUNET Technologies, Inc.)	703 204 8000	info@alter.net
713 The Black Box	713 480 2684	info@blkbox.com
713 Delta Design and Development, Inc.	800 763 8265	sales@deltaweb.com
713 ELECTROTEX, Inc.	713 526 3456	info@electrotex.com
713 I-Link, Ltd.	800 ILINK 99	info@i-link.net
713 Internet Connect Services, Inc.	512 572 9987	info@icsi.net
713 NeoSoft, Inc.	713 684 5969	info@neosoft.com
713 OnRamp Technologies, Inc.	214 746 4710	info@onramp.net
713 Phoenix DataNet, Inc.	713 486 8337	info@phoenix.net
713 South Coast Computing Services, Inc.	713 917 5000	info@houston.net
713 USiS	713 682 1666	admin@usis.com
714 Argonet	714 261 7511	postmaster@argonet.net
714 ArtNetwork	800 395 0692	info@artnet.net

714 Business Access Technologies	714 577 8978 Techs@batech.com
714 Cloverleaf Communications	714 895 3075 sales@cloverleaf.com
714 Cogent Software, Inc.	818 585 2788 info@cogsoft.com
714 CruzNet	714 680 6600 info@cruznet.net
714 DPC Systems Beach.Net	714 443 4172 connect@beach.net
714 Delta Internet Services	714 778 0370 info@deltanet.com
714 DigiLink Network Services	310 542 7421 info@digilink.net
714 EDM NetWORK	714 476 0416 info@edm.net
714 Electriciti	619 338 9000 info@powergrid.electriciti.com
714 Exodus Communications, Inc.	408 522 8450 info@exodus.net
714 InterNex Tiara	408 496 5466 info@internex.net
714 InterWorld Communications, Inc.	310 726 0500 sales@interworld.net
714 KAIWAN Internet	714 638 2139 info@kaiwan.com
714 Liberty Information Network	800 218 5157 info@liberty.com
714 Lightside, Inc.	818 858 9261 Lightside@Lightside.Com
714 The Loop Internet Switch Co.	213 465 1311 info@loop.com
714 NetQuest	714 379 8228 info@net-quest.com
714 Network Intensive	714 450 8400 info@ni.net
714 OutWest Network Services	818 545 1996 info@outwest.net
714 Primenet	602 870 1010 info@primenet.com
714 QuickNet, Inc.	714 969 1091 sales@quick.net
715 FullFeed Communications	608 246 4239 info@fullfeed.com
715 Minnesota OnLine	612 225 1110 info@mn.state.net
716 Blue Moon Online System Internet Svcs	716 447 5629 sales@net.bluemoon.net
716 BuffNET	800 463 6499 info@buffnet.net
716 E-Znet, Inc.	716 262 2485
716 epix	800 374 9669 karndt@epix.net
716 NYSERNet	800 493 4367 sales@nysernet.org
716 ServiceTech, Inc.	716 263 3360 info@servtech.com
716 VivaNET, Inc.	800 836 UNIX info@vivanet.com
717 epix	800 374 9669 karndt@epix.net
717 The Internet Cafe	717 344 1969 info@lydian.scranton.com
717 Keystone Information Access Systems	717 741 2626 office@yrkpa.kias.com
717 Microserve Information Systems	717 779 4430 info@microserve.com
717 Oasis Telecommunications, Inc.	610 439 8560 staff@oasis.ot.com

717 PenNet	717 368 1577 safrye@pennet.net
717 Red Rose SuperNet	800 222 2517 info@redrose.net
717 Spectra.net	607 798 7300 info@spectra.net
717 VoiceNet	800 835 5710 info@voicenet.com
717 You Tools Corp. / FASTNET	610 954 5910 info@fast.net
718 Advanced Standards, Inc. advn.com	212 302 3366 kolian@advn.com
718 Blythe Systems	212 226 7171 infodesk@blythe.org
718 BrainLINK	718 805 6559 info@beast.brainlink.com
718 bway.net / Outernet, Inc.	212 982 9800 info@bway.net
718 Creative Data Consultants (SILLY.COM)	718 229 0489 info@silly.com
718 escape.com - Kazan Corp	212 888 8780 info@escape.com
718 Ingress Communications, Inc.	212 679 2838 info@ingress.com
718 INTAC Access Corp.	800 504 6822 info@intac.com
718 Intellitech Walrus	212 406 5000 info@walrus.com
718 Intercall, Inc.	800 758 7329 sales@intercall.com
718 InterCom Online	212 714 7183 info@intercom.com
718 Internet QuickLink Corp.	212 307 1669 info@quicklink.com
718 Interport Communications Corp.	212 989 1128 info@interport.net
718 Lightning Internet Services, LLC	516 248 8400 sales@lightning.net
718 Long Island Information, Inc.	516 294 0124 info@liii.com
718 Long Island Internet HeadQuarters	516 439 7800 support@pb.net
718 Mnematics, Inc.	914 359 4546 service@mne.com
718 Mordor International BBS	201 433 4222 ritz@mordor.com
718 New World Data	718 962 1725 dmk@nwdc.com
718 Panix (Public Access uNIX)	212 741 4400 info@panix.com
718 Phantom Access Technologies, Inc.	212 989 2418 bruce@phantom.com
718 Pipeline New York	212 267 3636 info@pipeline.com
718 Real Life Pictures RealNet	212 366 4434 reallife@walrus.com
718 Spacelab.Net	212 966 8844 mike@mxol.com
718 ThoughtPort of New York City	212 645 7970 info@precipice.com
718 tunanet/InfoHouse	212 229 8224 info@tunanet.com
718 ZONE One Network Exchange	212 824 4000 info@zone.net
719 Colorado SuperNet, Inc.	303 296 8202 info@csn.org
719 Internet Express	719 592 1240 info@usa.net
719 Old Colorado City Communications	719 528 5849 thefox@oldcolo.com
719 Rocky Mountain Internet	800 900 7644 info@rmii.com

770 Digital Service Consultants, Inc.	770 455 9022 info@dscga.com
770 MindSpring Enterprises, Inc.	800 719 4332 info@mindspring.com
770 Paradise Communications, Inc.	404 980 0078 info@paradise.net
770 Random Access, Inc.	404 804 1190 sales@randomc.com
770 vividnet	770 933 0999 webadmin@vivid.net
801 I-Link, Ltd.	800 ILINK 99 info@i-link.net
801 Internet Technology Systems (ITS)	801 375 0538 admin@itsnet.com
801 NETConnect	800 689 8001 office@tcd.net
801 The ThoughtPort Authority, Inc.	800 ISP 6870 info@thoughtport.com
801 Utah Wired/The Friendly Net	801 532 1117 sales@utw.com
801 Vyzynz International	801 568 0999 info@vii.com
801 XMission	801 539 0852 support@xmission.com
802 The Plainfield Bypass	802 426 3963 questions@plainfield.bypass.com
802 SoVerNet, Inc.	802 463 2111 info@sover.net
803 A World of Difference, Inc.	803 769 4488 info@awod.com
803 CetLink.Net	803 327 2754 info@cetlink.net
803 Global Vision, Inc.	803 241 0901 info@globalvision.net
803 Hargray Telephone Company	803 686 5000 info@hargray.com
803 InteliNet	803 279 9775 administrator@intelinet.net
803 Interpath	800 849 6305 info@interpath.net
803 SIMS, Inc.	803 762 4956 info@sims.net
803 South Carolina SuperNet, Inc.	803 212 4400 info@scsn.net
803 SunBelt.Net	803 328 1500 info@sunbelt.net
803 Teleplex Communications, Inc.	803 585 PLEX info@teleplex.net
804 Widomaker Communication Service	804 253 7621 bloyall@widowmaker.com
805 The Catalina BBS InterNet Services fax->	805 687 1185 help@catalina.org
805 The Central Connection	818 735 3000 info@centcon.com
805 Cogent Software, Inc.	818 585 2788 info@cogsoft.com
805 Delta Internet Services	714 778 0370 info@deltanet.com
805 Fishnet Internet Services, Inc.	805 650 1844 info@fishnet.net
805 Instant Internet Corp. (InstaNet)	818 772 0097 charlyg@instanet.com
805 Internet Access of Ventura County	805 383 3500 info@vcnet.com
805 KAIWAN Internet	714 638 2139 info@kaiwan.com

805 KTB Internet Online	818 240 6600 info@ktb.net
805 Lancaster Internet (California)	805 943 2112 dennis@gargamel.ptw.com
805 Liberty Information Network	800 218 5157 info@liberty.com
805 The Loop Internet Switch Co.	213 465 1311 info@loop.com
805 Netport Internet Access	805 538 2860 info@netport.com
805 Network Intensive	714 450 8400 info@ni.net
805 OutWest Network Services	818 545 1996 OWInfo@outwest.com
805 Quantum Networking Solutions, Inc.	805 538 2028 info@qnet.com
805 Regional Alliance for Info Networking	805 967 7246 info@rain.org
805 Saigon Enterprises	818 246 0689 info@saigon.net
805 Silicon Beach Communications	805 730 7740 help@silcom.com
805 Tehachapi Mountain Internet	805 822 7803 info@tminet.com
805 ValleyNet Communications	209 486 8638 info@valleynet.com
805 WestNet Communications, Inc.	805 892 2133 info@west.net
806 HubNet	806 792 4482 info@HUB.ofthe.NET
806 OnRamp Technologies, Inc.	214 746 4710 info@onramp.net
807 Pronet Internet Services	807 622 5915 info@mail.procom.net
808 FlexNet, Inc.	808 732 8849 info@aloha.com
808 Hawaii OnLine	808 533 6981 support@aloha.net
808 Inter-Pacific Network Services	808 935 5550 sales@interpac.net
808 LavaNet, Inc.	808 545 5282 info@lava.net
808 Pacific Information Exchange, Inc.	808 596 7494 info@pixi.com
810 Branch Information Services	313 741 4442 branch-info@branch.com
810 Freeway, Inc. (tm)	616 347 2400 info@freeway.net
810 Great Lakes Information Systems	810 786 0454 info@glis.net
810 ICNET / Innovative Concepts	313 998 0090 info@ic.net
810 The Internet Ramp	800 502 0620 newaccts@tir.com
810 Michigan Internet Cooperative Association	810 355 1438 info@coop.mica.net
810 Mich.com, Inc.	810 478 4300 info@mich.com
810 Msen, Inc.	313 998 4562 info@msen.com
810 RustNet, Inc.	810 650 6812 info@rust.net
810 Voyager Information Networks, Inc.	517 485 9068 help@voyager.net
812 accessU.S., Inc.	800 638 6373 info@accessus.net

812 HolliCom Internet Services	317 883 4500 cale@holli.com
812 IgLou Internet Services	800 436 4456 info@iglou.com
812 World Connection Services	812 479 1700 info@evansville.net
813 Bay-A-Net	813 988 7772 info@bayanet.com
813 Centurion Technology, Inc.	813 538 1919 info@tpa.cent.com
813 CFTnet	813 980 1317 sales@cftnet.com
813 CocoNet Corp.	813 945 0055 info@coconet.com
813 CyberGate, Inc.	305 428 4283 sales@gate.net
813 Florida Online	407 635 8888 info@digital.net
813 Intelligence Network Online, Inc. x22 ->	813 442 0114 info@intnet.net
813 PacketWorks, Inc.	813 446 8826 info@packet.net
813 Shadow Information Services, Inc.	305 594 2450 admin@shadow.net
813 The ThoughtPort Authority, Inc.	800 ISP 6870 info@thoughtport.com
813 WebIMAGE, an internet presence provider	407 723 0001 info@webimage.com
814 North Coast Internet	814 838 6386 info@ncinter.net
814 Penncom Internet Co.	814 723 4141 admin@penn.com
814 PenNet	717 368 1577 safrye@pennet.net
815 American Information Systems, Inc.	708 413 8400 info@ais.net
815 BOSSNet Internet Services	608 362 1340 mbusam@bossnt.com
815 CIN.net Computerese Information Network	708 310 1188 info@cin.net
815 InterAccess Co.	708 498 2542 info@interaccess.com
815 The Software Farm	815 246 7295 info@softfarm.com
815 T.B.C. Online Data-Net	815 758 5040 info@tbcnet.com
815 Wink Communications Group, Inc.	708 310 9465 sales@winkcomm.com
816 fyi@unicom.net	913 383 8466 fyi@unicom.net
816 Interstate Networking Corp.	816 472 4949 staff@interstate.net
816 Primenet	602 870 1010 info@primenet.com
817 Association for Computing Machinery	817 776 6876 account-info@acm.org
817 CompuTek	214 994 0190 info@computek.net
817 Connection Technologies - ConnectNet	214 490 7100 sales@connect.net
817 Delta Design and Development Inc.	800 763 8265 sales@deltaweb.com
817 DFW Internet Services, Inc.	817 332 5116 info@dfw.net
817 OnRamp Technologies, Inc.	214 746 4710 info@onramp.net

817	Texas Metronet, Inc.	214 705 2900 info@metronet.com
818	ArtNetwork	800 395 0692 info@artnet.net
818	BeachNet Internet Access	310 823 3308 info@beachnet.com
818	The Central Connection	818 735 3000 info@centcon.com
818	Cogent Software, Inc.	818 585 2788 info@cogsoft.com
818	CruzNet	714 680 6600 info@cruznet.net
818	Cyberg8t Internet Services	909 398 4638 sales@cyberg8t.com
818	Cyberverse Online	310 643 3783 info@cyberverse.com
818	Delta Internet Services	714 778 0370 info@deltanet.com
818	DigiLink Network Services	310 542 7421 info@digilink.net
818	Exodus Communications, Inc.	408 522 8450 info@exodus.net
818	Flamingo Communications, Inc.	310 532 3533 sales@fcom.com
818	Instant Internet Corp. (InstaNet)	818 772 0097 charlyg@instanet.com
818	InterNex Tiara	408 496 5466 info@internex.net
818	InterWorld Communications, Inc.	310 726 0500 sales@interworld.net
818	KAIWAN Internet	714 638 2139 info@kaiwan.com
818	KTB Internet Online	818 240 6600 info@ktb.net
818	Leonardo Internet	310 395 5500 jimp@leonardo.net
818	Liberty Information Network	800 218 5157 info@liberty.com
818	Lightside, Inc.	818 858 9261 Lightside@Lightside.Com
818	The Loop Internet Switch Co.	213 465 1311 info@loop.com
818	Network Intensive	714 450 8400 info@ni.net
818	Online-LA	310 967 8000 sales@online-la.com
818	OutWest Network Services	818 545 1996 info@outwest.net
818	Primenet	602 870 1010 info@primenet.com
818	QuickCom Internet Communcations	213 634 7735 info@quickcom.net
818	Regional Alliance for Info Networking	805 967 7246 info@rain.org
818	Saigon Enterprises	818 246 0689 info@saigon.net
818	ViaNet Communications	415 903 2242 info@via.net
819	Information Gateway Services (Ottawa)	613 592 5619 info@igs.net
819	Interactive Telecom, Inc.	613 727 5258 info@intertel.net
819	Magma Communications, Ltd.	613 228 3565 info@magmacom.com
819	o://info.web	613 225 3354 kevin@magi.com
860	Connix: Connecticut Internet Exchange	860 349 7059 office@connix.com
860	imagine.com	860 527 9245 Postmaster@imagine.com

860 MCIX, Inc.	860 572 8720 info@mcix.com
860 Mindport Internet Services, Inc.	860 892 2081 staff@mindport.net
860 Paradigm Communications, Inc.	203 250 7397 info@pcnet.com
864 Global Vision, Inc.	803 241 0901 info@globalvision.net
901 accessU.S., Inc.	800 638 6373 info@accessus.net
901 A2ZNET	901 854 1871 webmaster@a2znet.com
901 ISDN-Net, Inc.	615 377 7672 jdunlap@rex.isdn.net
901 Magibox, Inc.	901 757 7835 info@magibox.net
901 U.S. Internet	615 522 6788 info@usit.net
902 Cycor Communications, Inc.	902 892 7354 signup@cycor.ca
903 Cloverleaf Technologies	903 832 1367 helpdesk@clover.cleaf.com
903 Delta Design and Development, Inc.	800 763 8265 sales@deltaweb.com
903 Phoenix DataNet, Inc.	713 486 8337 info@phoenix.net
903 Rapid Ramp, Inc.	903 759 0705 help@rapidramp.com
903 StarNet Online Systems	903 785 5533 lrhea@stargate.1starnet.com
904 CyberGate, Inc.	305 428 4283 sales@gate.net
904 Florida Online	407 635 8888 info@digital.net
904 Gulf Coast Internet Company	904 438 5700 info@gulf.net
904 Internet Connect Company	904 375 2912 info@atlantic.net
904 Jax Gateway to the World	904 730 7692 sales@gttw.com
904 MagicNet, Inc.	407 657 2202 info@magicnet.net
904 Polaris Network, Inc.	904 878 9745 staff@polaris.net
904 PSS InterNet Services	800 463 8499 support@america.com
904 SymNet	904 385 1061 info@symnet.net
904 WebIMAGE, an internet presence provider	407 723 0001 info@webimage.com
905 ComputerLink/Internet Direct	416 233 7150 info@idirect.com
905 Cycor Communications Inc.	902 892 7354 signup@cycor.ca
905 eagle.ca - Northumbria Associates	905 373 9313 info@eagle.ca
905 HookUp Communications	905 847 8000 info@hookup.net
905 iCOM Internet Services	905 522 1220 sales@icom.ca
905 InterLog Internet Services	416 975 2655 internet@interlog.com
905 Internet Access Worldwide	905 714 1400 info@iaw.on.ca

905 Internet Connect Niagara, Inc.	905 988 9909 info@niagara.com
905 Internex Online, Inc.	416 363 8676 support@io.org
905 Magic Online Services International, Inc.	416 591 6490 info@magic.ca
905 Neptune Internet Services	905 895 0898 info@neptune.on.ca
905 Network Enterprise Technology, Inc.	905 525 4555 info@netinc.ca
905 Times.net	905 775 4471 rfonger@times.net
905 Vaxxine Computer Systems, Inc.	905 562 3500 admin@vaxxine.com
906 Branch Information Services	313 741 4442 branch-info@branch.com
906 Mich.com, Inc.	810 478 4300 info@mich.com
906 Msen, Inc.	313 998 4562 info@msen.com
906 The Portage at Micro + Computers	906 487 9832 admin@mail.portup.com
907 Alaska Information Technology	907 258 1881 info@anc.ak.net
907 Internet Alaska	907 562 4638 info@alaska.net
907 Micronet Communications	907 333 8663 info@micronet.net
907 NorthWestNet	206 562 3000 info@nwnet.net
908 BLASTNET Internet Service	908 534 5881 mcp@blast.net
908 Castle Network, Inc.	908 548 8881 request@castle.net
908 CyberComm Online Services	908 506 6651 info@cybercomm.net
908 Crystal Palace Networking, Inc.	201 300 0881 info@crystal.palace.net
908 Digital Express Group	301 847 5000 info@digex.net
908 Eclipse Internet Access	800 483 1223 info@eclipse.net
908 I-2000, Inc.	800 464 3820 info@i-2000.com
908 INTAC Access Corp.	800 504 6822 info@intac.com
908 Intercall, Inc.	800 758 7329 sales@intercall.com
908 Internet For 'U'	800 NET WAY1 info@ifu.net
908 Internet Online Services	x226 -> 201 928 1000 help@ios.com
908 Lightning Internet Services, LLC	516 248 8400 sales@lightning.net
908 Openix - Open Internet Exchange	201 443 0400 info@openix.com
908 Planet Access Networks	201 691 4704 info@planet.net
908 TechnoCore Communications, Inc.	908 928 7400 info@thecore.com
908 Texel International	908 297 0290 info@texel.com
908 You Tools Corp. / FASTNET	610 954 5910 info@fast.net
909 Cogent Software, Inc.	818 585 2788 info@cogsoft.com
909 CONNECTnet Internet Network Services	619 450 0254 info@connectnet.com

909 CruzNet	714 680 6600 info@cruznet.net
909 Cyberg8t Internet Services	909 398 4638 sales@cyberg8t.com
909 DiscoverNet	909 335 1209 info@discover.net
909 DPC Systems Beach.Net	714 443 4172 connect@beach.net
909 Delta Internet Services	714 778 0370 info@deltanet.com
909 EmpireNet	909 787 4969 support@empirenet.com
909 InterWorld Communications, Inc.	310 726 0500 sales@interworld.net
909 KAIWAN Internet	714 638 2139 info@kaiwan.com
909 Keyway Internet Access	909 933 3650 sales@keyway.net
909 Liberty Information Network	800 218 5157 info@liberty.com
909 Lightside, Inc.	818 858 9261 Lightside@Lightside.Com
909 Network Intensive	714 450 8400 info@ni.net
909 Primenet	602 870 1010 info@primenet.com
909 Saigon Enterprises	818 246 0689 info@saigon.net
910 Interpath	800 849 6305 info@interpath.net
910 NetDepot, Inc.	770 434 5595 info@netdepot.com
910 Netpath, Inc.	910 226 0425 info@netpath.net
910 Red Barn Data Center	910 750 9809 tom@rbdc.rbdc.com
910 SpyderByte Communications	910 643 6999 info@spyder.net
910 Vnet Internet Access	704 334 3282 info@vnet.net
912 Hargray Telephone Company	803 686 5000 info@hargray.com
912 Homenet Communications, Inc.	912 329 8638 info@hom.net
912 Internet Atlanta	404 410 9000 info@atlanta.com
912 MindSpring Enterprises, Inc.	800 719 4332 info@mindspring.com
913 Flint Hills Computers, Inc.	913 776 4333 gil@flinthills.com
913 fyi@unicom.net	913 383 8466 fyi@unicom.net
913 Interstate Networking Corp.	816 472 4949 staff@interstate.net
913 Tri-Rivers Internet	913 826 2595 staff@tri.net
914 bway.net / Outernet, Inc.	212 982 9800 info@bway.net
914 Cloud 9 Internet	914 682 0626 info@cloud9.net
914 Computer Net	914 773 1130 paul@computer.net
914 Creative Data Consultants (SILLY.COM)	718 229 0489 info@silly.com
914 epix	800 374 9669 karndt@epix.net
914 GBN InternetAccess	201 343 6427 gbninfo@gbn.net

914 ICU On-Line	914 627 3800 info@icu.com
914 INTAC Access Corp.	800 504 6822 info@intac.com
914 I-2000, Inc.	800 464 3820 info@i-2000.com
914 InteleCom Data Systems, Inc.	401 885 6855 info@ids.net
914 Lightning Internet Services, LLC	516 248 8400 sales@lightning.net
914 Long Island Internet HeadQuarters	516 439 7800 support@pb.net
914 MHVNet (Computer Solutions by Hawkinson)	914 473 0844 info@mhv.net
914 Mnematics, Inc.	914 359 4546 service@mne.com
914 New World Data	718 962 1725 dmk@nwdc.com
914 NYSERNet	800 493 4367 sales@nysernet.org
914 Panix (Public Access uNIX)	212 741 4400 info@panix.com
914 Pipeline New York	212 267 3636 info@pipeline.com
914 TZ-Link Internet	914 353 5443 info@j51.com
914 WestNet Internet Services	914 967 7816 info@westnet.com
914 ZONE One Network Exchange	212 824 4000 info@zone.net
915 Delta Design and Development, Inc.	800 763 8265 sales@deltaweb.com
915 New Mexico Technet, Inc.	505 345 6555 granoff@technet.nm.org
915 Primenet	602 870 1010 info@primenet.com
915 TexNet Internet Services	915 857 1800 jcoving@tnis.net
915 WhiteHorse Communications ,Inc.	915 584 6630 whc.net.html
916 CASTLES Information Network	707 422 7311 info@castles.com
916 Connectus, Inc.	702 323 2008 info@connectus.com
916 Great Basin Internet Services	702 829 2244 info@greatbasin.com
916 mother.com	916 757 8070 info@mail.mother.com
916 InterStar Network Services	916 224 6866 gfrank@shasta.com
916 ORONET	916 477 6650 info@oro.net
916 NetLink Data-Communications, Inc.	916 447 3025 info@netlink.net
916 Psyberware Internet Access	916 645 9451 info@psyber.com
916 R C Concepts Foothill-Net	916 367 3818 sales@foothill.net
916 Sacramento Network Access	916 565 4500 info@sna.com
916 Sierra-Net	702 831 3353 giles@sierra.net
916 SnowCrest Computer Specialties	916 926 2526 root@snowcrest.net
916 Sutter Yuba Internet Exchange	916 755 1751 dave@syix.com
916 TTCI.net	916 895 1609 info@ttci.net
916 VFR, Inc.	916 652 7237 vfr@vfr.net
916 West Coast Online	707 586 3060 info@calon.com

916 Zocalo Engineering	510 540 8000 info@zocalo.net
917 ZONE One Network Exchange	212 824 4000 info@zone.net
918 Galaxy Star Systems	918 835 3655 info@galstar.com
918 Internet Oklahoma	918 583 1161 info@ionet.net
918 South Coast Computing Services, Inc.	713 917 5000 info@houston.net
919 Interpath	800 849 6305 info@interpath.net
919 MCS Internet Services	919 751 5777 shultz@mail.gld.com
919 Vnet Internet Access	704 334 3282 info@vnet.net
941 Centurion Technology, Inc.	813 538 1919 info@tpa.cent.com
941 Net Sarasota	941 371 1966 info@netsrq.com
941 PacketWorks, Inc.	813 446 8826 info@packet.net
941 USA Computers	941 939 5630 info@usacomputers.net
954 Acquired Knowledge Systems, Inc.	305 525 2574 info@aksi.net
954 ICANECT	305 621 9200 sales@icanect.net
954 Shadow Information Services, Inc.	305 594 2450 admin@shadow.net
954 Zimmerman Communications	954 584 0199 bob@zim.com
970 EZLink Internet Access	970 482 0807 ezadmin@ezlink.com
970 Frontier Internet, Inc.	970 385 4177 info@frontier.net
970 Rocky Mountain Internet	800 900 7644 info@rmii.com
970 Verinet Communications, Inc.	970 416 9152 info@verinet.com

FOREIGN

A listing of Internet service providers in countries other than the U.S. and Canada, sorted by country. Fields are country, service provider name, voice phone number, and e-mail address for more information.

Antigua/Barbuda Cable & Wireless (WI) Ltd.	+1 809 462 0840 scholla@candw.ag

Australia AusNet Services Pty., Ltd.	+61 2 241 5888 sales@world.net
Australia Byron Public Access	+61 18 823 541 admin@byron.apana.org.au
Australia Corporate Internet Pty., Ltd .	+61 2 391 3489 admin@corpnet.com.au
Australia DIALix Services	+61 2 948 6995 justin@sydney.dialix.oz.au
Australia Global Data Access	+61 9 421 1222 info@ednet.com.au
Australia Highway 1	+61 9 370 4584 info@highway1.com.au
Australia Hilink Communications Pty.	+61 3 9528 2018 info@hilink.com.au
Australia Hunter Network Association	+61 49 621783 mbrown@hna.com.au
Australia iiNet Technologies	+61 9 3071183iinet@iinet.com.au
Australia Kralizec Dialup Unix System	+61 2 837 1397 nick@kralizec.zeta.org.au
Australia Informed Technology	+61 9 245 2279 info@it.com.au
Australia The Message eXchange Pty., Ltd.	+61 2 550 5014 info@tmx.com.au
Australia Microplex Pty., Ltd.	+61 2 888 3685 info@mpx.com.au
Australia Pegasus Networks Pty., Ltd.	+61 7 257 1111 fwhitmee@peg.apc.org
Australia PPIT Pty., Ltd. (059 051 320)	+61 3 747 9823 info@ppit.com.au
Australia Stour System Services	+61 9 571 1949 stour@stour.net.au
AustraliaWinthrop Technology	+61 9 380 3564 wthelp@yarrow.wt.uwa.edu.au
Australia Zip Australia Pty., Ltd.	+61 2 482 7015 info@zip.com.au
Austria ARGE DATEN	+43 1 4897893info@email.ad.or.at
Austria EUnet EDV	+43 1 3174969info@austria.eu.net
Austria Hochschuelerschaft...	+43 1 586 1868 sysop@link-atu.comlink.apc.org
Austria Net4You	+43 4242 257367 office@net4you.co.at
Austria netwing	+43 5337 65315 info@netwing.at
Austria PING EDV	+43 1 3194336info@ping.at
Austria simon media	+43 316 813 8240 info@sime.com
Austria Vianet Austria, Ltd.	+43 1 5892920info@via.at
Bashkiria UD JV 'DiasPro'	+7 3472 387454 iskander@diaspro.bashkiria.su
Belarus Open Contact, Ltd.	+7 017 2206134 admin@brc.minsk.by
Belgium EUnet Belgium NV	+32 16 236099info@belgium.eu.net
Belgium Infoboard Telematics	+32 2 475 22 99 info@infoboard.be
Belgium INnet NV/SA	+32 14 319937info@inbe.net
Belgium KnoopPunt VZW	+32 9 2333 686 support@knooppunt.be
Belgium Netropolis Belgium	+32 2 6493693info@netropolis.be

Bulgaria EUnet Bulgaria	+359 52 259135 info@bulgaria.eu.net
Denmark DKnet / EUnet Denmark	+45 3917 9900info@dknet.dk
Finland Clinet, Ltd.	+358 0 437 5209 clinet@clinet.fi
Finland EUnet Finland, Ltd.	+358 0 400 2060 helpdesk@eunet.fi
France CalvaCom	+33 1 3463 1919 fb101@calvacom.fr
France French Data Network	+33 1 4797 5873 info@fdn.org
France Internet Way	+33 1 4143 2110 info@iway.fr
France OLEANE	+33 1 4328 3232 info-internet@oleane.net
France REMCOMP SARL	+33 1 4479 0642 info@liber.net
Georgia Mimosi Hard	+7 8832 232857 kisho@sanet.ge
Germany bbTT Electronic Networks	+49 30 817 42 06 willem@b-2.de.contrib.net
Germany ccn computer consultant net	+49 89 29164023 info@ccn.de
Germany EUnet Germany GmbH	+49 231 972 2222 info@germany.eu.net
Germany ILK INternet GmbH	+49 721 9100 0 info@ilk.de
Germany Individual Network e.V.	+49 441 980 8556 in-info@individual.net
Germany INS Inter Networking Systems	+49 2305 356505 info@ins.net
Germany Internet PoP Frankfurt	+49 69 94439192 joerg@pop-frankfurt.com
Germany ISC Dr.-Ing. Nepustil	+49 7123 93102 1 Info@Nepustil.NET
Germany Knipp Medien & Kommunikation	+49 231 9703 0 info@knipp.de
Germany Lemke & Fuerst GbR	+49 711 7189847 info@lf.net
Germany LyNet Kommunikation	+49 451 6101056 info@lynet.de
Germany MUC.DE e.V.	+49 89 324 683 0 postmaster@muc.de
Germany Onlineservice Nuernberg	+49 911 9933882 info@osn.de
Germany PFM News & Mail Xlink POP	+49 171 331 0862 info@pfm.pfm-mainz.de
Germany Point of Presence GmbH	+49 40 2519 2025 info@pop.de
Germany POP Contrib.Net Netzdienste	+49 521 9683011 info@teuto.de
Germany SpaceNet GmbH	+49 89 324 683 0 info@space.net
Germany TouchNET GmbH	+49 89 5447 1111 info@touch.net
Germany Westend GbR	+49 241 911879 info@westend.com
Ghana Chonia Informatica	+233 21 66 94 20 info@ghana.net
Greece Ariadne	+30 1 651 3392 dialup@leon.nrcps.ariadne-t.gr

Greece Foundation of Research	+30 81 221171 forthnet-pr@forthnet.gr
Greece Hellenic Informatics	+30 1 620 3040 info@hol.gr
Hong Kong Asia On-Line Limited	+852 2866 6018 info@asiaonline.net
Hong Kong Asia Pacific CompuNet, Ltd.	+852 2976 9995 info@ap.net.hk
Hong Kong Hong Kong SuperNet	+852 358 7924 trouble@hk.super.net
Hungary iSYS Hungary	+36 1 266 6090 info@isys.hu
Iceland SURIS / ISnet	+354 1 694747 isnet-info@isnet.is
Ireland Cork Internet Services	+353 21 277124 info@cis.ie
Ireland Ieunet Limited	+353 1 679 0832 info@ieunet.ie
Ireland Ireland On-Line	+353 91 592727 info@iol.ie
Israel ACTCOM	+972 4 676115 office@actcom.co.il
Israel Elronet	+972 313534 info@elron.net
Israel NetMedia, Ltd.	+972 2 795 861 info@netmedia.co.il
Israel NetVision, Ltd.	+972 550330 info@netvision.net.il
Italy Abacom s.a.s.	+39 434 660911 info@system.abacom.it
Italy I.NET S.p.A.	+39 2 26162258 info@inet.it
Italy ITnet S.p.A.	+39 10 6563324 info@it.net
Italy Spin	+39 40 8992 286 info@spin.it
Italy Tex.NET TELECOMUNICAZIONI	+39 574 35038 texnet@texnet.it
Italy Video On Line	+39 70 659 625 info@vol.it
Jamaica Jamaica Online Information	+1 809 960 8209 info@jol.com.jm
Japan Asahi Net	+81 3 3666 2811 info@asahi-net.or.jp
Japan Global OnLine	+81 3 5330 9380 info@gol.org
Japan HA Telecom Corp.	+81 58 253 7641 info@hatelecom.or.jp
Japan Internet Initiative Japan	+81 3 3580 3781 info@iij.ad.jp
Japan M.R.T., Inc.	+81 3 3255 8880 sysop@janis-tok.com
Japan TWICS	+81 3 3351 5977 info@twics.com
Japan Typhoon, Inc.	+81 3 3757 2118 info@typhoon.co.jp
Kazakhstan Bogas Soft Laboratory Co.	+7 322 262 4990 pasha@sl.semsk.su

Kuwait Gulfnet Kuwait	+965 242 6728 info@kw.us.com
Latvia LvNet-Teleport	+371 2 551133 vit@riga.lv
Latvia Versia, Ltd.	+371 2 417000 postmaster@vernet.lv
Lisboa Esoterica	716 2395 info@esoterica.com
Luxemburg EUnet Luxemburg	+352 47 02 61 361 info@luxemburg.eu.net
Mexico Datanet S.A. de C.V.	+52 5 1075400 info@data.net.mx
Mexico Internet de Mexico S.A.	+52 5 3602931 info@mail.internet.com.mx
Netherlands The Delft Connection	+31 15560079 info@void.tdcnet.nl
Netherlands Hobbynet	+31 365361683 henk@hgatenl.hobby.nl
Netherlands Holland Online	+31 71 40 16943 Sales@hol.nl
Netherlands Internet Access Foundation	+31 5982 2720 mail-server@iafnl.iaf.nl
Netherlands NEST	+31 206265566 info@nest.nl
Netherlands NetLand	+31 206943664 info@netland.nl
Netherlands NLnet (EUnet)	+31 206639366 info@nl.net
Netherlands Psyline	+31 80445801 postmaster@psyline.nl
Netherlands Simplex Networking	+31 206932433 skelmir@simplex.nl
Netherlands Stichting XS4ALL	+31 206225222 helpdesk@xs4all.nl
New Zealand Actrix Networks Limited	+64 4 389 6356 john@actrix.gen.nz
New Zealand Efficient Software Limited	+64 3 4738274 bart@dunedin.es.co.nz
Norway Oslonett A/S	+47 22 46 10 99 oslonett@oslonett.no
Poland ATM	+48 22 6106073 szeloch@ikp.atm.com.pl
Poland PDi Ltd. - Public Internet	+48 42 30 21 94 info@pdi.lodz.pl
Romania EUnet Romania SRL	+40 1 312 6886 info@romania.eu.net
Russia ELCOM	+7 092 223 2208 root@centre.elcom.ru
Russia GlasNet	+7 95 262 7079 support@glas.apc.org
Russia InterCommunications, Ltd.	+7 8632 620562 postmaster@icomm.rnd.su
Russia NEVAlink, Ltd.	+7 812 592 3737 serg@arcom.spb.su
Russia Relcom CO	+7 95 194 25 40 postmaster@ussr.eu.net

Russia SvjazInform	+7 351 265 3600 pol@rich.chel.su
Singapore Singapore Telecom Limited	+65 7308079 admin@singnet.com.sg
Slovakia EUnet Slovakia s.r.o.	+42 7 839 404 info@Slovakia.EU.net
Slovenia NIL, System Integration	+386 61 1405 183 info@slovenia.eu.net
South Africa Aztec	+27 21 419 2690 info@aztec.co.za
South Africa Internet Africa	+27 0800 020003 info@iaccess.za
South Africa The Internet Solution	+27 11 447 5566 info@is.co.za
Spain INTERCOM S.T.A.	+34 3 5802846 info@intercom.es
Spain OFFCAMPUS SL	+34 1 577 3026 infonet@offcampus.es
Spain Servicom	+34 93 580 9396 info@servicom.es
Sri Lanka Information Laboratories	+94 1 61 1061 info@infolabs.is.lk
Sweden NetGuide	+46 31 28 03 73 info@netg.se
Switzerland EUnet AG, Zurich	+41 1 291 45 80 info@eunet.ch
Switzerland EUnet SA, Geneva	+41 22 348 80 45 deffer@eunet.ch
Switzerland Internet ProLink SA	+41 22 788 8555 info@iprolink.ch
Switzerland SWITCH	+41 1 268 1515 postmaster@switch.ch
Tataretan KAMAZ, Inc.	+7 8439 53 03 34 postmaster@kamaz.kazan.su
Ukraine ConCom, Ltd.	+7 0572 27 69 13 igor@ktts.kharkov.ua
Ukraine Crimea Communication Centre	+380 0652 257214 sem@snail.crimea.ua
Ukraine Electronni Visti	+7 44 2713457 info%elvisti.kiev.ua@kiae.su
Ukraine PACO Links Int'l, Ltd.	+7 48 2200057 info@vista.odessa.ua
Ukraine UkrCom-Kherson, Ltd.	+7 5522 64098 postmaster@ukrcom.kherson.ua
United Kingdom Compulink (CIX Ltd)	+44 181 390 8446 cixadmin@cix.compulink.co.uk
United Kingdom CONNECT - PC User Group	+44 181 863 1191 info@ibmpcug.co.uk
United Kingdom Demon Internet Limited	+44 181 371 1000 internet@demon.net
United Kingdom The Direct Connection	+44 81 313 0100 helpdesk@dircon.co.uk
United Kingdom EUnet GB	+44 1227 266466 sales@britain.eu.net

United Kingdom ExNet Systems, Ltd.	+44 81 244 0077 info@exnet.com
United Kingdom Frontier Internet Services	+44 171 242 3383 info@ftech.net
United Kingdom GreenNet	+44 71 713 1941 support@gn.apc.org
United Kingdom Lunatech Research	+44 1734 791900 info@luna.co.uk
United Kingdom Pavilion Internet plc	+44 1273 606072 info@pavilion.co.uk
United Kingdom Planet Online, Ltd.	+44 113 234 5566 info@theplanet.net
United Kingdom Sound & Visions BBS	+44 1932 253131 info@span.com
United Kingdom Utopia! Internet, Ltd.	+44 121 5614621 sales@utopia.co.uk
United Kingdom WinNET (UK)	+44 181 863 1191 info@win-uk.ne
Venezuela Internet Comunicaciones c.a.	+58 2 959 9550 info@ccs.internet.ve

Appendix C—URL List

1-800-MUSIC-NOW
http://www.1800musicnow.mci.com

1 Mall
http://www.1mall.com/

1st Shopping Planet
http://www.shoppingplanet.com/

1 World Plaza
http://www2.clever.net/1world/plaza/shop.htm

Adobe
http://www.adobe.com
http://www.adobe.com/Amber/Index.html
http://w1000.mv.us.adobe.com/Amber/Index.html
http://w1000.mv.us.adobe.com/Amber/makepdf.html
http://w1000.mv.us.adobe.com/Acrobat/Exch.html

Aereal Serch
http://www.virtpark.com/theme/cgi-bin/serch.html

Aladdin Systems:
http://www.aladdinsys.com/ under Shareware/Freeware products

All-In-One Search Site
http://www.albany.net/allinone/

AlterDial/UUNet
info@uu.net www.uu.net www.alter.net

America Online, Inc.
info@aol.com
www.aol.com
ftp://mirror.aol.com/

American Internet Mall
http://www.ammall.com/

Anarchie
http://www.share.com/peterlewis/anarchie/anarchie.html

Apple
http://www.apple.com/
QuickTime VR: http://qtvr.quicktime.apple.com/
QuickTime Player: http://quicktime.apple.com/
http://www2.apple.com/documents/Internet.html

Beyond our Borders
http://www.freenet.hamilton.on.ca/Beyond.html

Canadian Free-Nets
http://www.synapse.net/~radio/freenet.htm

CBS Eye on the Net
http://www.cbs.com/

Center for Disease Control, Morbidity and Mortality Weekly Report
http://www.cdc.gov/epo/mmwr/mmwr_wk.html

Chaco
VR Scout VRML: http://www.chaco.com
VR Scout plugin: http://www.chaco.com/vrscout/
Jack O' Lantern: http://www.chaco.com/~glenn/jack/

Cheap & Easy
http://www.cheapandeasy.com

City.Net
http://www.city.net

C|Net Radio
http://www.cnet.com
http://www.cnet.com/Content/Radio/index.html
http://www.shareware.com/

C|Net Vendor Rolodex
http://www.cnet.com/Resources/Info/Vendor/index.html

Claris E-mailer
http://www.claris.com/products/ClarisE-mailer/index.html
http://www.claris.com/software/ClarisE-mailer/ClarisE-mailerTrial10v3.hqx
ftp.claris.com in the /pub/USA-Macintosh/Trial_Software/ folder

Cleveland Free-Net Telnet
freenet-in-a.cwru.edu
freenet-in-b.cwru.edu
freenet-in-c.cwru.edu

CMP Tech Web
http://techweb.cmp.com/

Community Network guide
http://http2.sils.umich.edu/~ckummer/community.html

Compaq Computer Corp.
http://www.compaq.com/

CompuServe Information Service
70006.101@ compuserve.com
www.compuserve.com

Connectix QuickCam
http://www.connectix.com/

ConnectSoft
http://www.connectsoft.com/
ftp.connectsoft.com in the directory /pub/emc25/.nd Windows 95

Cool Site of the Day
http://www.infi.net/cool.html

CUSeeMe
http://cu-seeme.cornell.edu/

Cyberian Outpost
http://cybout. com

Dallas Market Center
http://www.the-center.com/

David Singer's OS/2 Page of Pointers
http://index.almaden.ibm.com/

Dell Computer Corp.
http://www.us.dell.com

Dial-A-Book
http://dab.psi.net/DialABook/

Digital Equipment Corp.
http://www.digital.com/

DreamShop
http://www.dreamshop.com

Epicurious
http://www.epicurious.com/

Earthlink
http://www.earthlink.net\

Eudora
http://www.qualcom.com/ProdTech/quest/light.html
ftp.qualcomm.com/in the/Eudora/mac/directory

ESPN
http://espnet.sportszone.com/index.text.html

Excite!
http://www.excite.com

Fetch
wuarchive.wustl.edu

Firehorse
http://www.peg.apc.org/~firehorse/welcome.html

Forte FreeAgent
http://www.forteinc.com/forte/
FTP at papa.indstate.edu in the directory /winsock-l/news/

FREEnet INF-0001 General Information
http://www.free.net/FREEnet/INF/INF-0001.en.html

FreeNet Newsflash
http://www.freenet.vancouver.bc.ca/vrfa/newsflash/

Front Page, The
http://www.thefrontpage.com/

Galaxy
http://galaxy.tradewave.com

Georgia Tech Research Corporation
http://www.cc.gatech.edu/gvu/user_surveys/User_Survey_Home.html

GNN
http://gnn.com

Hewlett-Packard Co.
http://www.hp.com

Hot Wired
http://www.hotwired.com

IBM Corp.
http://www.ibm.com

IBM Personal Software Co.
http://www.austin.ibm.com/pspinfo/

Infomart
http://www.infomartusa.com/

InfoSeek
http://www.infoseek.com/

Integrated Data Systems VRealm plugin
http://www.ids-net.com/

Intel Corp.
http://www.intel.com

InterArt
http://www.interart.net/

Internal Revenue Service
http:// www.irs.ustreas.gov/prod/cover.html
http://www.irs.ustreas.gov/

Internet Mailing Lists Guides and Resources
http://www.nlc-bnc.ca/ifla/I/training/listserv/lists.htm

Internet Service Providers worldwide
http://www.celestin.com/pocia/index.html
http://thelist.com

Internet Telephony Page, The
http://rpcp.mit.edu/~asears/main.html
http://www.northcoast.com/savetz/voice-faq.html

Internet Underground Music Archive
http://www.iuma.com

InterRamp/PSI
interramp-info@psi.com
www.psi.net

Internet Valet
valet-info@svcdudes.com
http://www.svcdudes.com/

Liszt
http://www.liszt.com/

Live3D plugin
http://home.netscape.com/comprod/products/navigator/live3d/index.html

Lotus Development Corp.
http://www.lotus.com

Lycos
http://www.lycos.com

Macromedia
http://www.macromedia.com.

Macromedia Director
http://www.macromedia.com/Tools/Shockwave/sdc/Plugin/index.htm

Macromedia Shockwave
http://www.macromedia.com/Tools/Shockwave/sdc/Plugin/index.htm

MakeMusic.com
http://www.makemusic.com

McAffee
http://www. mcafee.com/

Michigan PC Archives
http://www.umich.edu/~archive/msdos/

Microsoft Corp.
http://www.microsoft.com

Microsoft Internet Explorer
http://www.microsoft.com/windows/ie/iexplorer.htm
http://www. microsoft.com/windows/ie/ieinfo.htm
ftp.microsoft.com in directory /Softlib/MSLFILES/

mIRC Web
http://sunsite.nijenrode.nl/software/mirc/index.html
ftp://ftp.demon.co.uk/pub/ibmpc/win3/winsock/apps/mirc/mirc392.zip

MIT FAQ FTP archive
ftp://rtfm.mit.edu/pub/usenet/news.answers/

Mosaic for Macintosh
http://www.ncsa.uiuc.edu/SDG/Software/MacMosaic/
ftp://ftp.ncsa.uiuc.edu/ in the /Mac/Mosaic directory

MTV, Music Television
http://www.mtv.com/

National Public Telecomputing Network (NPTN)s
http://www.nptn.org/

NCSA Mosaic
http://www.ncsa.uiuc.edu/SDG/Software/WinMosaic/HomePage.html
ftp.ncsa.uiuc.edu in the directory /Mosaic/Windows/ Win95/
http://www.ncsa.uiuc.edu /SDG/Software/WinMosaic/Features.htm
http://www.nptn.org/

NEC Corp.
http://www.nec.com

NetCom Internet Services
info@netcom.com
www.netcom.com

Netcom On-Line Communication Services
http://www.netcom.com

NetManatge
http://www.netmanage.com

Net.Radio
http://www.netradio.net

Netscape Comunications Corp.
http://home.netscape.com
http://www.netscape.com

Netscape plug-in page
http://home.netscape.com/comprod/products/navigator/version_2.0/
plugins/index.html

Netscape Web browser
http://home.netscape. com/comprod/mirror/index. html
ftp.netscape.com

NewsWatcher
ftp://ftp.acns.nwv.edu/pub/newswatcher/

New York Times Fax
http://nytimesfax.com/

Novell, Inc.
http://www.novell.com

Nuntius
ftp://ftp.ruc.dk/pub/nuntius/
http://www.shareware.com

OAK Software Depository
http://www.acs.oakland.edu/oak.html

OpenText
http://www.opentext.com

Oracle
http://www.oracle.com/

Oracle PowerBrowser
http://www.oracle.com/PowerBrowser/

O'Reilly & Associates and Trish Information Services
http://www.ora.com/survey/

Oxford's USENET Newsgroup
http://www.lib.ox.ac.uk/internet/news/

Paper, Inc.
http://www.paperinc.com/

Pathfinder
http://www.pathfinder.com

Performance Systems International Inc.
http://www.psi.net

Peter Lewis
ftp://ftp:share.com

Plugins and addons
http://home.netscape.com/comprod/products/navigator/version_2.0/plugins/index.html
http://www2.netscape.com/assist/helper_apps/windowhelper.html
http://charlotte.acns.nwu.edu/internet/helper/
http://wwwhost.cc.utexas.edu/learn/use/helper.html
http://www.ncsa.uiuc.edu/SDG/Software/WinMosaic/viewers.htm

Power Computing Corporation
http://www.powercc.com

Prodigy
freetrial@ prodigy.com
www.prodigy. com

Publically Accessible Mailing Lists
http://www.neosoft.com/internet/paml/index.html

Qualcomm
http://www.qualcomm. com/ ProdTech/quest/
ftp.qualcomm.com in the directory /Eudora/windows/light/
http://www.qualcomm.com/ ProdTech /quest/eudora.html
http://www.qualcomm.com/quest/

Quarterdeck
http://www.qdeck.com

QuickRes
http://www.windows.microsoft.com/windows/software/powertoy.htm

QuickTime VR
http://qtvr.quicktime.apple.com

RealAudio
http://www.realaudio.com/
2.0 Sites: http://www.realaudio.com/products/ra2.0/sites

SBI List
http//dkeep.com/sbi.htm

Search The List of Lists
http://catalog.com/vivian/interest-group-search.html

Shockwave Gallery
http://www.macromedia.com/Tools/Shockwave/Gallery/index.html.
http://www.shocker.com/shocker/

Shop-The-Net
http://www.shop-the-net.com/

Silicon Graphics, Inc.
http://www.sgi.com

Speek Freely Web
http://www.fourmilab.ch/netfone/windows/speak_freely.html

Spry, Inc.
http://www.spry.com

Storm Chaser Page
http://taiga.geog.niu.edu/chaser/chaser.html

Suck
http://suck.com

Sun Microsystems, Inc.
http://www.sun.com
HotJava: http://java.sun.com/
FTP: java.sun.com in directory /pub
http://www.gamelan.com/

Symantec's Anti-Virus Research Center
http://www.symantec.com/avcenter/avcenter.html

Telnet
http://www.shareware.com or http://vsl.cnet.com

TimesFax
http://nytimesfax.com/cgi-bin/tmp/login

Todd Rundgren's Freedom Fighters Home Base
http://www.iglou.com/scm/cgi-bin/todd.pl

UMass-Lowell PC Game Archives
ftp://ftp.ulowell.edu/msdos/Games

U of Michigan Mac Archives
ftp://grind.iscs.uiuwa.edu

Underground Music Archive
http://www.iuma.com/

USENET
http://www.indirect.com/user/steiners/usenet.html

USENET Graphics FAQs
http://www.cis.ohio-state.edu/hypertext/faq/usenet/graphics/top.html

Usenet Newsgroups Resources
http://scwww.ucs.indiana.edu/NetRsc/usenet.html

UT Mac Archive
http://wwwhost.uts.utexas.edu/mac/main.html

UUNET Technologies
http://www.uu.net

Vancouver Regional FreeNet Association
http://freenet.vancouver.bc.ca/vrfa/

Virtual Tourist
http://www.vtourist.com/webmap/

VREAM
http://www.vream.com

VREAM WIRL
http://www.vream.com/3dl1.html

VRML
http://www.vrml.org/

VRML Review
http://www.imaginative.com/Chuck/vrml/

VRML Site of the Week
http://www.virtus.com/modmonth.html

VR Scout
http://www.chaco.com/vrscout/

Washington U. PC Archives
ftp://ftp.wustl.edu/systems/ibmpc

WeatherNet
http://cirrus.sprl.umich.edu/wxnet/
http://taiga.geog.niv.edu/chaser/chaser.html

WebCrawler
http://www.webcrawler.com

WebFX
http://www.paperinc.com

WinVN
http://www.ksc.nasa.gov/software/winvn/winvn.html
ftp.coast.net in directory /SimTel/win3/winsock for Windows 3.1/3.11
/SimTel/win95/winsock for Windows 95

WinZip
http://www.winzip.com/

WIRL Virtual Reality Browser
http://www.vream.com

Xing Technology Corporation
http:// www.xingtech.com/

Yahoo!
http://www.yahoo.com.
http://www. yahoo.com/Computers_and_Internet/Internet/

ZD Net: http://www.zdnet.com

Ziff-Davis/ZD Net
http://www.zdnet.com

Index

I

J

K

L

M

N

P

Q

R

S

SIZZLER by TOTALLY HIP (Freeware)
Totally Hip's Sizzler plug-in allows simultaneous viewing and interaction with Web pages while streaming animation is delivered over the Web. It let's you view Quicktime animation before completely downloading it.

TALKER (Freeware)
The Talker plug-in enables Web pages to talk to Mac and PowerMac users, using Netscape and Apple Corporation's "English text-to-Speech" software.

STUFF-IT EXPANDER (Freeware)
Stuff-it Expander is the most simple, efficient way to expand compressed and encoded files that you may have downloaded from the Internet.

About the CD-ROM

The enclosed CD has all the software you'll need to get yourself up and running on the Net! Versions of shareware and freeware applications include:

NETSCAPE NAVIGATOR 2.0 (Commercial)
Netscape's famous World Wide Web browser lets you surf the Net! Only available if you subscribe to EarthLink Network TotalAccess. See below.

EUDORA LIGHT by QUALCOMM (Freeware)
Eudora Light is the freeware version of Eudora Pro--the Net's most popular e-mail client software.

ACROBAT AMBER READER by ADOBE (Freeware)
The "Amber" version of the Acrobat Reader lets you view, navigate, and print Portable Document Format (PDF) files right in your Navigator window.

EARTHLINK NETWORK TOTALACCESS (Commercial)
The cornerstone of the CD disc is a full installation of Earthlink Network TotalAccess. If you choose to load this software, you can use EarthLink Network as your Internet provider; if so, it will load Netscape Navigator for you.

ENVOY PLUG-IN by TUMBLEWEED SOFTWARE (Freeware)
The Envoy plug-in lets users view embedded or entire Envoy documents from within Netscape Navigator.

LIGHTNING STRIKE by INFINET OP (Freeware)
Lightning Strike is an optimized wavelet image codec plug-in for Netscape 2.0. It provides higher compressing ratios, smaller image files, faster transmissions, and improved image quality.

REAL AUDIO by PROGRESSIVE NETWORKS (Freeware)
RealAudio provides live and on-demand real-time audio over 14.4Kbps or faster connections to the Internet.

SHOCKWAVE FOR DIRECTOR by MACROMEDIA (Freeware)
The Shockwave plug-in lets users interact with Director presentations right in a Netscape Navigator window.